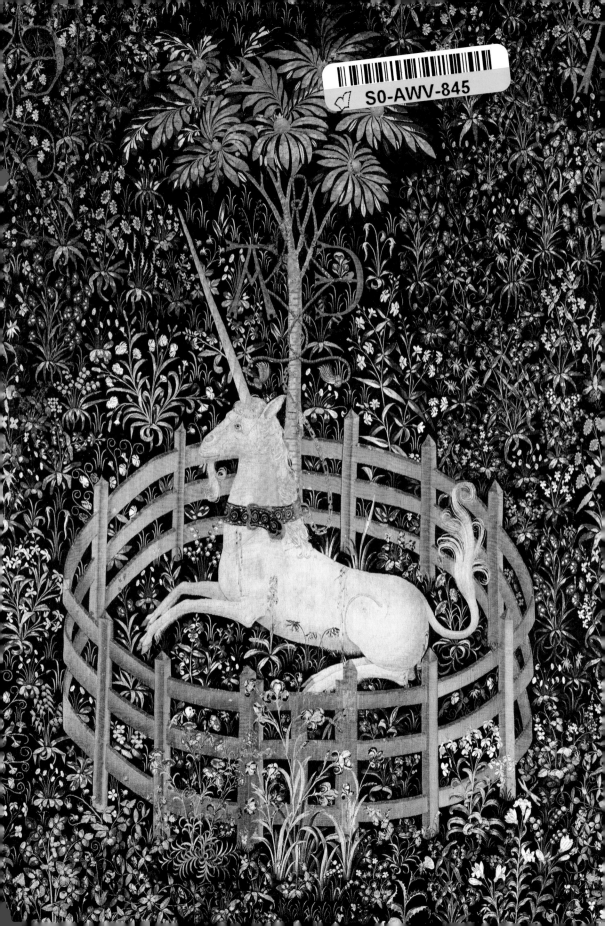

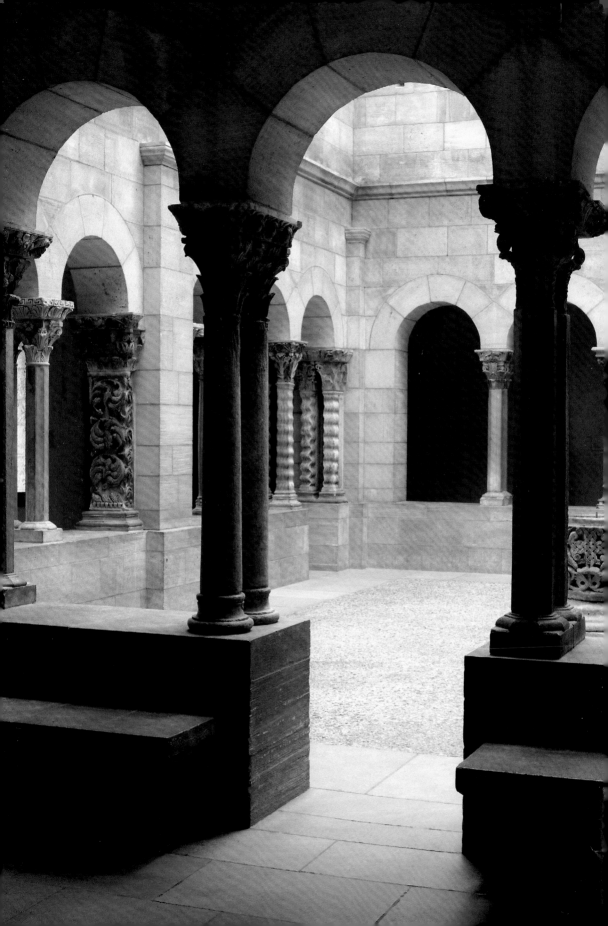

THE CLOISTERS
MEDIEVAL ART AND ARCHITECTURE

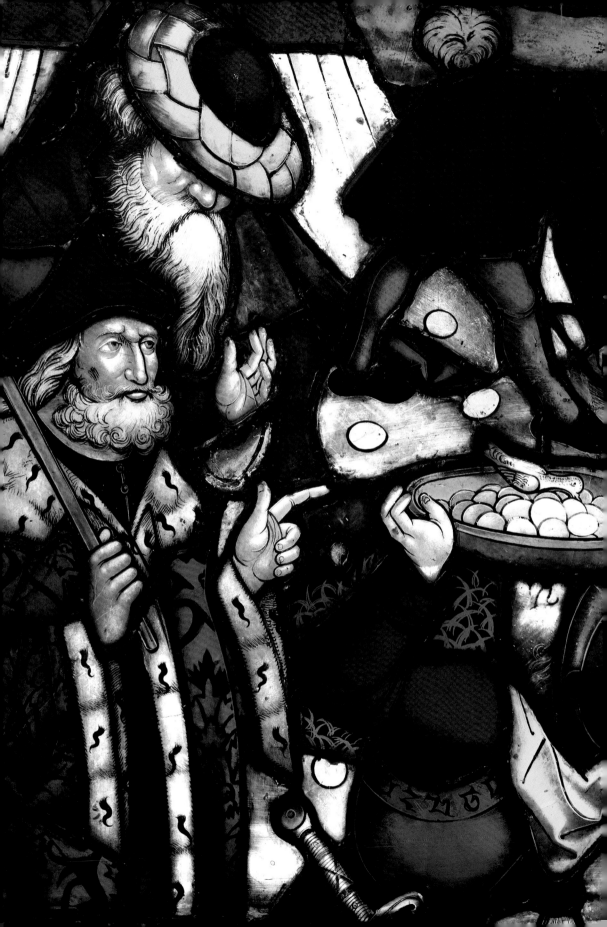

Contents

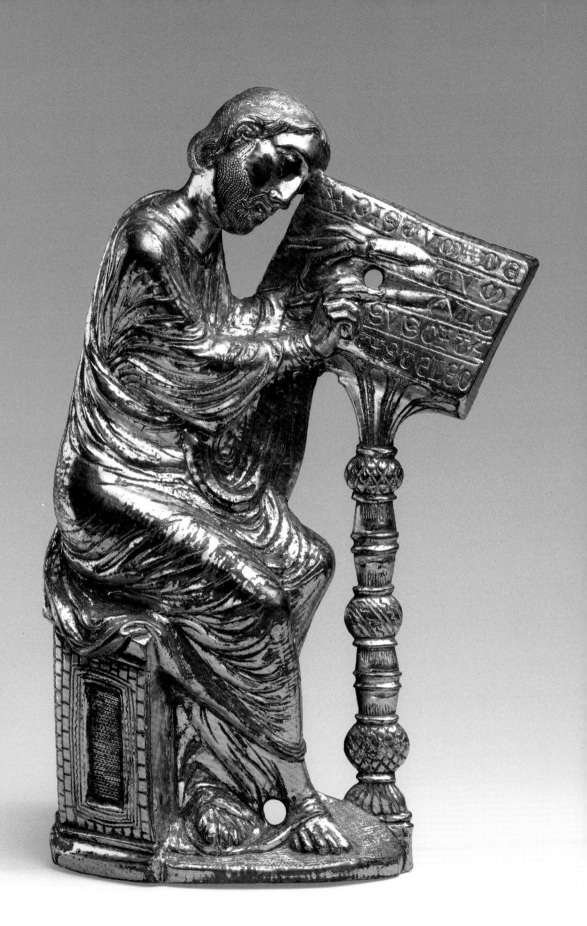

Director's Foreword

In May 1938 The Cloisters opened to the public as a branch of the Metropolitan Museum dedicated to the arts of the Middle Ages. Since that time The Cloisters has continued to grow, broadening and deepening its world-renowned holdings as well as undergoing renovations and reinstallations not only to preserve the fabric of the building but also to reflect new scholarship and to better serve visitors. With this expanded, updated, and completely redesigned edition of *The Cloisters: Medieval Art and Architecture* we celebrate the seventy-fifth anniversary of a unique and vibrant institution.

An introduction by co-authors Peter Barnet, Michel David-Weill Curator in Charge, Medieval Art and The Cloisters, and Nancy Wu, Museum Educator, The Cloisters, outlines the fascinating history of The Cloisters. It is generously illustrated with both historical and recent photography and sets the stage for the chronological survey of the collection that follows. Through the presentation and discussion of 144 master works, readers can explore Medieval styles and traditions and gain a better understanding of the historical and political environments that gave rise to them.

I would like to thank Peter Barnet and Nancy Wu, as well as other Museum staff past and present, for their work on this and earlier editions of The Cloisters guidebook.

Thomas P. Campbell
Director, The Metropolitan Museum of Art

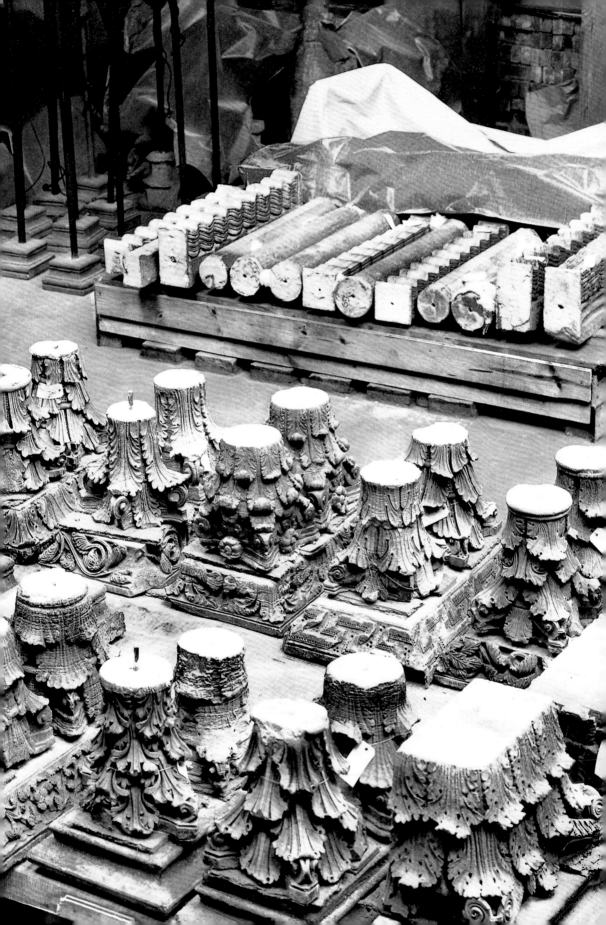

INTRODUCTION

The Cloisters, a branch of The Metropolitan Museum of Art, houses an extraordinary collection of art and architecture from medieval Europe, particularly from the Romanesque and Gothic periods. Students and enthusiasts of the Middle Ages have long made pilgrimages to The Cloisters to appreciate the collection's remarkable richness and broad scope. Many visitors also come to enjoy the Museum's magnificent setting, overlooking the Hudson River, and to experience its unique design concept, which incorporates subtle transitions between indoor and outdoor, past and present.

The history of The Cloisters begins with George Grey Barnard (1863–1938), an American sculptor trained at the Art Institute of Chicago and at the Académie des Beaux-Arts in Paris. From 1905 to 1913 Barnard was living with his family in a small village near Fontainebleau, where he was at work on a commission for the facade of the Pennsylvania state capitol building, in Harrisburg. To supplement his income, he became a casual art dealer and, later, an adroit collector, amassing in just a few years an impressive ensemble of medieval objects. Among his acquisitions were portions of four cloisters from southern France—Saint-Michel-de-Cuxa, Saint-Guilhem-le-Désert, Trie-sur-Baïse, and elements once thought to have come

from Bonnefont-en-Comminges—that would eventually form the architectural core of The Cloisters.

Barnard's interest in acquiring medieval sculpture stemmed from his frustrated attempts to introduce his students at New York's Art Students League, where he had taught in the late 1890s, to the beauty of medieval stone carving. He resolved to found a medieval museum "where the 'spirit of Gothic' could once more cast its spell." Barnard's timing was propitious, for at the turn of the twentieth century medieval architectural fragments were still available to the interested collector. Many such objects had become separated from their original settings as a result of pillage or vandalism, first during the sixteenth-century Wars of Religion and later in the French Revolution. Less violent causes, such as extensive renovations undertaken by owners—often a reflection of changing tastes—also contributed to the dispersal or destruction of art works. By the time Barnard began dealing in and collecting antiques, most of the fragments he was acquiring had already been displaced from their original sites. Some he found in private residences or dealers' showrooms, but others had been hidden from view or even abandoned in fields.

In 1913 Barnard entered into negotiations with Mme Baladud de Saint-Jean for at least ten arches from

Columns and capitals from Saint-Guilhem-le-Désert awaiting reinstallation in the new Cloisters, 1936

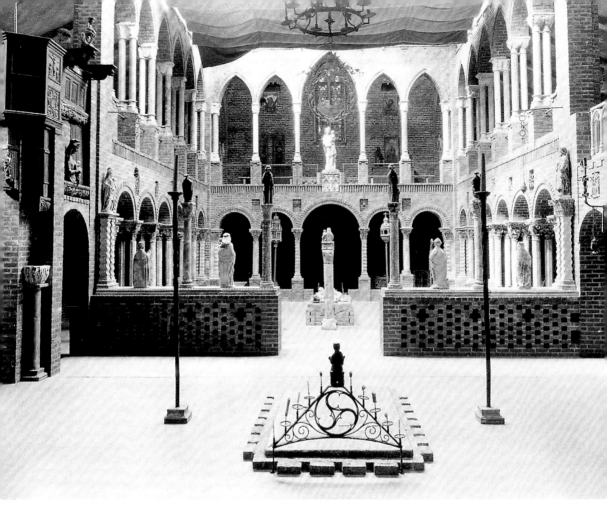

Interior views of George Grey Barnard's original Cloisters Museum, ca. 1925

Saint-Michel-de-Cuxa then decorating her bathhouse in Prades. The proposed sale alarmed local residents, however, as it did officials in Paris, who were already vexed by Barnard's earlier acquisitions. As a result, in late December of that year, shortly before the French senate passed a law designed to impede the export of historical monuments, Barnard shipped his entire collection to New York. He built a home for his antiquities at 698 Fort Washington Avenue and West 190th Street in Upper Manhattan. His new Cloisters Museum (above and right), essentially a barnlike brick structure

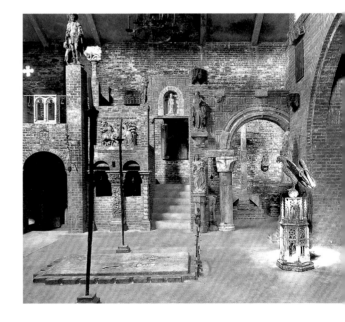

with a pitched roof, opened in December 1914 "for the benefit of the widows and orphans of French sculptors." Four years later, at the end of World War I, Barnard's energies were diverted to yet another ambitious plan: to build a national peace memorial showcasing the achievements of world architecture. Although never realized, the project consumed so much of Barnard's capital he was forced to put his museum up for sale. In 1925 John D. Rockefeller Jr. (1874–1960) provided funds for The Metropolitan Museum of Art to purchase the Barnard collection, and in May of the following year Barnard's Cloisters reopened as a branch of the Metropolitan (below).

Over the next few years Rockefeller helped enlarge The Cloisters' holdings through gifts and initiated plans to better accommodate the ever-growing collection. He purchased a tract of land just north of Fort Washington Avenue, part of which had previously been occupied by the estate of C. K. G. Billings (p. 12), and in 1927 he contracted Olmsted Brothers (the firm of Central Park architect Frederick Law Olmsted's sons) to landscape the area. They created what is now Fort Tryon Park (part of the New York City Parks and Recreation system), which Rockefeller donated to the city in 1930 with the condition that four acres be set aside for the future Cloisters Museum. Rockefeller also presented some seven hundred acres of the Palisades, the imposing bluffs on the west side of the Hudson River opposite

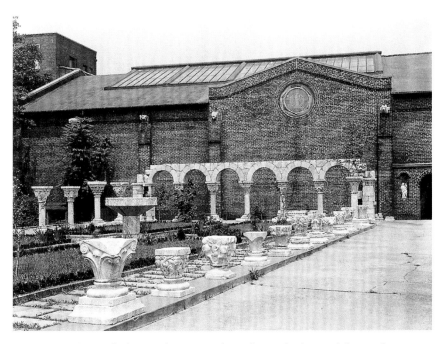

Exterior view of Barnard's Cloisters, showing an early installation of architectural elements from Saint-Michel-de-Cuxa, 1926

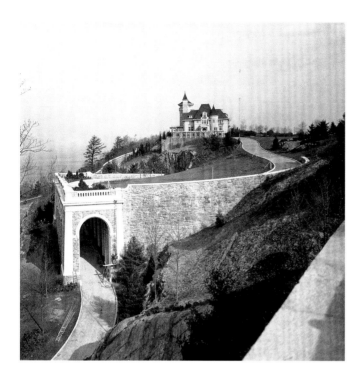

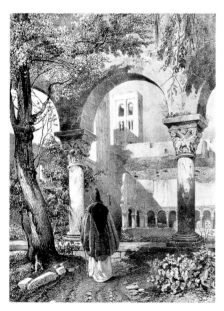

Baron I. J. Taylor (1789–1879). *Ruines de Saint-Michel-de-Cuxa*, 1834. Lithograph, from *Voyages pittoresques et romantiques dans l'ancienne France* (Paris, 1820–78)

the Museum, to the State of New Jersey, thereby preserving the remarkably pristine vista still treasured by visitors to

The Cloisters. On a clear day the spectacular view stretches south to the George Washington Bridge and as far north as the Tappan Zee Bridge.

In 1931 the design for a new building was entrusted to architect Charles Collens (1873–1956), who had recently completed Riverside Church on the Upper West Side of Manhattan. By a fortunate coincidence, at the same time the new Cloisters was under construction (1935–38), New York City was extending its subway system to 190th Street, allowing excavated Manhattan schist to be used for the Museum's rampart walls. Similarly, the Belgian cobblestones paving the exterior grounds and driveways had been retired from the Wall Street area. Granite quarried near New London, Connecticut, was selected for the exterior facing, and Doria limestone from Genoa, Italy, was used on the interior.

Rockefeller had initially envisioned the new Cloisters as a castle-like structure modeled loosely on Kenilworth, in England, but he quickly realized that the predominantly religious content of the collection called for a style more evocative of medieval ecclesiastical architecture. To that end, Collens, working with Metropolitan curators Joseph Breck (1885–1933) and James J. Rorimer (1905–1966), surveyed numerous monuments in southern France for inspiration. The five-story tower, for example, is reminiscent of those in the region around Cuxa (opposite), while the entirely modern Gothic Chapel bears a resemblance to thirteenth-century chapels at Carcassonne and Monsempron. The dimensions of some individual stone blocks and the designs for roof and floor tiles were likewise patterned after ones from Europe. In fact, many European medieval monuments influenced aspects of The Cloisters' design, but none served as an exact model for any part of the Museum. In the final plan, Collens incorporated all four of Barnard's original cloisters as well as several other major architectural elements from medieval France, including an arcade from Froville (in Lorraine; see p. 182), a chapter house from the Cistercian abbey in Pontaut, and a Romanesque chapel from Langon.

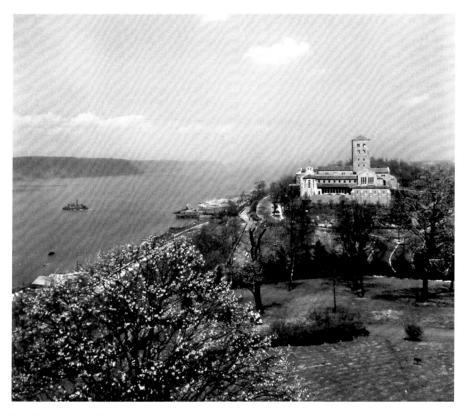

The Cloisters viewed from the south, ca. 1938

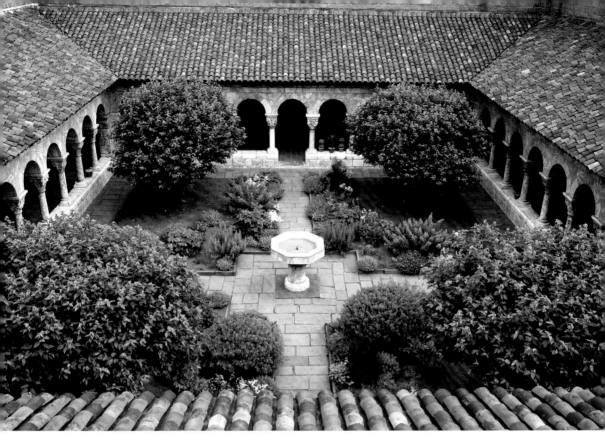

View of Cuxa Cloister garden from the tower

Within the galleries of the new Cloisters the atmosphere was intended to be intimate, with minimal ornamentation, limited artificial lighting, and even an occasional burning candle. Some of the galleries reflected the original functions of the architectural fragments they incorporated, whereas others provided a neutral and sympathetic setting for the works on display. When the Museum opened in May 1938, Lewis Mumford, writing in the *New Yorker*, praised The Cloisters as "one of the most thoughtfully studied and ably executed monuments we have seen in a long time." Louvre curator Germain Bazin hailed it as "the crowning achievement of American museology."

Three of the newly reconstructed cloisters (Cuxa, "Bonnefont," and Trie) incorporated gardens, an idea explored first by Joseph Breck in 1926, when he fashioned a garden court at Barnard's old museum with fragments from Cuxa. Curators James Rorimer and, later, Margaret Freeman (1899–1980) pursued Breck's vision of re-creating historical gardens. Rorimer personally surveyed catalogues of terracotta pots, and Freeman collected plant specimens from Cuxa in France. Their efforts to make The Cloisters' gardens aesthetically pleasing as well as educational were immediately seized upon by horticultural enthusiasts, and in 1939 the gardens were included on a list published by the Herb Society of America of "Botanic Gardens and Herbaria devoted especially to medicinal plants and other herbs for flavor, fragrance or household use." Today the gardens at The Cloisters are overseen by staff horticulturists who, like curators, are continually researching the species that grow there and adding new ones to the mix.

The Cuxa Cloister garden (opposite), with its central fountain, was conceived as a typical monastic enclosed garden. Footpaths intersecting in a cross shape divide it into equal quadrants, each planted with a fruit tree in the center and flowering plants along the border.

The "Bonnefont" Cloister garden (below), overlooking an expansive view of the Hudson River and Fort Tryon Park, was designed with herbs and other useful plants in mind. The space is organized symmetrically, with four quince trees situated around a fifteenth-century Venetian wellhead, and plantings that are divided into small, geometrically shaped beds. The Trie Cloister garden offers yet another, less formal design approach. A tall fountain stands at the center of a rectangular plot, amid a profusion of plants evocative of the rich foliage on many backgrounds of late medieval tapestries.

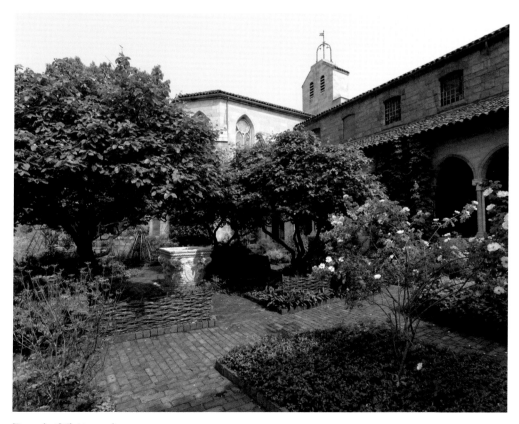

"Bonnefont" Cloister garden

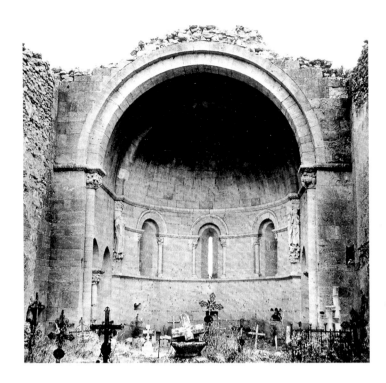

Apse from the church of San Martín at Fuentidueña before relocation to The Cloisters, ca. 1950s

John D. Rockefeller Jr. remained intimately involved with the new Cloisters, proposing ideas to the curators and the architect and donating more objects from his personal collection, including, in 1937, six of the seven famed Unicorn Tapestries. His generosity culminated in 1952 with a significant endowment that assured the continued growth of the collection for years to come. In 1948 the original Hall of the Unicorn Tapestries was reconfigured into two smaller galleries to accommodate the newly acquired Nine Heroes Tapestries, a rare surviving set from the Late Gothic period. The 1950s saw the acquisition of the Merode Altarpiece and the arrival of the apse from the church of San Martín at Fuentidueña, on permanent loan from the Spanish government (above). The installation of the apse required that the original Special Exhibition Room be reconfigured as a churchlike gallery space, which opened to the public in 1961. The superb acoustics of the Fuentidueña Chapel, as it is known today, quickly became apparent, and for more than fifty years it has proved a popular venue for concerts of early music. The renovation and expansion of the Treasury, which contains such splendid liturgical and devotional objects as the twelfth-century ivory "Cloisters Cross" and the fourteenth-century Hours of Jeanne d'Evreux, were completed in 1988 to mark the Museum's fiftieth anniversary.

Today The Cloisters continues to enhance its holdings and improve its facilities. The gallery housing the Unicorn Tapestries was refurbished in the late 1990s, including new lighting installed above the long-shut (now reopened) wood louvered ceiling panels. The flat glass-tile roof and opaque plexiglass that had covered Saint-Guilhem Cloister since 1938 were similarly replaced in 2002 with a pyramidal skylight and a ceiling of transparent panels that allow natural light to filter softly into the interior. These updates were followed in quick succession by the renovations of the Boppard Room in 2004, the Early Gothic Hall in 2006, and the Merode Room in 2007. More recently, in 2009, the Late Gothic Hall reopened after extensive restoration of the fifteenth-century limestone windows from Sens (see p. 182). The early sixteenth-century tapestry from Burgos, off view for decades, was reintroduced into this gallery amid a new installation of late medieval sculpture and painting. While these and other renovations help the Museum meet the latest in museological standards, they also occasionally reveal lost original design details, such as a small window hidden for decades behind a tapestry in the Boppard Room and now open once again onto a view of Cuxa Cloister.

As we adapt twenty-first-century technology to The Cloisters' unique setting, we do so in part to better accommodate the visiting public. At the same time, mindful of the contemplative atmosphere originally envisioned for the Museum, we seek a balance between accessibility and tranquillity. The number of didactic panels and wall texts, for example, has historically been kept to a minimum. Now, though, visitors can rely on random-access digital audioguides for information on highlights and major themes of the collection without intruding on the serene ambience in the galleries. Maintaining a respectful setting, especially given the spiritual resonance of much of the collection, remains a paramount concern at The Cloisters as we pursue our core missions: to preserve and protect the monuments of medieval art in our care; to elucidate those works through creative educational programming; to provide vigilant stewardship of The Cloisters' landmark physical facilities; and to continue collecting masterworks of medieval art at the highest levels of quality.

Note to Reader

All works of art featured here are in the permanent collection of The Metropolitan Museum of Art, but some may be off view on occasion for conservation or curatorial reasons. In object headings, information on country or culture of origin is generally listed in the following order: Country, Region (Province or Département), Town or City. Place-names within Catalonia are given in Catalan; Castilian spellings are used for all other locations in Spain. Dimensions are in inches followed by centimeters. Unless otherwise noted, height precedes width precedes depth.

Biblical citations are from the Douay-Rheims Version. When the events and persons from the Hebrew Bible that appear in the works of art are used in a Christian typological context, the traditional term Old Testament has been retained.

The Cloisters

Main Level

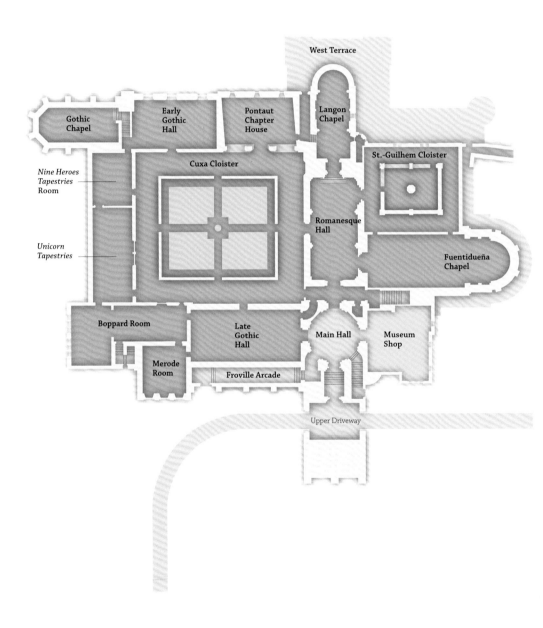

West Terrace

Gothic Chapel

Early Gothic Hall

Pontaut Chapter House

Langon Chapel

St.-Guilhem Cloister

Nine Heroes Tapestries Room

Cuxa Cloister

Romanesque Hall

Unicorn Tapestries

Fuentidueña Chapel

Boppard Room

Late Gothic Hall

Main Hall

Museum Shop

Merode Room

Froville Arcade

Upper Driveway

Lower Level

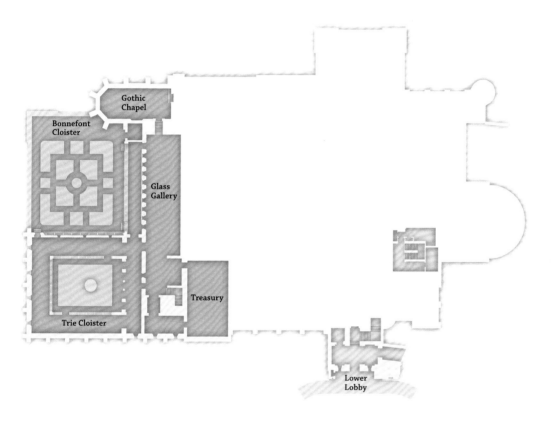

Gothic Chapel

Bonnefont Cloister

Glass Gallery

Treasury

Trie Cloister

Lower Lobby

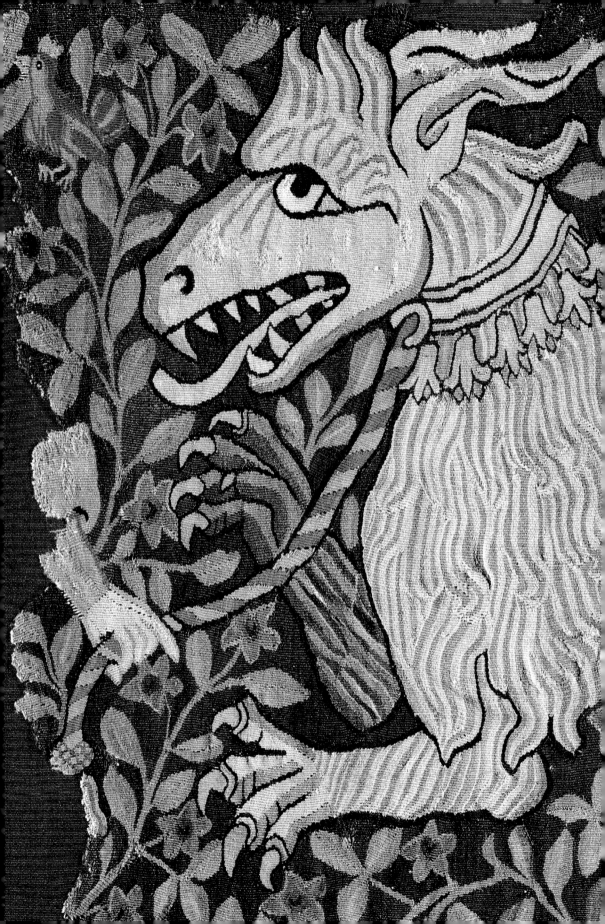

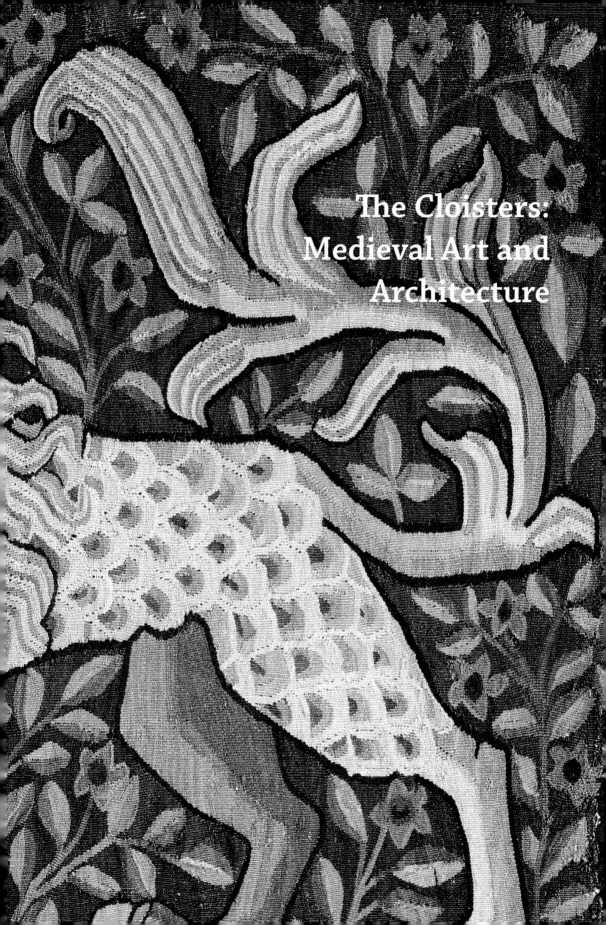

The Cloisters:
Medieval Art and
Architecture

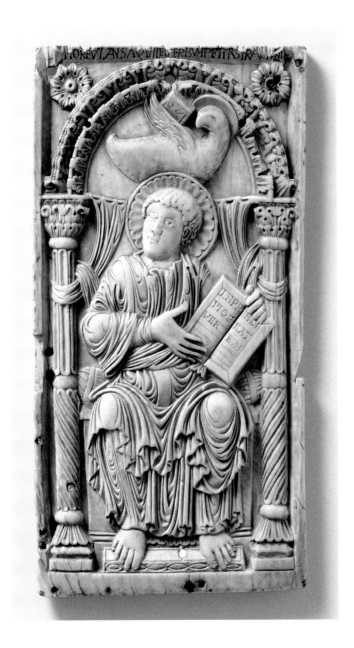

Plaque with Saint John the Evangelist

Germany, North Rhine-Westphalia, Aachen, early 9th century
Elephant ivory, 7¼ @ 3¾ in. (18.4 @ 9.5 cm)
The Cloisters Collection, 1977 (1977.421)

Although the core of The Cloisters' collection is devoted to Romanesque and Gothic art, the Museum houses several important early medieval treasury objects, such as this exquisite ivory plaque from the time of Charlemagne (r. as emperor 800–814), the so-called Carolingian period. On the plaque, which was probably carved in Aachen, Charlemagne's capital, we see a youthful Saint John the Evangelist sitting in richly carved classical garb. He is flanked by elaborate columns that support an arch framing his symbol, the eagle, and holds an open book bearing the words from the beginning of his Gospel: IN PRINCI/PIO ERAT/VERBVM (In the beginning was the Word). A second inscription, taken from a poem by the fifth-century Roman poet Sedulius, is found on the upper border: MORE VOLANS AQVILE VERBVM PETIT ASTRA [IOHAN]NI[S] (Flying like an eagle the word of John aspires to Heaven). Although the original function of the plaque is not known, most surviving ivories from the Carolingian period once decorated covers of ecclesiastical volumes. The imagery and inscriptions on this example suggest that the plaque likely adorned the cover of a Gospel book.

Plaque with Scenes at Emmaus

France, Lorraine (Moselle), Metz, ca. 850–900
Elephant ivory, 4½ @ 9¼ in. (11.5 @ 23.5 cm)
The Cloisters Collection, 1970 (1970.324.1)

Carved during or soon after the reign of Charlemagne's grandson Charles the Bald (r. 840–77), this plaque reflects a later phase of Carolingian art. The figures, represented in lively poses, gesture broadly to convey the narrative. At left is Christ, identified by the halo, appearing after the Resurrection to two of his disciples on the road to Emmaus (Luke 24:13–32). At right we see the Supper at Emmaus, when Christ reveals his identity to the two disciples, set within a detailed representation of the town, including an elaborate gate and city walls. The horizontal format of the plaque suggests that it originally formed the front or back of a box whose other panels were decorated with additional scenes from the life of Christ (probably following the Resurrection). The elegant outer border was no doubt inlaid with a contrasting material. The plaque belongs to a stylistically related group of ivories from the second half of the ninth century traditionally associated with the city of Metz, where Charles the Bald had his court.

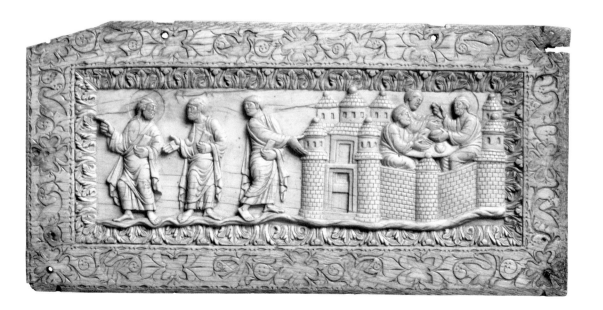

Bursa Reliquary

North Italy, early 10th century
From the treasury of the Benedictine abbey
of Saint Peter at Salzburg, Austria
Bone, paint, copper gilt, and sycamore,
7¾ @ 7⅜ @ 3¼ in. (19.7 @ 18.6 @ 8.3 cm)
The Cloisters Collection, 1953 (53.19.2)

The crisply carved, flat decoration of this
reliquary recalls the style and ornamental
vocabulary seen frequently in large-scale stone
carving throughout northern Italy. Its shape
is also reminiscent of a *bursa*, a purse made of
precious textiles in which saints' relics were
carried. The openwork patterns of the bone
plaques were originally silhouetted against
gilded copper foil, creating a delicate interplay
of light and shadow. In his twelfth-century
treatise *On Divers Arts*, the German monk
Theophilus recommended a similar decorative
approach to the ivory carver: "Delicately draw
little flowers or animals, or birds, or dragons
linked by their necks and tails, pierce the
grounds with fine tools and carve with the
best and finest workmanship that you can.
After doing this, fill the hole inside with a
piece of oak covered with gilded copper sheet
so that the gold can be seen through all the
[pierced] grounds."

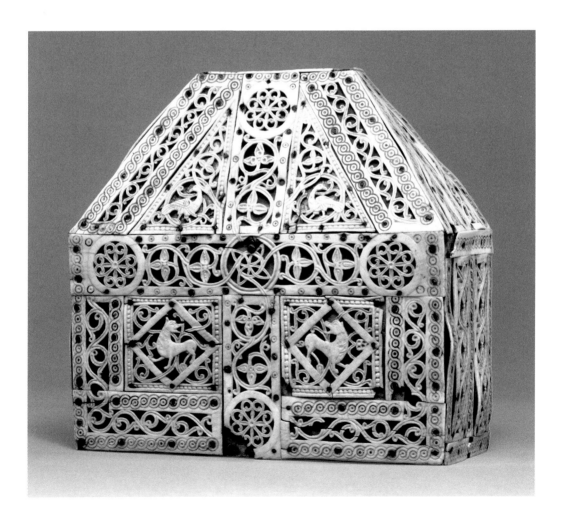

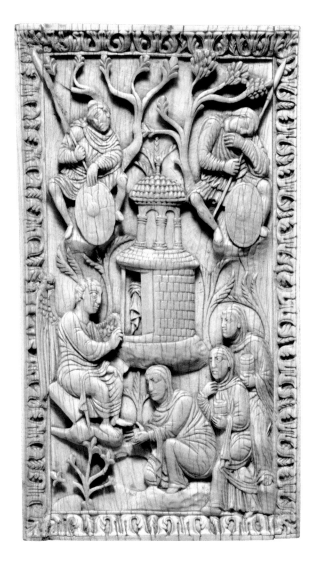

Plaque with the Holy Women at the Tomb

North Italy (Milan?), early 10th century
Elephant ivory, 7½ @ 4¼ in. (19 @ 10.8 cm)
Purchase, The Cloisters Collection and Lila
Acheson Wallace Gift, 1993 (1993.19)

Like the ivory plaque with Saint John the Evangelist carved about one hundred years earlier (p. 22), this plaque was probably made to decorate a book cover. At the center of the dramatic scene is the Holy Sepulchre, with the burial shroud of Jesus visible through the open door of the circular building. The soldiers— who the Bible says were "struck with terror, and became as dead men" (Matthew 28:4)—are seen behind the tomb, as the Holy Women approach with their ointment jars. The latter are greeted by the winged angel, sitting atop the lid of the sarcophagus, who informs them that Christ has risen from his grave. The figures, particularly in the upper portion of the ivory, are boldly carved and deeply undercut. The strong, symmetrical composition and the masterful carving make this ivory a powerful piece of relief sculpture.

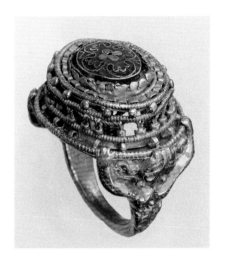

Ring

Germany, ca. 950–1050
Gold with cloisonné enamel, DIAM. ¾ in. (1.7 cm)
The Cloisters Collection, 2004 (2004.274)

One of the most opulent and technically complex gold rings from the early Middle Ages, this intricate piece of jewelry bears witness to the high degree of sophistication at the court of the Ottonian emperors, who ruled central Europe from 936 to 1024. Two feline beasts support the bezel; at top is an elliptical floral design in gold cloisonné enamel, with a central cruciform shape in white enamel framed by a green field with four crescent-shaped petals in blue glass. Typical of Ottonian goldsmithing, the multiple elements of the ring are soldered together to create a rich, microarchitectural form. In addition to enamel, the varied fabrication techniques include granulation, swabbed and twisted wires, ribbons of bent wire, and cast, punched, and chased elements. Within the lowest register of the bezel are small rings to contain strung pearls—now lost—within a slot.

Cylindrical Box

Spain, Andalucía (Córdoba), ca. 950–975
Elephant ivory, H. 4⅝ in. (11.7 cm);
DIAM. 4⅛ in. (10.5 cm)
The Cloisters Collection, 1970 (1970.324.5)

During the tenth century most of the Iberian peninsula was ruled by the Muslim Umayyad dynasty. This exquisitely carved cylindrical box, cut from the cross section of an elephant's tusk, is one of the most accomplished works of a master from the palace of the Córdoban caliph Abd al-Rahman III (r. 912–61). Unlike pyxes, their Western Christian counterparts, which held consecrated bread for the Mass, Islamic examples were exclusively secular and used to store jewelry and cosmetics. The pairing of birds, lions, and gazelles amid richly carved vine scrolls is typical of dense, symmetrical Islamic design, which strongly influenced the decoration of Romanesque ivories and

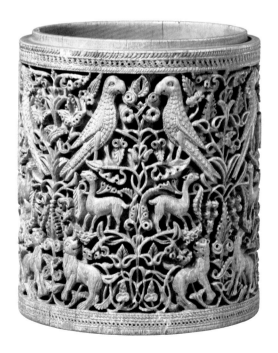

illuminated manuscripts. The missing lid of this example was likely shaped as a low dome with a finial on top, and it probably would have had an inscription on it, perhaps giving a date or the name of the owner.

———————————

Plaque with Saint Aemilian

Master Engelram and his son Redolfo
Spain, Castilla-León, 1060–80
From the monastery church of San Millán
de la Cogolla, near Logroño
Elephant ivory with glass inlay, 6⅝ @ 3 in. (16.8 @ 7.6 cm)
The Cloisters Collection, 1987 (1987.89)

The relics of the sixth-century Spanish saint Aemilian were housed in an ornate shrine crafted of ivory, gold, and gems. We are remarkably well informed about the reliquary, which was made on the occasion of the translation (or transport) of the saint's relics from the monastery of Suso to the church of San Millán de la Cogolla, dedicated in 1067. Although the reliquary was damaged during the Napoleonic invasion of Spain in 1809, we know from a 1601 description that The Cloisters' plaque decorated the roof of the shrine. On it we see the saint tending his sheep in the bottom register, while above he receives a blessing from the hand of God at the top of a mountain.

In addition to this plaque, several other ivories from the shrine survive in European and American collections. One, in the State Hermitage Museum, Saint Petersburg, depicts the ivory carver and his assistant in the workshop and bears an inscription that identifies them as Master Engelram and his son Redolfo. Such images of artists were rare in this period, as was the practice of identifying artists by name.

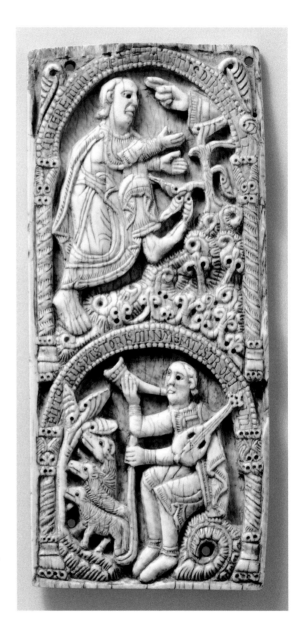

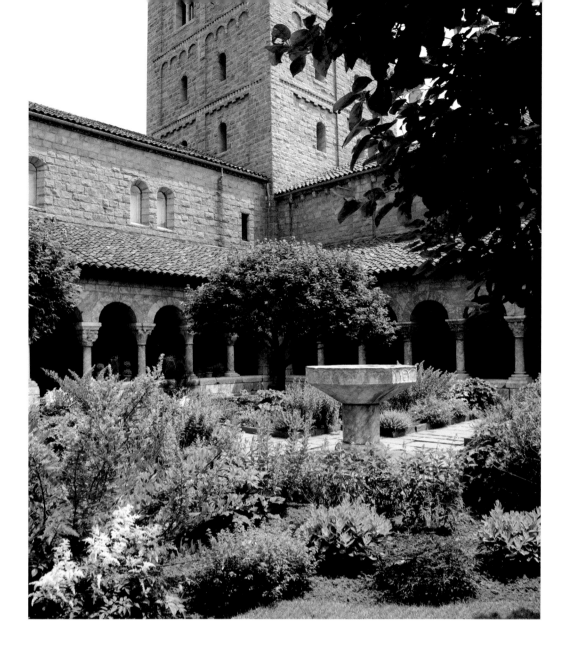

Cloister from Saint-Michel-de-Cuxa

Catalonia, ca. 1130–40
From the Benedictine monastery of Saint-Michel-de-Cuxa
(Sant Miquel de Cuixà), near Perpignan, France
Marble, 90 @ 78 ft. (27.4 @ 23.8 m)
The Cloisters Collection, 1925 (25.120.398–.954)

The cloister is the nucleus of monastic daily
life. Often square or rectangular in shape, it is
essentially an open-air courtyard bordered by
covered walkways connecting it to the other
important spaces of the monastery, such as the
church, chapter house, dormitory, and refectory.

Most of the fragments with which this cloister
is reconstructed come from the Benedictine
abbey of Saint-Michel-de-Cuxa, in the eastern
Pyrenees (the central fountain is believed to be
from the abbey of Saint-Génis-des-Fontaines).
Saint-Michel-de-Cuxa was founded in the ninth
century by monks from the nearby abbey of
Saint-André-d'Exalada. The original cloister,
probably constructed during the abbacy of
Gregory (1130–46), was almost twice the size
of the present reconstruction. Many of the
capitals bear wild or fanciful creatures, from

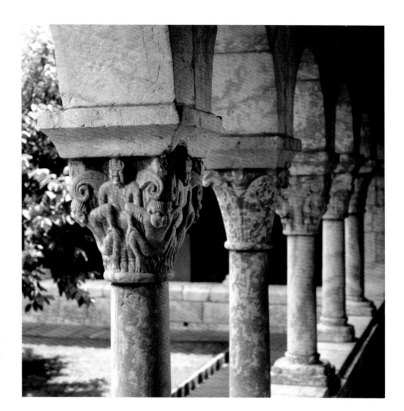

Detail of capitals

below
Columns and capitals
from Saint-Michel-de-
Cuxa on display in the
garden of Pierre-Yon
Vernière, Aniane,
France, before 1906

crouching apes supported by naked men to
monstrous heads devouring claw-footed arms.
In his *Apologia to Abbot William* (1125), the
prominent theologian and reformer Bernard of
Clairvaux noted the popularity of such hybrid
and outlandish beings and criticized them as
distractions from monastic contemplation.

Saint-Michel-de-Cuxa was confiscated in
1789 by the French state and sold in 1791; its
sculpture began to be dispersed soon afterward
(right). For the reconstruction at The Cloisters,
Languedoc marble was quarried from the
same mountainous region between Ria and
Villefranche where the twelfth-century masons
at Cuxa would have obtained their material.
The layout of the garden approximates a typical
monastic garth, like that depicted on the ninth-
century plan for the Benedictine monastery
in Saint-Gall, Switzerland. A crab apple tree
stands in the center of each quadrant of grass,
bordered by flowers and herbs. This ornamental
garden mixes plants known in the Middle Ages,
such as lady's-mantle and columbine—which
can also be found on the Unicorn Tapestries

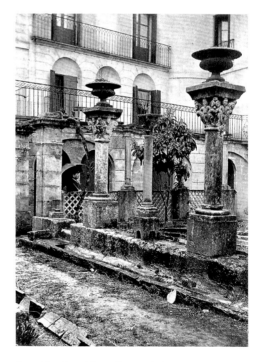

(pp. 168–75)—with modern varieties to assure
a continuous and bountiful display of blooms
from April through October.

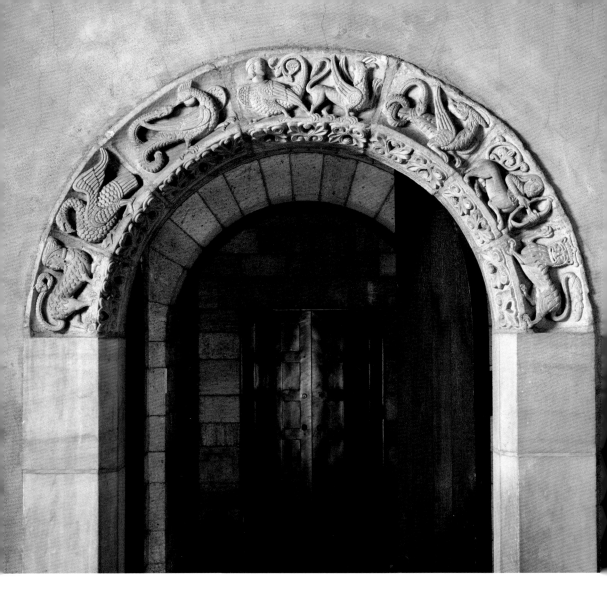

Narbonne Arch

France, Languedoc-Roussillon (Aude), ca. 1150–75
Said to come from Narbonne
Marble, 38 @ 74 @ 11¼ in. (96.5 @ 188 @ 28.6 cm)
John Stewart Kennedy Fund, 1922 (22.58.1a)

This semicircular arch comprises seven stone
blocks (known as voussoirs) decorated with
eight real and fantastic animals: left to right,
a manticore ("man-eater" in Persian, with the
face of a man, the body of a lion, and the tail
of a scorpion); a pelican (symbol of Christ); a
basilisk (dragon with a serpent's tail, signifying
the power to kill); a harpy (half-woman, half-
bird creature whose sweet song lures men

to their deaths); a griffin (with the body of a
lion and the head and wings of an eagle); an
amphisbaena (serpent with a head at either
end); a centaur (with the head and torso
of a man and lower body of a horse); and a
crowned lion. These are all animals familiar
from medieval bestiaries, texts compiled in the
twelfth century describing such creatures and
explaining their moral and religious associations.

The closest parallel to the carving style of
the arch can be found in the nave capitals of the
mid-twelfth-century church of Saint-Paul-Serge
in Narbonne, but the original location of the
arch remains unknown.

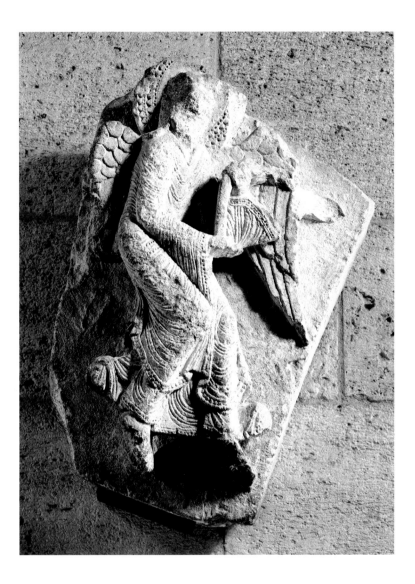

Angel from Saint-Lazare at Autun

France, Burgundy (Saône-et-Loire), ca. 1130
From the former north transept portal of the
cathedral of Saint-Lazare at Autun
Limestone, 23 @ 16½ in. (58.4 @ 41.9 cm)
The Cloisters Collection, 1947 (47.101.16)

Seemingly afloat in midair, this angel was
once a voussoir on the north transept portal
of the cathedral of Saint-Lazare in Autun,
Burgundy. His elongated body is accentuated
with fine drapery folds, the sleeves and hem
of his garment are decorated with beaded
borders, and the feathers of his wings are
articulated with deep lines. The fragmentary
state of the voussoir no longer allows for a sure
identification of the object held by the angel, in
all probability a liturgical or musical instrument.
The angel is one of a handful of physical
remains of the twelfth-century portal, which
was replaced with a Baroque doorway in 1776.
The fine, calligraphic carving style bears a strong
resemblance to the celebrated Eve figure from
the lintel of the same portal, now at the Musée
Rolin in Autun.

Enthroned Virgin and Child

France, Burgundy (Saône-et-Loire),
vicinity of Autun, 1130–40
Birch with paint and glass, H. 40½ in. (102.9 cm)
The Cloisters Collection, 1947 (47.101.15)

Despite the loss of the Christ Child's head,
three legs of the Virgin's throne, and most of
the original painted decoration, this sensitive
carving manifests enormous sculptural power.
The conception of the Virgin's elongated
face and the treatment of the drapery folds
compare closely to the well-known architectural
sculptures of the cathedral of Saint-Lazare in
Autun, including the relief of an angel in The
Cloisters' collection (p. 31). Indeed, one of the
sculpture's owners, Abbot Victor Terret of
Autun, believed it came from a local church,
perhaps Saint-Lazare. Surviving traces of paint
reveal that the Virgin's tunic was forest green
with vermilion cuffs, and her veil was a dark
lapis lazuli blue. The Child's tunic retains traces
of yellow, and his undergarment was red; the
book he holds shows evidence of blue on the
front cover and white and black on the sides.
The Virgin's hair was black, and both eyes were
originally inlaid with pupils of blue glass (only
the proper right eye is original).

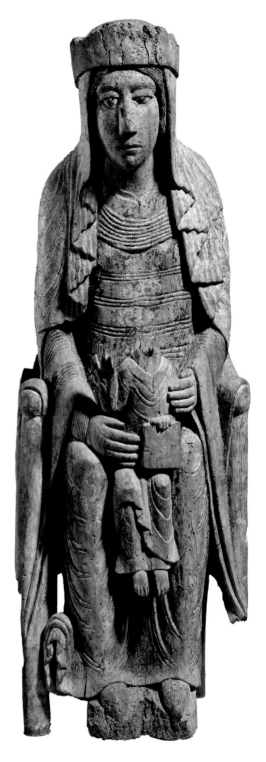

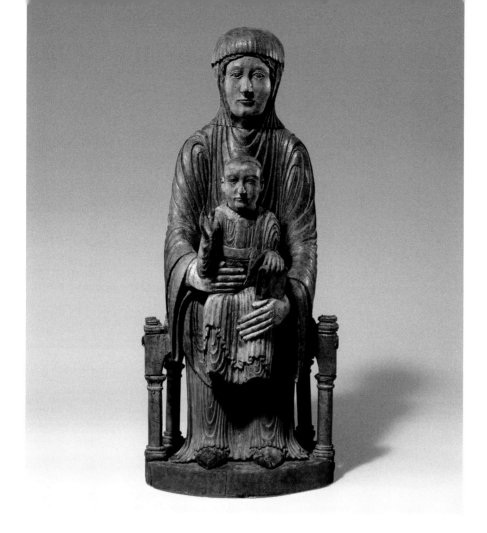

Enthroned Virgin and Child

France, Auvergne (Puy-de-Dôme), 1150–1200
Said to come from the chapel of Saint-Victor at
Montvianeix, near Vichy
Walnut with paint, tin leaf, and traces of linen,
H. 27 in. (68.6 cm)
The Cloisters Collection and James J. Rorimer
Memorial Fund, 1967 (67.153)

The Christ Child seated in a frontal pose on the
Virgin's lap is a sculptural type known as the
Throne of Wisdom, or Sedes Sapientiae (see also
The Cloisters' Burgundian version, opposite).
This seemingly straightforward arrangement
actually conveys complex theological ideas,
specifically the medieval tenet that Christ, like
his ancestors King David and King Solomon,
embodied wisdom and justice. Mary thus serves
as his "throne," and Christ holds an open book
emblematic of his divine wisdom. Sculptures like
this one frequently functioned as reliquaries; in
fact, X-radiography has revealed the presence of
a small sealed cavity under Mary's left shoulder
that appears to contain a relic.

Recent treatment and study in the Museum's
conservation laboratory have enabled us to
reconstruct the original painted decoration of
the sculpture. The Virgin's mantle was once dark
blue (lapis lazuli darkened by a gray underlayer)
and was further embellished with small lozenge-
shaped elements of tin leaf that were intended
to appear as gold. Beneath her blue mantle the
Virgin wore a red robe. That same red, also
decorated with tin leaf, is found on the Child's
himation (the overgarment that falls over his
shoulder), while his tunic (now light green) was
originally a darker green with red lining. Both
throne and base were painted in imitation of
colored marbles and precious stones.

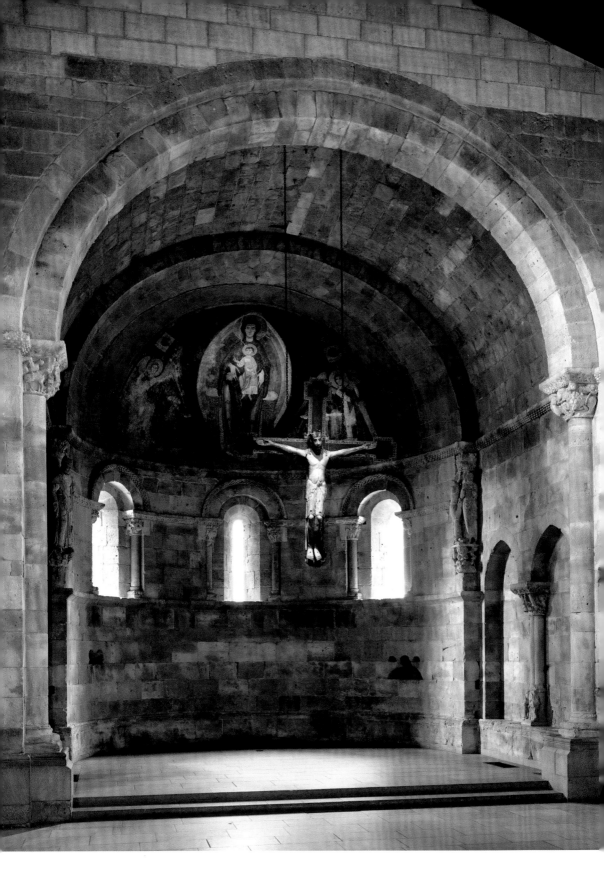

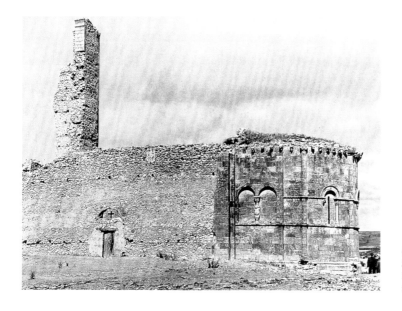

Church of San Martín at Fuentidueña, 1955

Apse from San Martín at Fuentidueña

Spain, Castilla-León (Segovia), ca. 1175–1200
From the church of San Martín at Fuentidueña, near Segovia
Limestone, H. to top of barrel vault: 29 ft. 8½ in. (905.5 cm); max. interior W.: 22 ft. ½ in. (672 cm)
Exchange Loan from the Government of Spain, 1958 (L.58.86)

The church of San Martín stood in the village of Fuentidueña in north-central Spain, a region largely uninhabited, though claimed intermittently by Christian and Muslim forces, from the eighth through the eleventh century. Little is known about the building's history. By the nineteenth century, the apse—a term that most often describes a semicircular space terminating at the east end of a church, where the altar is situated—was the only part of the church surviving in fair condition (above). In 1957 the Spanish government agreed to lend it permanently to The Cloisters. The apse is covered by a barrel vault and a half-dome, with three small windows piercing the exterior wall. Flanking the window zone are two columns fronted with figures: on the left, Saint Martin, bishop of Tours (ca. 316–397), and on the right, the Annunciate Angel and Mary. Below a triumphal arch are two attached columns whose capitals depict the Adoration of the Magi (left) and Daniel in the Lions' Den (right). To accommodate the reconstructed apse,

which comprises 3,300 stone blocks (below), the former Special Exhibition Room was partially demolished. The new gallery, which opened to the public in 1961, was designed to simulate a single-aisle nave with no projecting transepts, a plan characteristic of twelfth-century Segovian architecture.

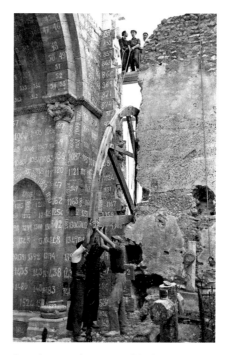

Fuentidueña apse being prepared for shipment to New York, 1958

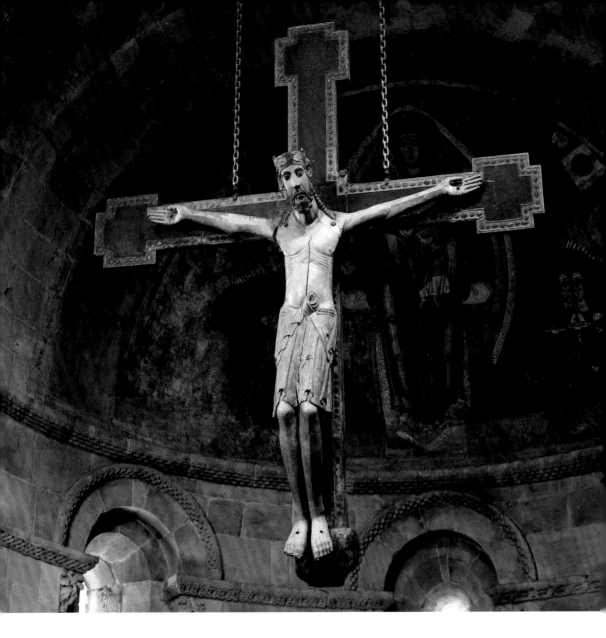

Crucifix

Spain, Castilla-León (Palencia), ca. 1150–1200
White oak, paint, gilding, and applied stones (corpus);
red pine and paint (cross), 102½ @ 81¾ @ 15¾ in.
(260.4 @ 207.6 @ 40 cm)
Samuel D. Lee Fund, 1935 (35.36a, b)

This monumental crucifix represents Christ
in a characteristically twelfth-century manner:
triumphant over death, with his eyes open,
and crowned. The patterns of his beard and rib
cage are boldly carved, as is the drapery of the
loincloth, and much of the painted and gilded
decoration is original. The reverse is embellished
with a painted image of the Lamb of God
(Agnus Dei) at the center and symbols of the
Four Evangelists at the terminals, suggesting
that the cross was intended to hang away from
the wall and be seen from both sides. The high
quality of the carving and the generally fine
state of preservation make this crucifix one of
the most important Romanesque examples of
its type. There are conflicting accounts about
the original location of the crucifix; it has been
said to be from the convent of Santa Clara at
Astudillo, near Palencia, but the source of the
information is not reliable.

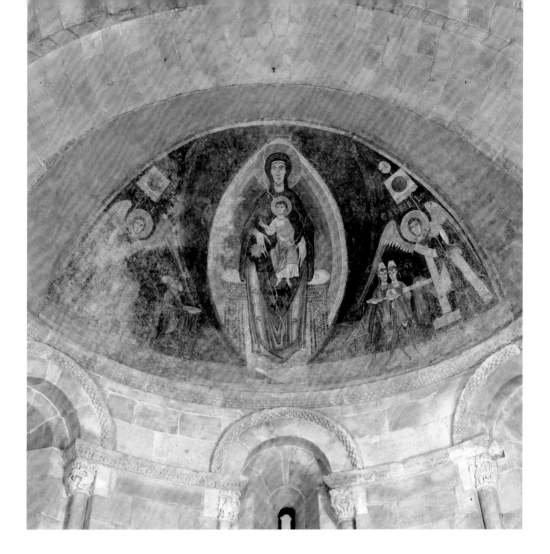

The Virgin and Child in Majesty and the Adoration of the Magi

Attributed to the Master of Pedret
Catalonia (Lleida), ca. 1100
From the church of Era Mare de Diu de Cap d'Aran,
near Tredòs, Spain
Fresco transferred to canvas, 10 ft. 7 in. @
19 ft. 5¼ in. (323@ 593 cm)
The Cloisters Collection, 1950 (50.180a–c)

Attributed on stylistic grounds to the so-called Master of Pedret, this fresco comes from the apse of the church of the Virgin near Tredòs, in the Catalan Pyrenees. At its center are the Enthroned Virgin and Child framed by a mandorla (an almond-shaped aureole). Flanking this central group, but on a smaller scale, are Archangels Michael (left) and Gabriel (right) in rigidly frontal poses. Only the Three Magi at the bottom—Melchior, Balthasar, and Gaspar—display any considerable agility or movement. The composition clearly intends to delineate the hierarchy of the figures. An Italo-Byzantine influence is evident in the representation of the bejeweled throne and the flaming wings of the archangels; the latter, in fact, are dressed in imperial Byzantine costumes.

The central group of the Virgin and Child was purchased by the Museum in 1950, followed soon after by the other two fragments (Michael and Melchior on one; Gabriel, Balthasar, and Gaspar on the other). When the Fuentidueña apse (pp. 34–35) came to The Cloisters, the fresco fragments were mounted on its half-dome to evoke their original setting.

The Adoration of the Magi

Spain, Castilla-León (Burgos), ca. 1175–1200
From the church of Nuestra Señora de la Llana
at Cerezo de Riotirón, near Burgos
Limestone, H. left to right. 48¾ in. (123.8 cm);
52¼ in. (134 cm); 53¾ in. (136.5 cm); 51 in. (129.5 cm)
The Cloisters Collection, 1930 (30.77.6–.9)

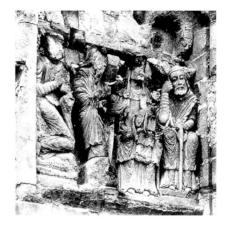

Adoration group as installed on the south facade of
Nuestra Señora de la Llana, ca. 1920s

Despite some visible damage, the masterful
carving in this Adoration scene is still apparent
in the swirling drapery folds and majestic
postures of the figures. We see two of the Magi
approaching the Virgin and Child (whose head
is missing) from the left, while Joseph sits on
the right with his head resting on his hand.
The church of Nuestra Señora de la Llana at
Cerezo de Riotirón, in ruins since 1924, no
longer provides evidence either for the group's
twelfth-century disposition or for the original
placement or presence of the third wise man,
but it is possible the group was intended for a
tympanum. However, the earliest photograph
of it, taken in the 1920s (above), already shows
the ensemble inserted in a recessed space not
likely to have been its original setting. Comparisons with surviving regional sculptures have
identified the hand of the sculptor, who,
although anonymous, created this Adoration
group in his mature style.

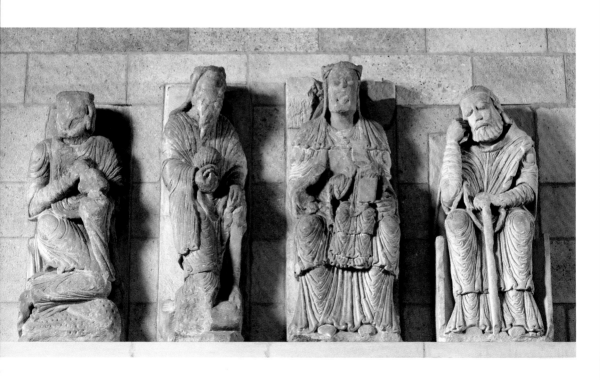

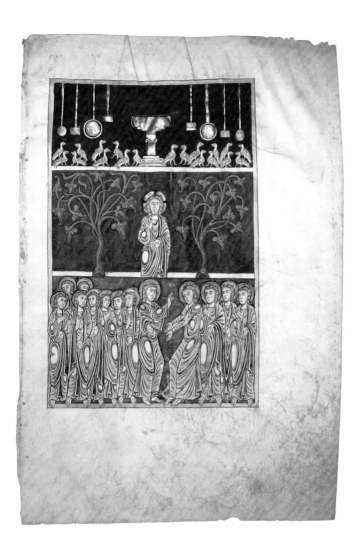

Commentary on the Apocalypse of Saint John

Spain, Castilla-León (Burgos), ca. 1180
Probably from the Benedictine monastery
of San Pedro de Cardeña
Tempera, gold, and ink on parchment,
17½ @ 11⅞ in. (44.4 @ 30 cm)
Purchase, The Cloisters Collection, Rogers and
Harris Brisbane Dick Funds, and Joseph Pulitzer Bequest,
1991 (1991.232.1–.14)

In about 776 the Spanish monk Beatus of
Liébana compiled a commentary on the biblical
Revelation of Saint John, commonly known as
the Apocalypse. Boldly illuminated manuscripts
of Beatus's text are among the masterworks of
early medieval Spanish art. This miniature, one
of fourteen leaves from such a manuscript in
the Museum's collection, depicts the imagery
in Revelation 6:9–11, or the opening of the fifth
seal. The horizontal bands of intense color
behind the images are characteristic of Beatus
manuscripts. In the blue register at top we see
an altar table with hanging votive offerings and
doves, representing the souls of the dead, on
either side; in the middle register an image of
the blessing Christ is flanked by trees; a crowd
of martyrs fills the bottom register. The drapery
of the figural decoration, which seems to cling to
the bodies in the "damp-fold" style, is consistent
with Spanish work of the period, as seen on the
twelfth-century carved figures of the Adoration
of the Magi group from Cerezo de Riotirón
(opposite), also in The Cloisters' collection.

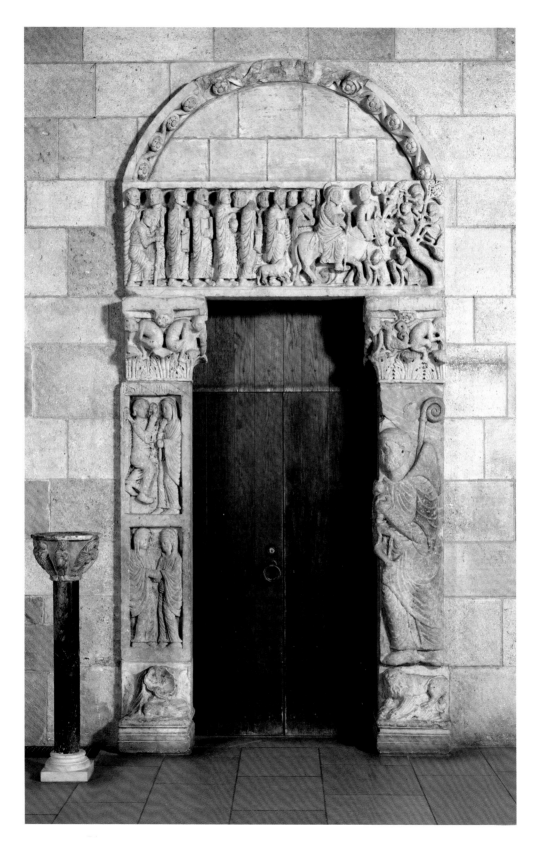

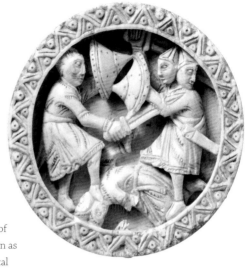

Game Piece with Hercules Slaying the Three-Headed Geryon

Germany, Lower Rhineland, Cologne, ca. 1150
Walrus ivory, DIAM. 2¾ in. (7 cm)
The Cloisters Collection, 1970 (1970.324.4)

This carved disk was originally part of a set of thirty pieces made for the board game known as "tables," a precursor of backgammon. Classical and biblical themes are seen frequently on surviving tablemen, including episodes from the stories of Hercules and Samson, suggesting that these ancient heroes often represented opposing sides in the game. Here, Hercules, at left, is shown killing the three-headed monster Geryon—his tenth Labor. The monster, now slain, is represented again at the bottom of the scene. Like many other examples, this tableman retains traces of paint. Color allowed one side to be easily distinguished from the other side, which was often left unpainted.

Doorway from San Leonardo al Frigido

Workshop of Biduinus
Italy, Tuscany, ca. 1175
From the church of San Leonardo al Frigido, near Massa
Carrara marble, 13 ft. 2 in.@ 76 in. (400@ 190 cm)
The Cloisters Collection, 1962 (62.189)

The church of San Leonardo al Frigido is situated near the juncture of roads leading to two great pilgrimage destinations of the Middle Ages: Rome and Santiago de Compostela, in northwestern Spain. In 1879 this doorway was still standing at the entrance to the ruined church, but by 1893 it was in Countess Benkendorff-Schouvaloff's villa near Nice. In 1962 it was found in pieces in a field near that city (right) and was purchased by the Museum.

The stone carvings decorating the doorway are from different periods and by different sculptors. The two doorposts are recarved from an antique sarcophagus (excluding the capitals and bases), with scenes of the Annunciation and Visitation on the left, and, on the right, a depiction of Leonard, patron saint of prisoners, holding a miniature figure with chained feet. The bases are

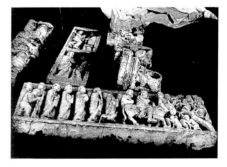

Elements of the San Leonardo doorway abandoned near Nice, ca. 1962

postmedieval. On the lintel, which some have attributed to the workshop of the Pisan sculptor Biduinus, is the Entry into Jerusalem (Matthew 21:1–9): Jesus, riding a donkey, is greeted by four children in a tree, while two others lay garments on the road before him. The apostles, some holding objects and some singing, walk with a tonsured Leonard in a liturgical procession. That Leonard, a locally revered saint, is included in the procession seems to invite viewers to imagine themselves walking alongside Jesus on a spiritual pilgrimage to Jerusalem.

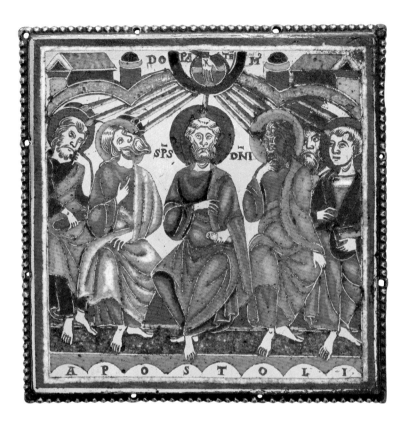

Plaque with the Pentecost

South Netherlands, Meuse valley, ca. 1150–60
Champlevé enamel and copper gilt,
4⅛ @ 4⅛ in. (10.3 @ 10.3 cm)
The Cloisters Collection, 1965 (65.105)

The dignified figure of Saint Peter, flanked by other apostles, sits at the center of this exceptionally fine, well-preserved plaque. The hand of God appears above him radiating red and white lines. The scene represented here is the Pentecost, when, fifty days after Easter, the apostles were gathered and "suddenly there came a sound from heaven, as of a mighty wind coming, and it filled the whole house where they were sitting. And there appeared to them parted tongues as it were of fire, and it sat upon every one of them" (Acts 2:2–3).

The plaque is one of a group of twelve enamels, all measuring close to ten centimeters square, divided among the Metropolitan and several European museums. The group depicts scenes from the Old and New Testaments and must have originally decorated a large object in a church, such as an altarpiece or a pulpit. Together they demonstrate the high quality achieved by Mosan enamelers as well as the complexity of the monuments they created. As seen here, the faces of the apostles are fluidly engraved in a style that recalls drawing in pen and ink, while the drapery and architectural elements are marvelously rendered in a rich palette of more than twelve colors. The translucency of some of the enamel allows for the reflective play of light off the metallic foil beneath.

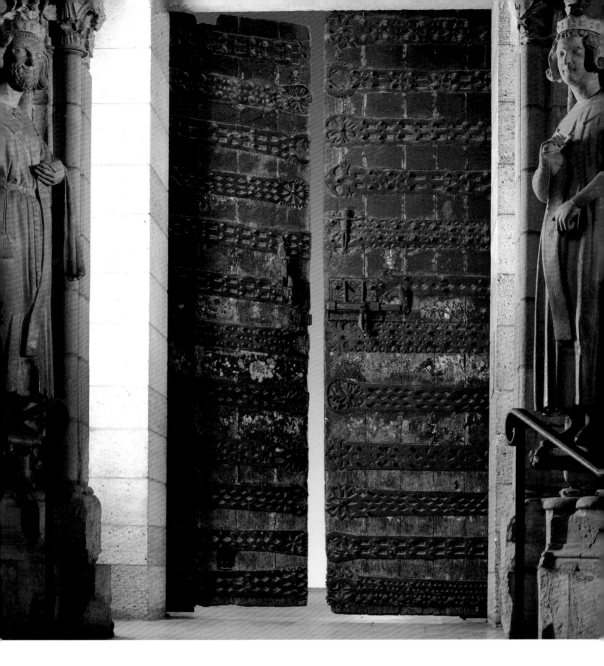

Pair of Doors with Ironwork

France or Spain, Pyrenees, 12th century
Oak and iron, 9 ft. 6 in. @ 39½ in. @ 2 in.
(289.6 @ 100.3 @ 5.1 cm)
The Cloisters Collection, 1925 (25.120.291, .292)

When closed and bolted, these massive doors
provided considerable defense against weapons
such as battering rams and other war machines.
Their vertically arranged oak planks are rein-
forced with spiked iron bands on the exterior
and crossbeams on the interior. Except for the
fifteenth-century lock, the doors and ironwork
are believed to have come from a twelfth-
century building in the Pyrenees. The twenty-
four iron bands affixed horizontally to the doors
are pierced with geometric patterns such as
diamonds, dots, and rectangles. The terminals
of the bands are decorated with fanciful motifs
resembling animal heads, treetops, or wheels.
The wheel-shaped terminal directly above the
lock contains an image of the crucified Christ.

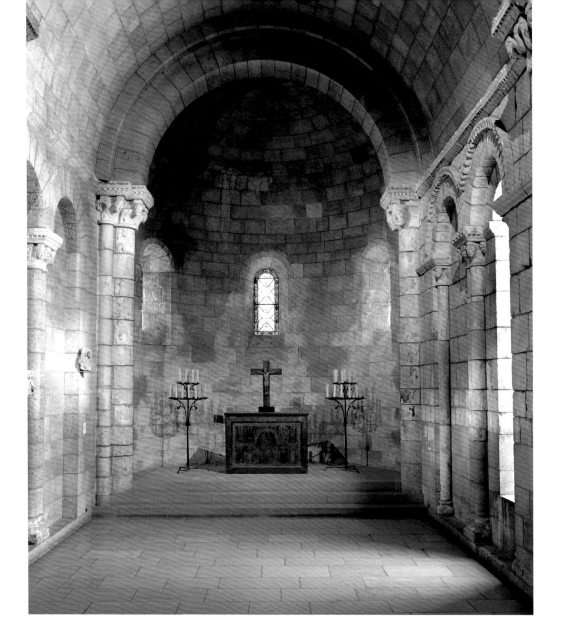

Chapel from Notre-Dame-du-Bourg at Langon

France, Aquitaine (Gironde), after 1126
From the church of Notre-Dame-du-Bourg
at Langon, near Bordeaux
Limestone, 22 ft. 4½ in. @ 16 ft. 5½ in.
(682 @ 502 cm) overall
Rogers Fund, 1934 (34.115.1–.269)

Parts of this chapel-like gallery were constructed
with twelfth-century limestone blocks from the
church of Notre-Dame-du-Bourg at Langon,
southeast of Bordeaux. According to one
seventeenth-century document, the small
parish church—which had a single-aisle nave,
slightly projecting transepts, and a semicircular
apse—was founded in 1126 as a dependency
of the nearby abbey of Notre-Dame-de-la-
Grande-Sauve (see p. 59). Seven capitals from
the crossing and choir of Langon are installed in
this gallery, all of them decorated with human
heads or figures carved almost in the round.
The crowned female bust on one of the capitals
has often been identified as Queen Eleanor of
Aquitaine (1122?–1204), one of the most remarkable women of the Middle Ages. However,
other than a trip she took to the region with her

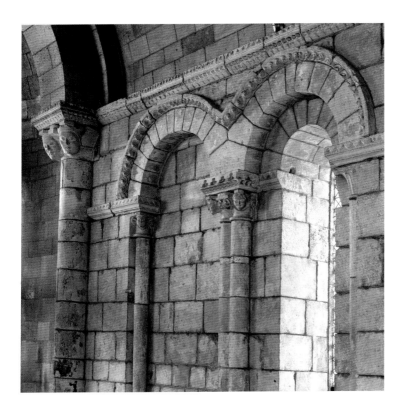

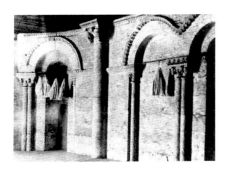

the French Revolution. By the early nineteenth century the choir had been divided into two levels: the lower served as a stable, while the upper became a dance hall, then a theater. When the Museum purchased the chapel fragments in 1934, the upper level was being used to store tobacco (left). The reconstructed chapel is about three-quarters of its original size.

husband, King Henry II of England (r. 1154–89), in the 1150s—when they might have spent one night at the nearby Notre-Dame-de-la-Grande-Sauve—there is no documentary evidence that Eleanor ever visited Langon or that the bust was intended to portray her. The blind arches lining the walls (above, top) and the predominantly geometric patterns decorating the abaci, arches, and cornices (right) are all characteristic of late twelfth-century architecture in western France.

Like many religious monuments in France, Notre-Dame-du-Bourg suffered repeated damage, especially from the Hundred Years' War and

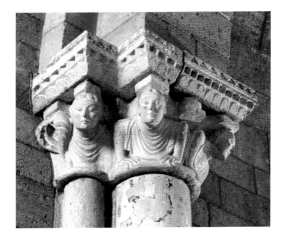

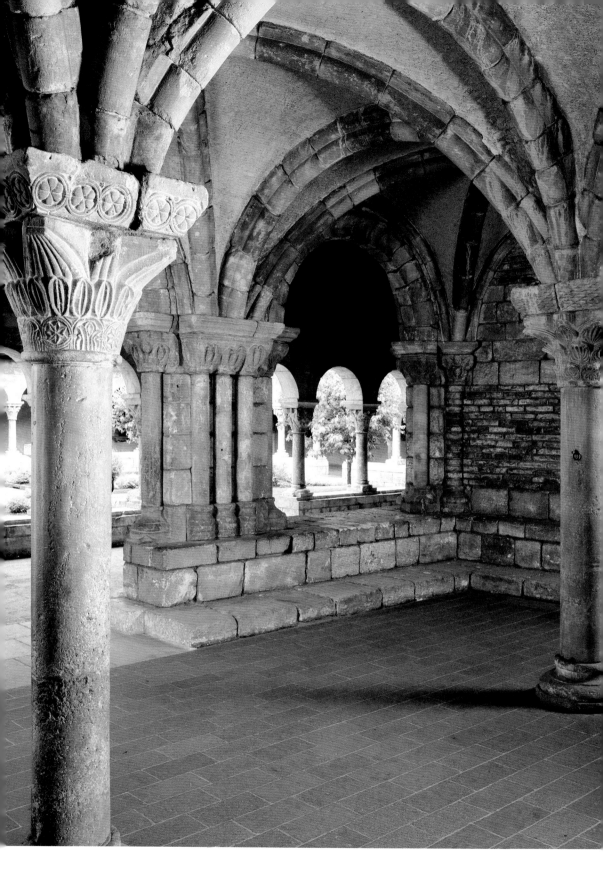

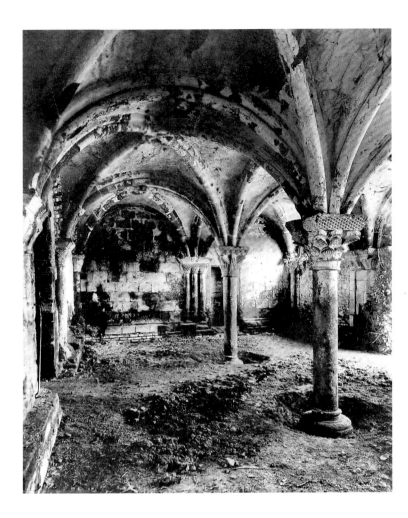

Chapter
house from
Pontaut
serving as a
stable, 1930

Chapter House from Notre-Dame-de-Pontaut

France, Aquitaine (Landes), 12th century
From the Cistercian abbey of Notre-Dame at Pontaut,
south of Bordeaux
Limestone, brick, and plaster, 37 ft. 9 in. @
25 ft. 4 in. (11.5 @ 7.7 m)
The Cloisters Collection, 1935 (35.50)

Notre-Dame-de-Pontaut, south of Bordeaux, was founded in 1115 as a Benedictine abbey but became a Cistercian house in 1151. As in most medieval monasteries, much of the abbey's liturgical and administrative business was conducted in the chapter house, where monks attending daily meetings would have sat on the continuous stone bench running along the walls. The chapter house was also the location for certain liturgies and rituals, such as the annual reenactment of Jesus washing the feet of his disciples before Easter. The walls of this chamber are constructed of limestone and brick and lined with engaged columns, each surmounted by a capital decorated with plant, animal, or geometric motifs. Two freestanding monolithic columns support the rib vaults above (opposite). Typical of monastic plans, the room opens onto the cloister walk through three large arches (pp. 48–49).

Much of Notre-Dame-de-Pontaut was damaged during an attack by the Huguenots in 1569, including the floor above the chapter house, where the dormitory might have been located. Following the sale of the monastic buildings to a local family, the chapter house was converted into a stable (above). It was purchased in 1932 by Parisian dealer Paul Gouvert, who sold it to the Metropolitan two years later. Although the tile floor and the plaster vaults are modern replacements, the rest of the chapter house has been reconstructed with original materials.

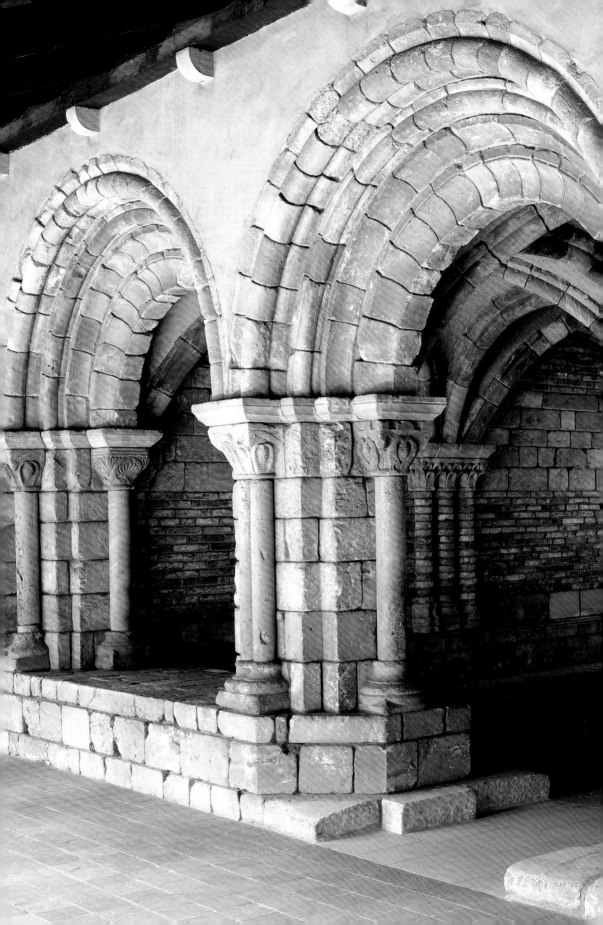

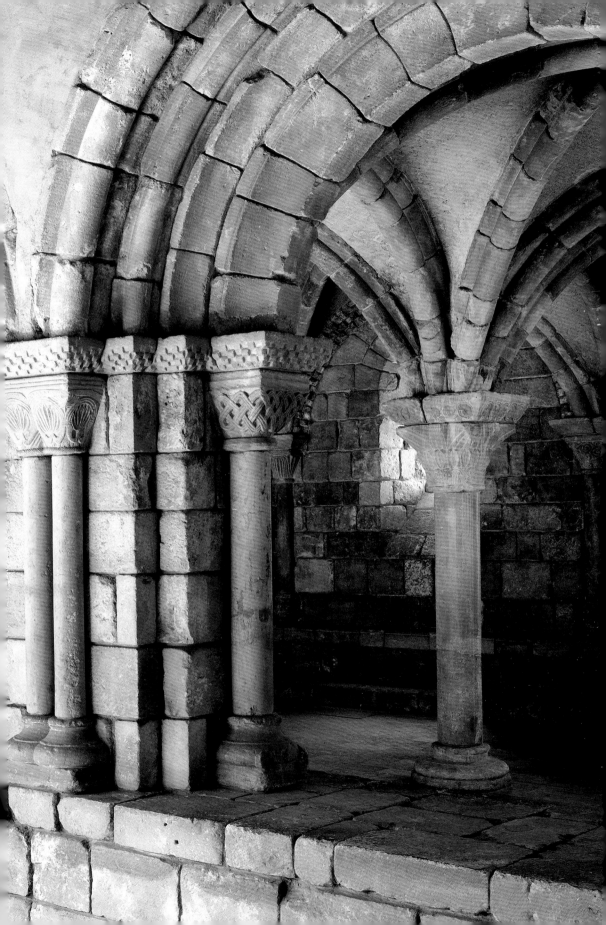

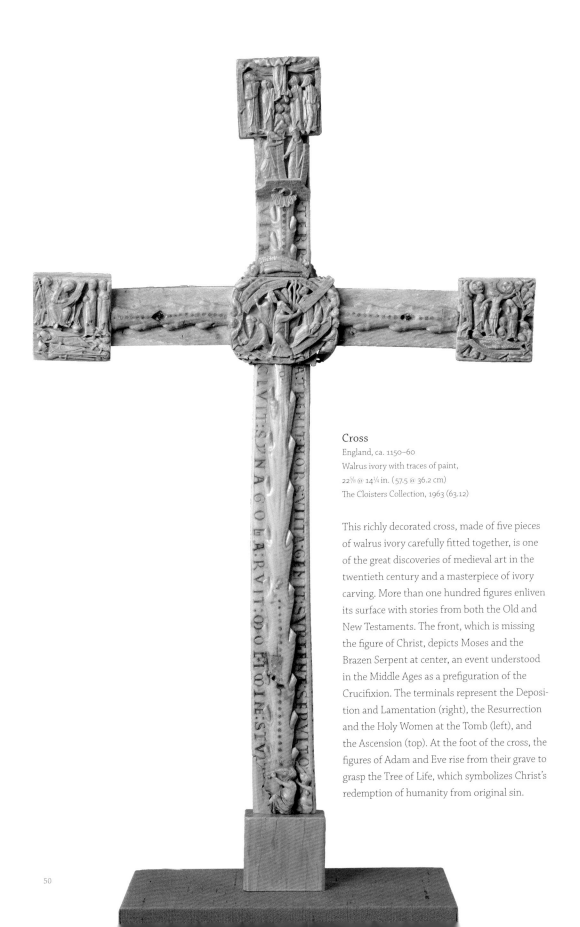

Cross

England, ca. 1150–60
Walrus ivory with traces of paint,
22⅝ @ 14¼ in. (57.5 @ 36.2 cm)
The Cloisters Collection, 1963 (63.12)

This richly decorated cross, made of five pieces
of walrus ivory carefully fitted together, is one
of the great discoveries of medieval art in the
twentieth century and a masterpiece of ivory
carving. More than one hundred figures enliven
its surface with stories from both the Old and
New Testaments. The front, which is missing
the figure of Christ, depicts Moses and the
Brazen Serpent at center, an event understood
in the Middle Ages as a prefiguration of the
Crucifixion. The terminals represent the Deposition and Lamentation (right), the Resurrection
and the Holy Women at the Tomb (left), and
the Ascension (top). At the foot of the cross, the
figures of Adam and Eve rise from their grave to
grasp the Tree of Life, which symbolizes Christ's
redemption of humanity from original sin.

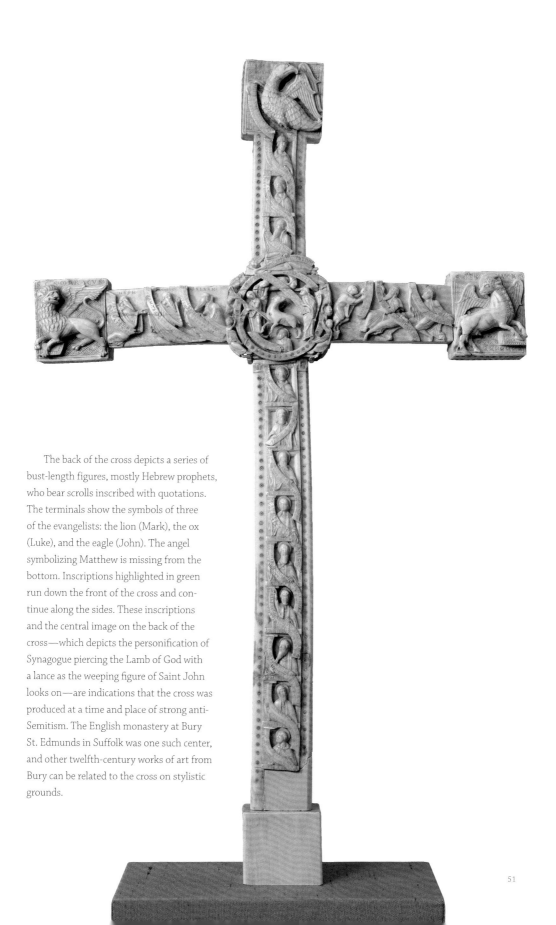

The back of the cross depicts a series of bust-length figures, mostly Hebrew prophets, who bear scrolls inscribed with quotations. The terminals show the symbols of three of the evangelists: the lion (Mark), the ox (Luke), and the eagle (John). The angel symbolizing Matthew is missing from the bottom. Inscriptions highlighted in green run down the front of the cross and continue along the sides. These inscriptions and the central image on the back of the cross—which depicts the personification of Synagogue piercing the Lamb of God with a lance as the weeping figure of Saint John looks on—are indications that the cross was produced at a time and place of strong anti-Semitism. The English monastery at Bury St. Edmunds in Suffolk was one such center, and other twelfth-century works of art from Bury can be related to the cross on stylistic grounds.

Martyrdom of Saint Lawrence

England, Kent, ca. 1175–80
From Christ Church Cathedral at Canterbury
Pot-metal glass and vitreous paint,
25½ @ 12⅝ in. (65 @ 32 cm)
The Cloisters Collection, 1984 (1984.232)

In scenes of his martyrdom Saint
Lawrence is most often depicted
stretched out on a gridiron (or grill).
Here, however, Lawrence is shown in
an attitude of supplication, an image
inspired by the writings of Saint
Augustine and Saint Ambrose. These
doctors of the church contended that
Saint Lawrence overcame the exter-
nal fire—the red flames seen licking
at his feet—by the power of three
fires within: the ardor of faith, the
love of Christ, and the true knowledge of God. These internal fires are
represented by the two horizontal

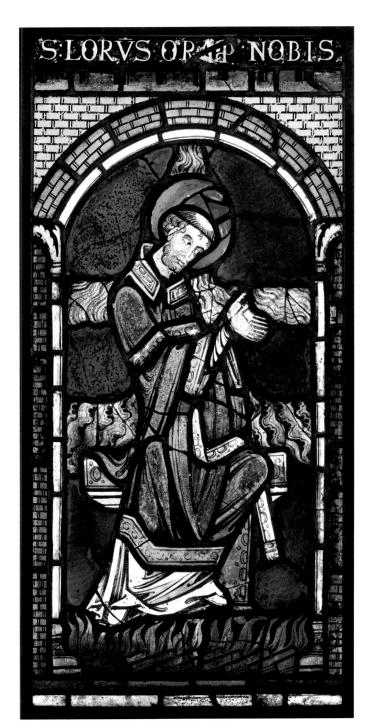

bands of rose-colored flame and the flame above Lawrence's head.

In its architecture and decoration, including an important program of stained-glass windows, Christ Church Cathedral at Canterbury is a major monument of the transitional style between Romanesque and Gothic that emerged about 1200. The importance of Canterbury increased dramatically after the murder of its archbishop, Thomas Becket, in 1170. Becket was canonized only three years later, and his tomb quickly became an important destination for pilgrims.

Plaque with Censing Angels

France, Limousin (Haute-Vienne),
Limoges, ca. 1170–80
Champlevé enamel and copper gilt,
4⅜ @ 8¾ in. (11 @ 22.1 cm)
The Cloisters Collection, 2001 (2001.634)

The two mournful, half-length angels on this plaque are set against stylized clouds and a brilliant gilt background engraved in a delicate scrolling pattern known as vermiculé. As they swing censers, the angels incline their heads to look down on what once was the crucified figure of Christ below. The plaque originally decorated what must have been one of the largest crosses produced in the prolific workshops of Limoges. The power of the design, the richness of the enameling, the control of the engraving, and the fine stippled decoration that accents the gilded lines of copper testify to the extraordinarily accomplished work made in that city by the end of the twelfth century. Judging from the size of surviving Limoges crosses, it is estimated that the cross embellished with this plaque would have stood at least four feet high. Although no cross of a size even approaching that survives, documents attest to the presence of monumental enameled crosses in Limoges and the surrounding area. Three other surviving pieces from the cross are known: from the bottom, a plaque depicting Adam rising from his tomb (Museo Sacro Vaticano, Vatican City), and from the lateral terminals the mourning figures of Saint John the Evangelist and the Virgin (British Museum, London).

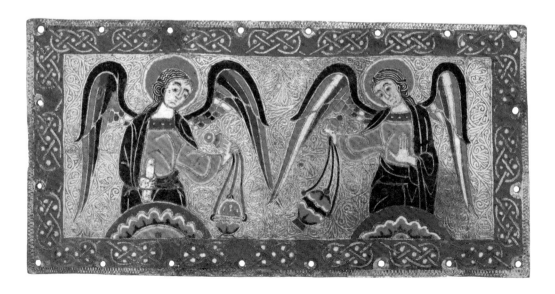

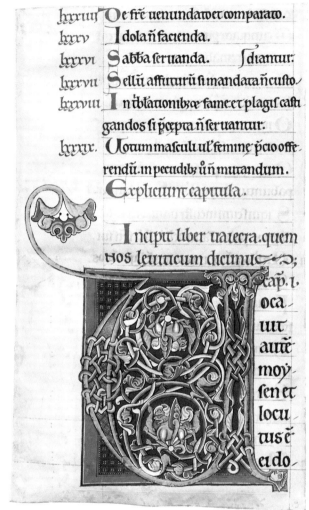

Initial *V* from a Bible

France, Burgundy (Yonne), ca. 1175–95
From the abbey at Pontigny
Tempera on parchment, 10⅞ @ 6 in.
(27.5 @ 15.2 cm)
The Cloisters Collection, 1999 (1999.364.2)

The Bible that originally contained this initial and a second example at The Cloisters has been lost. Both initials were removed from the manuscript, undoubtedly by an admiring collector, sometime during the nineteenth century. The *V*, which encloses two energetic lions amid vibrant foliage, marked the opening of the book of Leviticus: "Vocavit autem Moysen et locutus est ei Dominus de tabernaculo" (And the Lord called Moses, and spoke to him from the tabernacle).

Impressively large multivolume Bibles (some nearly twenty inches or more in height) are among the greatest achievements of twelfth-century manuscript illumination, and the Cistercian abbey of Pontigny in the diocese of Sens—where the Bible that once contained this initial came from—was renowned in the twelfth century for its collection. The monastery was a haven for the exiled English prelate Thomas Becket after his dispute with King Henry II of England and just before his martyrdom in Canterbury Cathedral in 1170. During the French Revolution the library at Pontigny was confiscated, the fate of so much French ecclesiastical art.

Reliquary Cross

France, Limousin (Haute-Vienne), Limoges, ca. 1180
Probably from the abbey of Grandmont, near Limoges
Silver gilt, rock crystal, and glass cabochons; wood core,
11¾ @ 4⅞ @ 1 in. (29.8 @ 12.5 @ 2.5 cm) with tang
Purchase, Michel David-Weill Gift, The Cloisters
Collection, and Mme. Robert Gras Gift, in memory
of Dr. Robert Gras, 2002 (2002.18)

This well-preserved, double-armed silver reliquary cross is bejeweled on both sides with more than sixty glass cabochons. The surface is further embellished with twisted wire, beading, repoussé florets, and engraved concentric circles. The relics, showcased in the gilded rectangular plaque at the intersection of the upper arm and set behind rock crystal cabochons on the principal face of the cross, are identified in inscriptions engraved on the sides. The most important is a piece of the True Cross, which was reputedly found in the fourth century by Helena, mother of Constantine the Great, and was thought to be the actual cross on which Jesus was crucified. That relic, along with the double-arm form of the cross (derived from early Byzantine examples), underscores the well-known connections with the Holy Land that existed in central France during the twelfth century as a result of the Crusades. Some Romanesque churches in the region, for example, incorporated domes in imitation of the Holy Sepulchre in Jerusalem.

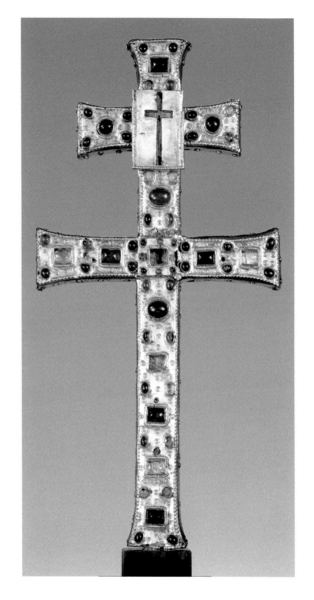

Cloister from Saint-Guilhem-le-Désert

France, Languedoc-Roussillon (Hérault),
late 12th–early 13th century
From the Benedictine monastery of
Saint-Guilhem-le-Désert, near Montpellier
Limestone, 30 ft. 3 in. @ 23 ft. 10 in. (922 @ 726 cm)
The Cloisters Collection, 1925 (25.120.1–.134)

Approximately 140 elements, including columns, pilasters, and capitals, mostly from the abbey of Saint-Guilhem-le-Désert, were used to reconstruct this cloister. The village of Saint-Guilhem-le-Desért is situated in a region of France with abundant remains of classical monuments, and the carving of these pieces reveals this considerable influence—evident, for example, in the use of acanthus leaves and meander patterns. Deep, cylindrical drill holes create a marvelous contrast of light and shadow on the carved surfaces of the stone. Nature also inspired some of the decorative motifs, among them the bark of tree trunks, intricate scrolling leaves and tendrils, and wavy patterns. In addition to a plethora of foliate designs, a few of the capitals are embellished with narrative scenes, such as the Presentation in the Temple and the Mouth of Hell (p. 58).

The cloister was part of a Benedictine monastery founded in 804 by Guilhem, duke of Aquitaine, count of Toulouse, and later saint (canonized 1066). A regular stop on the pilgrimage route to Santiago de Compostela in northwestern Spain, the abbey suffered severe damage during the Wars of Religion and the French Revolution. By about 1850 some archi-

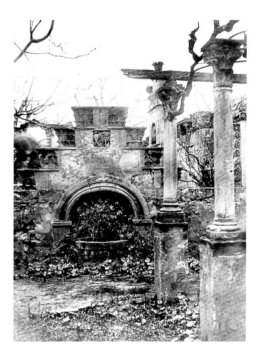

Architectural elements from Saint-Guilhem-le-Désert on display in the garden of Pierre-Yon Vernière, Aniane, France, before 1906

tectural and sculptural components of the cloister had been purchased by Pierre-Yon Vernière, a local judge, for display in his garden (above). In 1906 his heir sold the fragments, which were soon purchased by George Grey Barnard. Although installed here at eye level, the elements may have come from both levels of what had been a two-story cloister; the nearly complete dispersal of the cloister sculptures makes it impossible to trace each piece's original location. The carving style is typical of sculptures created at the turn of the thirteenth century.

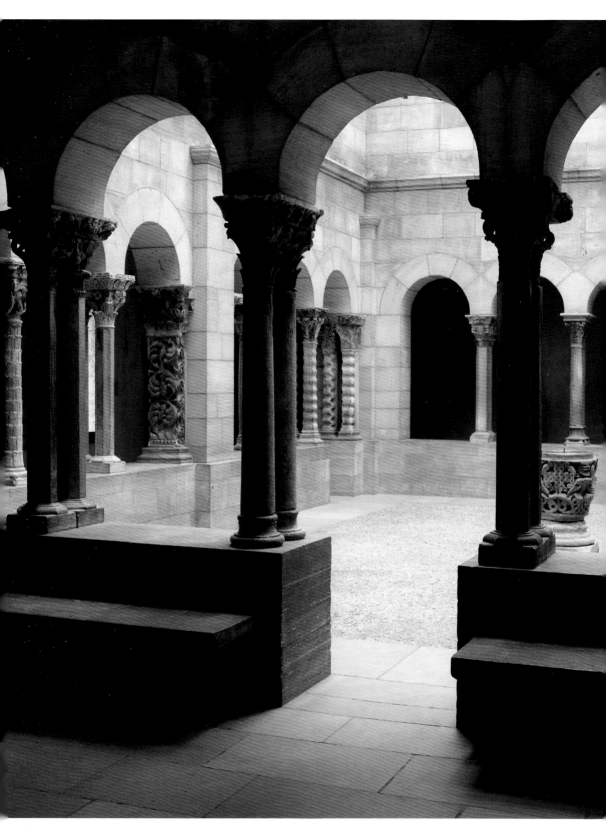

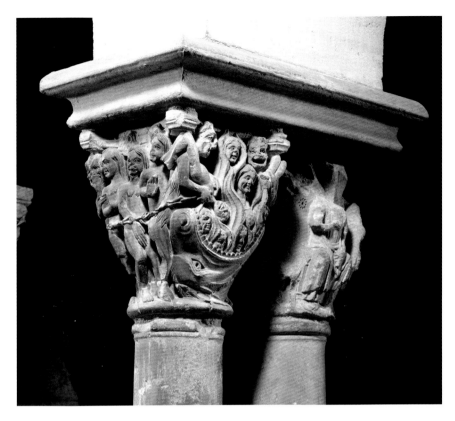

Details of capitals from Saint-Guilhem Cloister, showing the Mouth of Hell and acanthus leaves

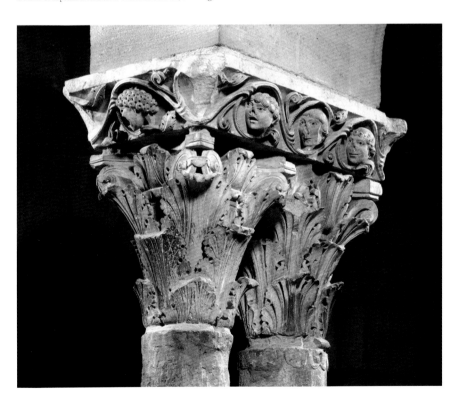

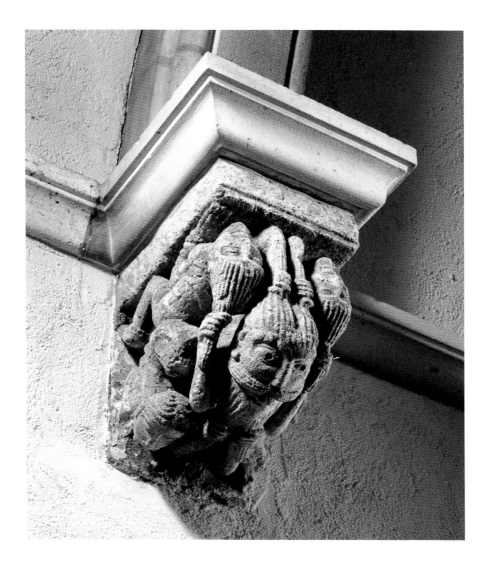

Corbel

France, Aquitaine (Gironde), 1150–1200
From the abbey of Notre-Dame-de-la-Grande-Sauve,
near Bordeaux
Limestone, 32 @ 15⅜ @ 18½ in. (81.3 @ 39.1 @ 47 cm)
Gift of George Blumenthal, 1934 (34.21.2)

Decorated with acrobatically intertwined figures pulling at one another's hair, this corbel belongs to a group from the Benedictine monastery of Notre-Dame-de-la-Grande-Sauve. They once supported the exterior cornice of the twelfth-century church and are embellished with a wide range of patterns and motifs. Many are still at the abbey; others are in different French and American collections. As a group, the corbels reveal a preference for acanthus leaves, a stylized rendering of anatomy, and a calligraphic treatment of hair, mane, and other linear details. Of the ten corbels now at The Cloisters, two are decorated with foliate motifs. Several of the others display more mischievous activities, such as hair or beard pulling and mouth poking, and a few are even sexually suggestive, perhaps an allusion to humanity's inner demons and licentious fantasies. Corbels like these enjoyed a lasting popularity and can be found on the exterior of many medieval churches.

Torso of Christ

France, Auvergne (Haute-Loire), late 12th century
Said to come from the abbey at Lavaudieu
Poplar with paint, tin leaf, and traces of parchment,
43 @ 13¾ @ 9½ in. (109.2 @ 34.9 @ 24.1 cm)
The Cloisters Collection, 1925 (25.120.221)

This fragmentary but sensitively carved
sculpture was for many years considered to be
from a crucifix. The position of Christ's body,
however, which is bent slightly at the waist,
suggests that the work more likely was one
of a group of sculptures that represented the
Deposition, or the removal of Christ's body
from the Cross. Despite major losses, the torso
retains great sculptural power arising from the
careful modeling of the body and the rhythmic
patterns of the drapery. When discovered by
George Grey Barnard near Lavaudieu, the piece
was being used in a field as a scarecrow. The
arms, legs, and (probably) head were originally
separate elements held in place by dowels in
mortise-and-tenon joints. The original paint
is obscured by a later medieval overpainting.
Examination has revealed that the loincloth
was originally painted with a layer of lapis
lazuli blue studded with applied tin leaf and a
brilliant red lining.

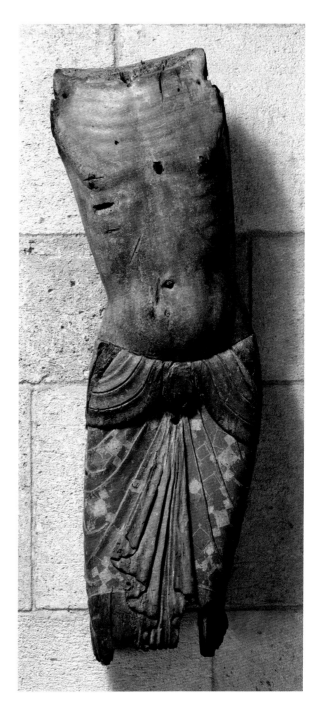

Altar Frontal

Catalonia (Lleida), ca. 1225
From the church of Santa María de Ginestarre,
near Esterri de Cardós, Spain
Wood with gesso, canvas, and paint, 37¾ @
58 @ 2¾ in. (95.9 @ 147.3 @ 7 cm)
The Cloisters Collection, 1925 (25.120.256)

The altar, before which the Mass is celebrated,
is the most important piece of liturgical
furnishing within a church. In a large church
there are often many altars—the high altar,
in the choir, and several more in various
chapels and other spaces. At the center of
this altar frontal from the church of Santa
María de Ginestarre, near Esterri de Cardós,
are the Enthroned Virgin and Child encircled
by a mandorla, which is supported by four

angels (the bottom two damaged). Eight
apostles, haloed and standing under round
arches, accompany the central group. Painted
inscriptions along the upper border give the
names of six saints: Simon, Jude, Matthew,
John, Thomas, and Barnabas. The composition
is surrounded by a procession of prancing
lions, each enclosed in a roundel. The bottom
edge is missing.

This altar frontal was decorated using a
technique that sought to imitate the gold or
silver frontals made for large cathedrals or
wealthy monasteries. To achieve the luxurious
appearance of the enamels and gemstones
often set into more elaborate examples, the
design was molded in low relief in gesso and
then embellished with paint.

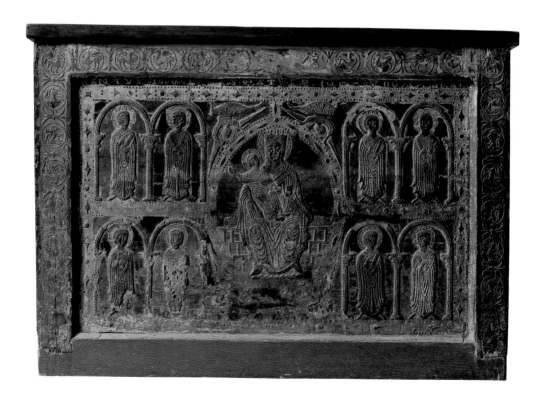

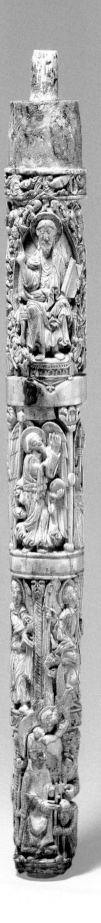

Segment of a Crosier Shaft

North Spain, late 12th century
Elephant ivory, H. 11¼ in. (28.6 cm);
DIAM. 1⅜ in. (3.5 cm)
The Cloisters Collection, 1981 (1981.1)

Richly carved, this ivory shaft was once a
section of a crosier, the staff carried by bishops
and abbots as a symbol of their office. The
carving is divided into four zones. At the
top, Christ is enthroned within a mandorla
embellished with bust-length figures of the
Elders of the Apocalypse. On the reverse of
that register, the Virgin and Child appear
enthroned within another mandorla. Filling
the two middle registers are angels dressed
as deacons. They are set within arcades, and
each carries an orb and a staff surmounted by
a lantern. The lower register depicts an angel
presenting a miter to an enthroned bishop as a
kneeling, secular donor hands him his crosier.
Because the bishop is not represented as a
saint, it seems likely that the scene refers to
the installation of a historical bishop.

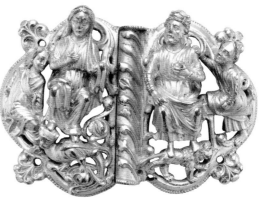

Bowl of a Drinking Cup
England or Scandinavia, late 12th century
Silver, silver gilt, and niello, H. 2¾ in. (7 cm);
DIAM. 6¾ in. (17.1 cm)
The Cloisters Collection, 1947 (47.101.31)

With its lively nude male figures and dragons
entwined in foliage, this bowl was likely part of
a secular drinking cup rather than a ciborium
(a vessel that holds the Host) or a chalice for
use in the Mass, as was once thought. Between
the principal compartments inhabited by the
nude figures and dragons are smaller areas with
basilisks. The heads of the men and beasts are in
high relief, and the bands between the compartments and the palmette frieze below the rim
are crisply rendered. The decoration of the bowl
has parallels in twelfth-century English art, but
similar pieces have also been found in Sweden.
This example was discovered near the Ob' River
in Siberia, an indication of how objects in the
Middle Ages sometimes circulated far from their
place of manufacture.

Clasp
South Netherlands, Meuse valley, ca. 1200
Gilt copper alloy, 2⅛ @ 2⅞ @ ⅝ in. (5.4 @ 7.3 @ 1.6 cm)
The Cloisters Collection, 1947 (47.101.48)

Exquisitely decorated and probably destined
for secular use, this clasp depicts an enigmatic
scene. A crowned male figure holding an orb is
enthroned at right, his feet resting on the back
of a lion, as a kneeling attendant places a hand
on his shoulder. On the other side is a veiled
female figure, also accompanied by an attendant,
resting her feet on a basilisk. Although the
couple has sometimes been seen as Solomon
and Sheba or as Esther and Ahasuerus,
no conclusive identification has emerged.

Compositionally, the figures recall late twelfth-
century depictions of the Coronation of the
Virgin. The stylistic features of the clasp, such
as the drapery drawn tight around the figures
and the foliage they inhabit, can be compared to
goldsmith works produced in the Meuse valley
about 1200.

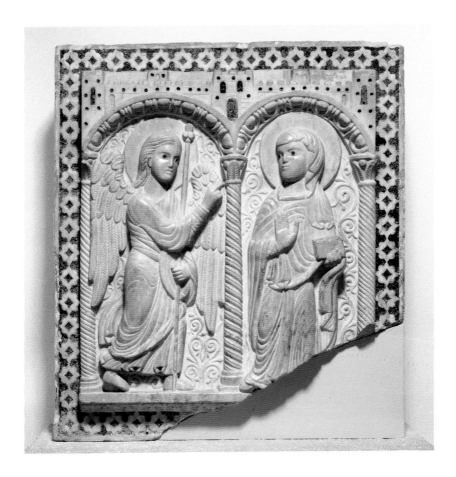

Relief with the Annunciation

Italy, Tuscany, ca. 1180–1200
From the church of San Piero Scheraggio in Florence
Carrara marble and verde di Prato (a form of serpentine),
26½ @ 24 @ 4¾ in. (67.3 @ 61 @ 12.1 cm)
The Cloisters Collection, 1960 (60.140)

The pulpit was a prominent element in the
medieval church. It was usually raised on columns above the choir and, during the Middle
Ages, used for readings from the Gospels and
the Epistles. In this panel from a pulpit, the
Archangel Gabriel announces to the Virgin that
she will be the mother of Christ. The figures
appear beneath an elaborate arcade supported
by twisted columns; the arches are embellished
with egg-and-dart molding and surmounted by
a design evoking a city wall. The marble relief,
with its decorative border inlaid with serpentine,
is characteristic of Tuscan sculpture at the end
of the Romanesque period (about 1200). It
is one of seven figurative carvings from a

rectangular pulpit originally in the Florentine
church of San Piero Scheraggio (now incorporated into the Uffizi). In 1782 the other six
panels were moved to the suburban church
of San Leonardo at Arcetri.

Lion

Spain, Castilla-León (Burgos), ca. 1200
From a room above the chapter house of the
monastery of San Pedro de Arlanza, near Burgos
Fresco transferred to canvas, 7 @ 11 ft. (213 @ 335 cm)
The Cloisters Collection, 1931 (31.38.1a, b)

The Benedictine monastery of San Pedro de
Arlanza, in northern Spain, was founded in
912 by Fernán González, count of Castile. A
two-story square structure stood southeast of
the monastic church. The ground level of that
building served as the chapter house; the room
on the upper level, the so-called Tower of the

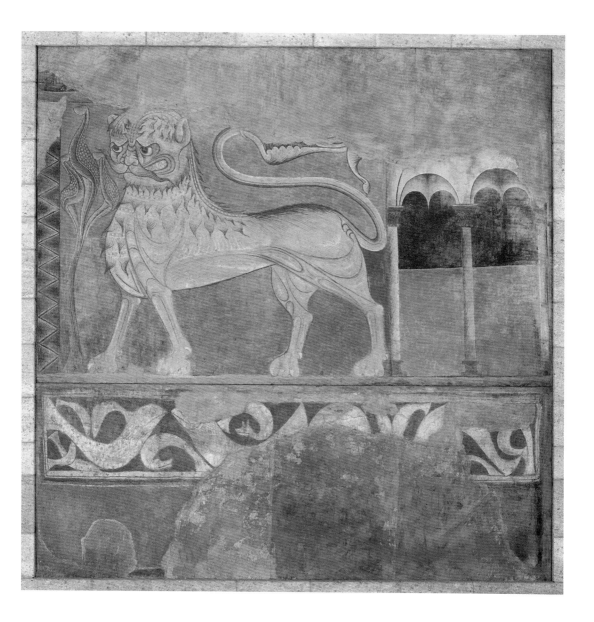

Treasure (Torro del Tesoro), was decorated with an extensive fresco cycle, including this mustachioed, prancing lion. The beast is framed within a rectangular field set against a background of solid bands of earth tones. Human and animal figures, both realistic and fantastic, fill the horizontal borders below the lion and its companion piece, which depicts a winged dragon. The Cloisters' lion was half of an imposing pair of lions on the east wall (the other is in the Museu Nacional d'Art de Catalunya, Barcelona). The Cloisters' dragon faced a griffin (also in Barcelona) across a double window on the south wall.

Although the date for the construction of the building is unknown, the style and subject matter of the frescoes suggest they were executed in the early thirteenth century. The frescoes were hidden beneath a layer of plaster applied as part of an eighteenth-century renovation and were only rediscovered in 1894, when a fire destroyed some of the plaster. By that time the monastery was already in private hands. The frescoes, along with everything else on-site, were removed and sold in the late 1920s to different institutions and private collectors.

Doorway from Notre-Dame at Reugny

France, Auvergne (Allier), late 12th century
From the church of Notre-Dame at Reugny,
near Clermont-Ferrand
Limestone, 14 ft. 9¾ in. @ 11 ft. 2⅝ in. (452 @ 342 cm)
Gift of George Blumenthal, 1934 (34.120.1–.120)

This doorway once stood on the west façade of
the small Augustinian priory of Notre-Dame at
Reugny (below), not far from Clermont-Ferrand
in central France. The two pairs of columns
flanking the door have molded archivolts above
them, which form a gently pointed arch typical
of the mid- to late twelfth century. A five-lobed
arch crowns the door opening; on the tips of its
four cusps are the symbols of the Four Evangelists, and four flowerlike decorations adorn the
spandrels in between. The remnant of a statue
is visible on the right jamb.

The doorway belongs to a sizable yet little-
known group of polylobed doorways, typically
having about three to seven lobes, found in central France. Sometime after 1920 this example
was sold to George Blumenthal, who installed
it in his Paris home as the main entrance to
his freestanding "Salle de Musique." In 1934
Blumenthal donated the doorway to The
Cloisters, where it now stands at the entrance
to the Saint-Guilhem Cloister.

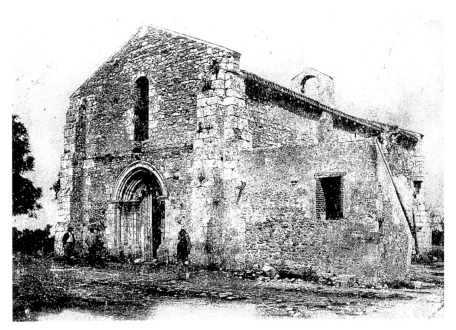

Priory of Notre-Dame at Reugny, 1920

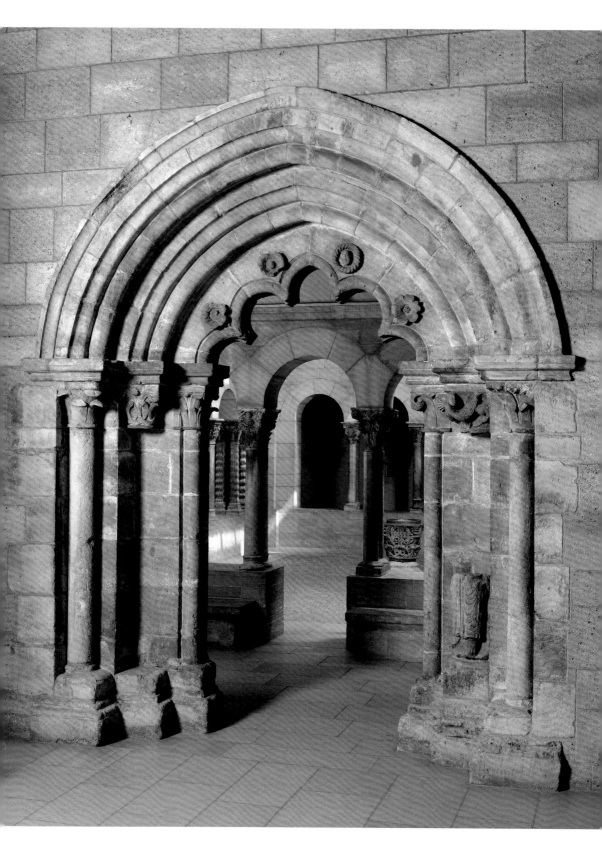

Doorway from Moutiers-Saint-Jean

France, Burgundy
(Côte-d'Or), ca. 1250
From the abbey of Moutiers-
Saint-Jean, near Dijon
Limestone with traces of paint,
15 ft 5 in. @ 12 ft. 7 in. (4.7 @ 3.8 m)
The Cloisters Collection, 1932 (32.147)
The Cloisters Collection, 1940
(40.51.1, .2)

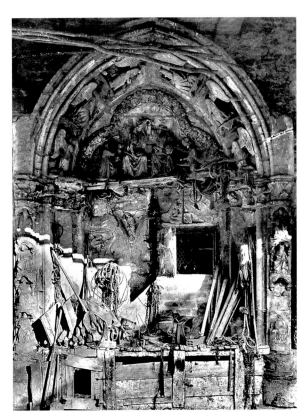

Doorway from Moutiers-Saint-Jean fitted into a farm building, 1920s

Framed by a trefoil arch, the tympanum of this doorway is decorated with the Coronation of the Virgin attended by two kneeling angels. Six other kneeling angels on the surrounding archivolt hold liturgical instruments. On each side of the door is a row of biblical figures in niches. Two large crowned figures, identified in a 1567 description as the Merovingian kings Clovis and Clothar, stand before the jamb columns. According to the same document, the doorway, from the monastery of Moutiers-Saint-Jean, probably served as the south transept portal, facing the cloister.

Founded in the sixth century by followers of Saint John of Réome, Moutiers-Saint-Jean and its archives suffered severe damage during the Wars of Religion and the French Revolution. Our knowledge of the abbey and its physical appearance can be gleaned only from the handful of drawings produced by the Maurist brothers whose congregation took over the monastery in the mid-1630s. In 1797 the surviving remains of the monastery were sold into private hands; it was probably during this period that the doorway, without the royal figures, was refitted for a farm structure (above). In the 1920s the owner of the farm sold the doorway, which entered The Cloisters' collection in 1932. The figures of Clovis and Clothar, decapitated probably in the sixteenth century and variously reassembled since, were acquired from a different owner eight years later.

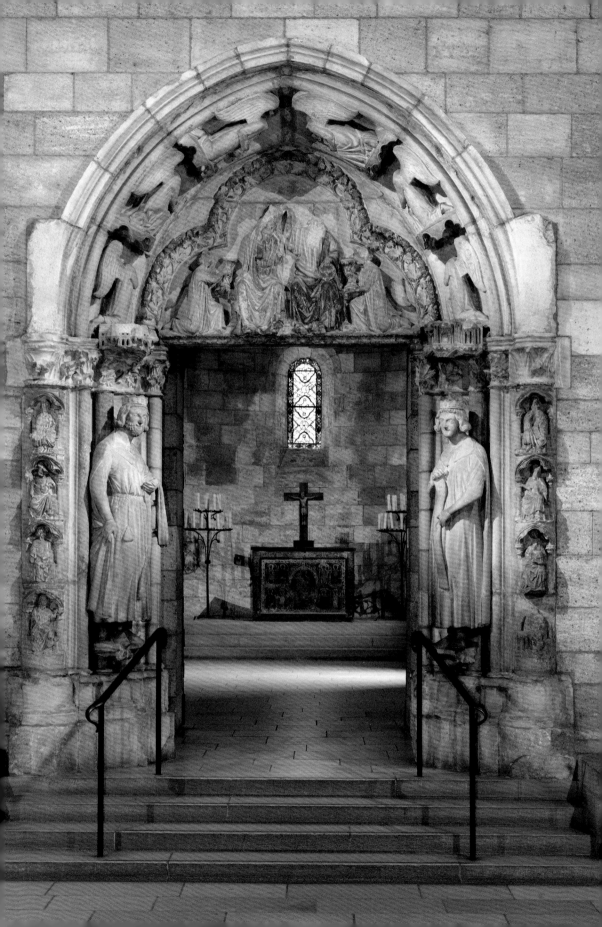

Theodosius Arrives at Ephesus

France, Normandy (Seine-Maritime), ca. 1200–1205
From the nave aisle of the cathedral of Notre-Dame
at Rouen
Pot-metal glass and vitreous paint,
25 @ 28⅛ in. (63.5 @ 71.5 cm)
The Cloisters Collection, 1980 (1980.263.4)

This panel is part of an extensive cycle depicting the legend of the Seven Sleepers, who, having converted to Christianity during the time of the Roman emperor Decius (r. 249–51), hid in a cave near Ephesus in Asia Minor to avoid being persecuted. As Roman soldiers sealed the cave with a boulder, God answered their prayers for safety by putting the group into a deep sleep. Awakening two centuries later in the reign of the Christian emperor Theodosius II (r. 408–50), one of the Seven Sleepers tried to buy bread with an obsolete gold coin and was thought to be a thief. Only after the Sleepers had been brought before the authorities was their story recognized as a miracle.

The cycle was originally made for side-aisle windows in the nave of the cathedral of Notre-Dame in Rouen in the early thirteenth century. Chapels were added to the side aisles in the 1270s, so the glass was refitted in the windows of the new chapels. This one depicts Theodosius arriving at Ephesus to visit the Sleepers. The lively gestures and vivid colors attest to the superb quality of the glass, ranked among the best cycles of the period.

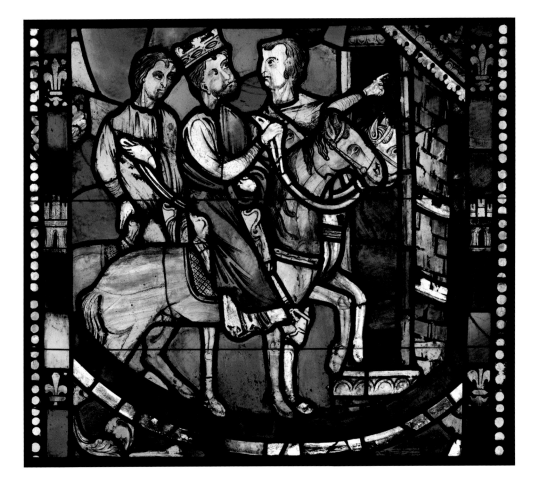

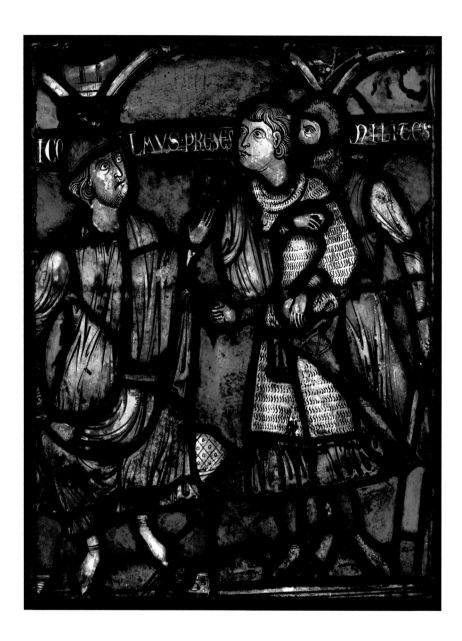

Scene from the Life of Saint Nicholas

France, Picardy (Aisne), ca. 1200–1210
From the cathedral of Saint-Gervais-Saint-
Protais at Soissons
Pot-metal glass and vitreous paint,
21⅜ @ 16 in. (54.2 @ 40.7 cm)
The Cloisters Collection, 1980 (1980.263.2)

This panel illustrates an early episode in the
life of Saint Nicholas, soon after he was elected
bishop of Myra in Asia Minor in the fourth century. Here, two knights falsely accused of trea-
son are condemned to death by the consul.

A third knight, the right arm of the consul, and
the beginning of the inscription—[S N]ICO/ LAVS:
PR[A]ESES/ MILITES (Nicholas protects the soldiers)—were lost when the panel was cut down
at an undetermined time.

The panel and another at The Cloisters probably came from an ambulatory chapel dedicated to
Saint Nicholas in the cathedral of Soissons, whose
choir was under construction in the 1190s. The
elegant figural style and flowing drapery patterns
exemplify a classicizing trend found in northern
France at the turn of the thirteenth century.

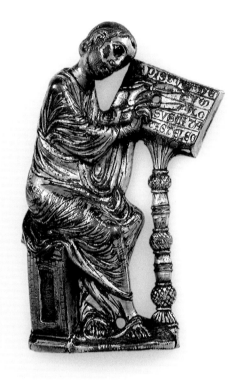
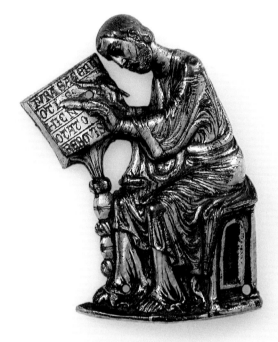

Evangelists Mark and Luke

France, Limousin (Haute-Vienne), Limoges, ca. 1220–30
Probably from the abbey of Grandmont, near Limoges
Gilded copper and glass, Mark (.1): 6⅞ @ 4⅜ @ 1¼ in.
(17.4 @ 11.2 @ 3.1 cm); Luke (.2): 6½ @ 4¾ @ 1⅜ in.
(16.5 @ 12.1 @ 3.6 cm)
Purchase, The Cloisters Collection, Michel David-Weill
Gift, and Gifts of J. Pierpont Morgan and George
Blumenthal, by exchange, 2012 (2012.70.1, .2)

Limoges metalworkers were justly famous for
their accomplishments in champlevé enamel,
but these figures in high relief demonstrate that
they were adept sculptors as well. Each relief was
raised from a single sheet of copper and finely
engraved before gilding. This pair represents
two of the Four Evangelists and likely decorated
the frontal of the high altar at the abbey of

Grandmont, where, with Saints John and
Matthew, they would have surrounded the central image of Christ in Majesty. The Grandmont
altar frontal was demolished in 1790; several
documents dated before the French Revolution
inform us that in addition to Christ in Majesty
surrounded by the evangelists, the frontal
included figures of the Twelve Apostles. Only
the evangelists Mark and Luke and some of the
apostles survive—one of these, Saint James, is
in the Metropolitan Museum (17.190.123). The
sculptural quality of the figures conveys the
intensity of the act of writing the Gospels and
is matched by sophisticated Latin inscriptions
that allude to the symbols of the evangelists:
the lion for Mark and the ox for Luke.

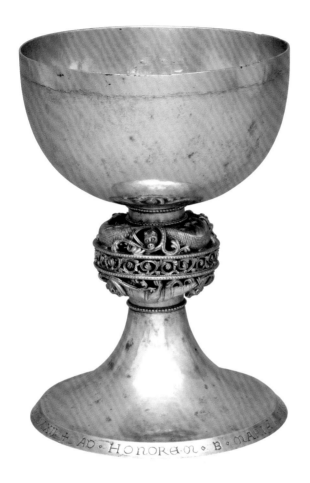

Chalice

Northern Europe, possibly Meuse valley,
dated 1222
Silver and silver gilt, H. 7½ in.
(19.1 cm); DIAM. 5⅜ in. (13.7 cm)
The Cloisters Collection, 1947 (47.101.30)

The Latin inscription on the foot of the chalice reads: AD HONOREM B. MARIE VIRGINIS F. BERTINUS ME FECIT AO MCCXXII (In honor of the Blessed Virgin Mary brother Bertinus made me in the year 1222). The inscription is remarkable because historians of medieval art rarely have the advantage of a date or the name of a patron or maker. It is all the more frustrating, then, that brother Bertinus has not been further identified, and that the place where this chalice was manufactured thus remains unknown. The style, apparent in the richly decorated knop with encircling dragons, is closely related to the metalwork production in the Meuse valley, in present-day Belgium. Mosan metalworkers were widely admired, though, so it is possible the chalice was produced elsewhere in northern Europe by a silversmith imitating the Mosan style.

Arm Reliquary

South Netherlands, Meuse valley, ca. 1230
Silver and silver gilt over wood core, niello,
and gems, 25½ @ 6½ @ 4 in. (64.8 @ 16.5 @ 10.2 cm)
The Cloisters Collection, 1947 (47.101.33)

Documents tell us that reliquaries in the form
of hands and arms were made beginning in the
early Middle Ages. Traditionally such reliquaries
contained relics of the part they represented. In
this example the hand gestures in benediction,
with the thumb and first two fingers raised.
The sanctity of the relics, regardless of their
type, would have served to increase the sacral
power of this gesture. The two large holes in
the arm served as cavities for the relics (now
lost) and were probably originally covered with
rock crystals. The reliquary is distinguished
artistically by a series of fine filigree and niello
plaques, which compare closely with Mosan
work of about 1230. Some of the niello plaques
are purely decorative in pattern, but five near
the top represent figurative images such as
Saints Peter and Paul.

Chalice, Paten, and Straw

Germany, Upper Rhineland, probably
Freiburg im Breisgau, ca. 1230–50
From the Benedictine monastery of Saint Trudpert
at Münsterthal, near Freiburg im Breisgau
Silver, silver gilt, niello, and jewels
Chalice: H. 8 in. (20.3 cm); DIAM. 7¾ in. (19.7 cm)
Paten: DIAM. 8¾ in. (22.2 cm)
Straw: H. 1 in. (2.5 cm); L. 8½ in. (21.6 cm);
DIAM. ¼ in. (0.6 cm)
The Cloisters Collection, 1947 (47.101.26–.28)

Chalice, paten, and straw were all used to cele-brate the Eucharist, the commemoration of Christ's sacrifice by the taking of consecrated bread and wine believed to be transformed into his body and blood during Mass. The chalice contained the consecrated wine, which was sipped with the straw to prevent spilling even a drop, and the paten held the bread. The four

Old Testament scenes represented in relief on the foot of this chalice were seen as prefigurations of the New Testament scenes on the knop above: Moses and the Burning Bush (the Annunciation); the Flowering of Aaron's Rod (the Nativity); Noah's Ark (the Baptism of Christ); and Moses and the Brazen Serpent (the Crucifixion). The niello decoration on the exterior of the bowl represents Christ enthroned with the standing figures of the Twelve Apostles. The paten includes a half-length figure of Christ holding a chalice and the Host. He is flanked by the Old Testament figures Abel, offering a lamb, and Melchisedech, clad as a bishop and raising a chalice. The fourth figure on the paten is Saint Trudpert, who holds a martyr's palm, indicating that this set of imple-ments comes from the monastery of Saint Trudpert, near Freiburg im Breisgau.

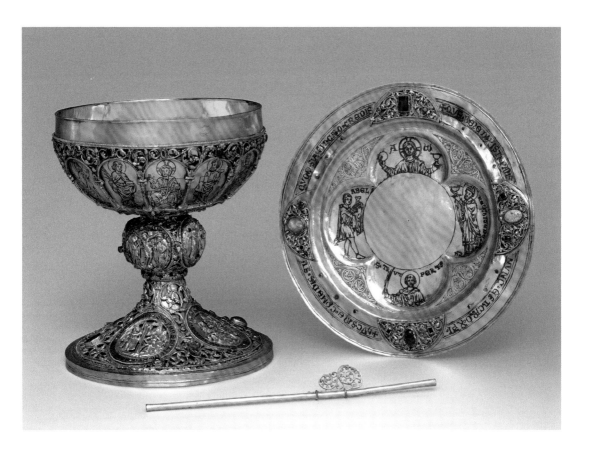

Virgin

Alsace (modern France), ca. 1250
From the former choir screen of the
cathedral of Strasbourg
Sandstone with original paint and
gilding, H. 58½ in. (148.6 cm)
The Cloisters Collection, 1947 (47.101.11)

The monumental choir screen at Strasbourg
Cathedral, where this almost lifesize statue of
the Virgin once stood, was demolished in 1682 in
response to changing liturgical practices. A 1630
woodcut by Isaac Brunn (ca. 1590–after 1657)
shows the original appearance of the screen,
which stood at the juncture of the nave and
crossing. It was constructed with two parallel
rows of seven arches. Above the arches was
a parapet platform decorated with openwork
quatrefoils from which announcements were
made and sermons delivered. The standing
statues, including this Virgin, were installed
between the gabled arches facing the nave.
Another image from about 1660 (opposite, top)
shows our statue as the fourth figure from the
left. To her right was the Christ Child (now
missing) sitting on a rosebush, a symbol of
the Virgin as a "rose without thorns." The now
armless Virgin gazes gently at the viewer. The
tender expression on her face and the cascading
drapery of her robe combine to create a sense
of realism that is at once elegant and engaging.
The statue is all the more remarkable because
much of its painted decoration survives, a
reminder that most Gothic sculpture was
embellished this way.

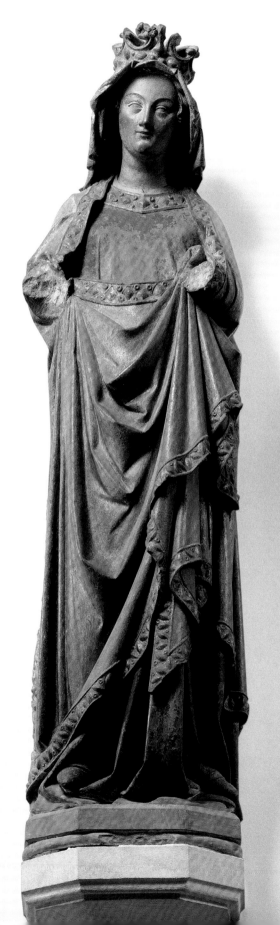

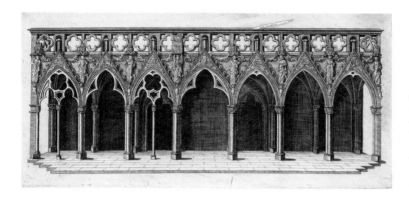

Jean-Jacques Arhardt (active 17th century). *Choir Screen of Strasbourg Cathedral*, ca. 1660. Engraving, 7⅛ @ 14⅝ in. (18 @ 37 cm). The Elisha Whittelesey Collection, The Elisha Whittelesey Fund, 1951 (51.501.6551 [8])

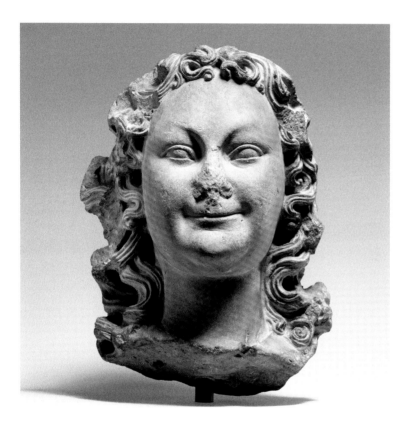

Head

France, Île-de-France, Paris, ca. 1250
Limestone, H. 9⅝ in. (24.5 cm)
Purchase, Michel David-Weill Gift, 1990 (1990.132)

Scientific analysis of the limestone used for this engaging head, perhaps that of an angel, confirms that it is the same as the stone with which the cathedral of Notre-Dame in Paris was built. The sensitive carving of the smiling face and the deeply cut, lively treatment of the hair link the head to the sculpture on the cathedral's north transept, which dates to about 1245. The well-preserved surface, however, suggests that the head was originally from an interior ensemble, possibly the cathedral's massive jubé, or choir screen (destroyed in the seventeenth century), or, alternatively, the interior of a transept. The head could also have come from another Parisian church of the mid-thirteenth century.

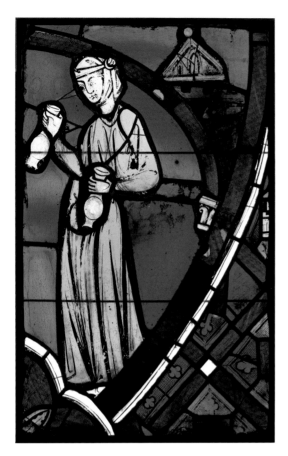
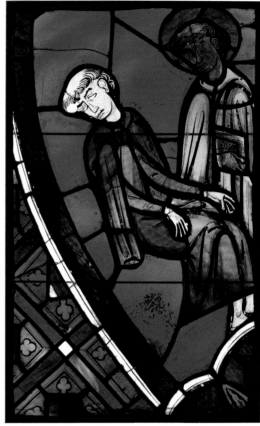

Two Scenes from the Legend of Saint Germain of Paris

France, Île-de-France, Paris, 1247–50
From the former Lady Chapel of the Benedictine
abbey of Saint-Germain-des-Prés in Paris
Pot-metal glass and vitreous paint,
25⅛ @ 15¾ in. (63.8 @ 40 cm) each
The Cloisters Collection, 1973 (1973.262.1, .2)

Prior to its demolition in 1802, the Lady Chapel
of the royal abbey of Saint-Germain-des-Prés
was glazed with an extensive program of stained
glass. Legends of the Virgin Mary, Saint Vincent
of Saragossa, and Saint Germain of Paris, on
color-saturated glass, occupied the seven windows in the apse. Ornamental grisaille glass
decorated windows along the straight bays. The
two panels at The Cloisters depict scenes from
the legend of Germain and the history of his
relics. In the first panel, a servant girl appears

carrying two wine flasks, one of which contains
poison. Unaware of the danger, she serves the
wine to Germain and his unfortunate companion, who drinks the poison and dies instantly.
In the second panel, a dreaming monk is reas-
sured by Germain himself that the saint's relics
would remain unharmed during the imminent
Norman invasion.

As originally arranged, each narrative scene
in the Lady Chapel would have included four
glass panels forming a complete oval. Some of
these ovals constituted one scene, while in others the top and bottom halves contained one
scene each. The ovals were arranged vertically
and interlocked by a single quatrefoil at every
contact point. The Lady Chapel's windows were
probably made by an itinerant workshop whose
stained glass can be traced to several sites in the
Île-de-France.

Enthroned Virgin and Child

France, Île-de-France, Paris, ca. 1260–80
Elephant ivory with traces of paint and gilding,
7¼ @ 3 in. (18.4 @ 7.6 cm)
Purchase, The Cloisters Collection and
Michel David-Weill Gift, 1999 (1999.208)

Paris emerged as the cultural capital of
western Europe during the reign of King
Louis IX (1226–70), a time when ivory became
an important medium for sculpture. Ivory
had often been a scarce commodity during
the earlier Middle Ages, but it appears that
a continuous supply of African elephant
ivory was available in Paris beginning about
the middle of the thirteenth century until
nearly the end of the fourteenth. The delicate
features of this Virgin and the sensitively
carved folds of her mantle reveal the
extraordinary skill of Parisian ivory carvers.
Even though the head of the Christ Child is
a modern replacement and the statuette has
lost all but traces of its original painted and
gilded decoration, the work still conveys the
intimate communication between mother
and child intended by the sculptor.

Diptych with the Coronation of the Virgin and the Last Judgment

France, Île-de-France, probably Paris, ca. 1260–70
Elephant ivory, 5 @ 5⅛ in. (12.7 @ 13 cm)
The Cloisters Collection, 1970 (1970.324.7a, b)

The new market for ivory carving that arose in Paris during the reign of Louis IX was fueled at least in part by the growing demand for works of art to be used for private devotion. The diptych form, seen here, proved ideal because it is highly portable, with the fragile carving protected inside the closed leaves. Thus ivory diptychs, rare in western Europe before the thirteenth century, became relatively commonplace by the fourteenth century.

This example is extraordinary for the fine quality of its deeply carved figures and the vivid imagery. At right, in the upper register, is Christ enthroned in Judgment and displaying the wounds from his Crucifixion. Angels appear bearing the Instruments of the Passion, and the Virgin and Saint John kneel in supplication. Below, trumpeting angels herald the rising of the dead, and the damned are hurled into the Mouth of Hell in the lower right corner. The Coronation of the Virgin is depicted in the upper section of the left leaf, while in the lower section we see the saved—including a friar followed by a king, a pope, and another cleric—being led by an angel up a ladder to heaven.

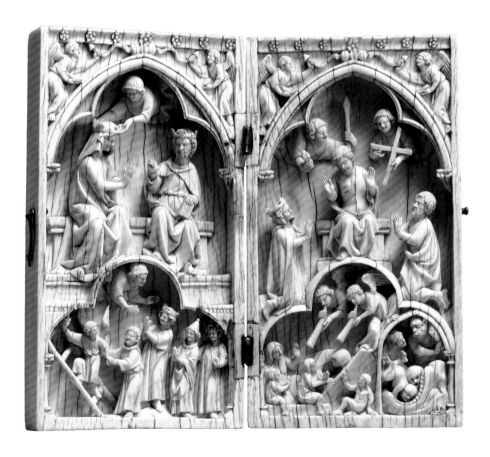

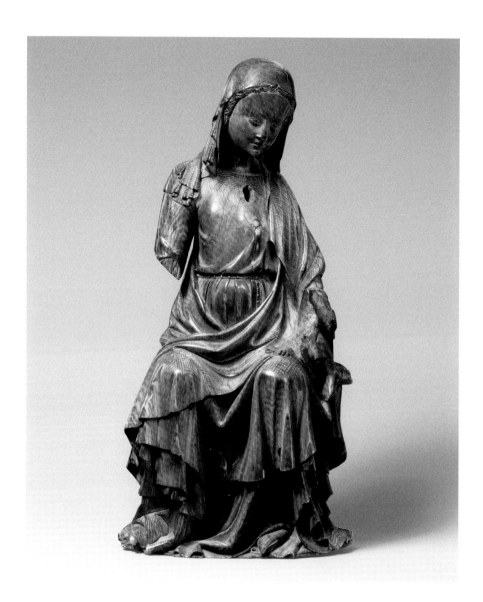

Enthroned Virgin and Child

England, probably London, ca. 1300
Elephant ivory, 10¾ @ 5⅜ @ 3¾ in.
(27.3 @ 13.5 @ 9.6 cm)
The Cloisters Collection, 1979 (1979.402)

Gothic ivory carving first emerged in Paris and
in northern France, but by about 1300 other
centers had begun to appear. Although English
ivories are comparatively rare, stylistic comparisons with architectural sculptures and with
some ivories displaying English coats of arms
indicate that this grand statuette was probably

carved there. Most of the figure of the Christ
Child is now missing, but the remaining part
of his leg by the Virgin's left knee suggests that
he was probably carved in a lively pose. The
cavity in the Virgin's chest may have originally
held a jewel, and she was probably seated on a
throne made of a different material. The unusually dark color of the ivory might be the result of
an application of walnut oil—as recommended
by the twelfth-century monk Theophilus in his
treatise *On Divers Arts*—or an effect of exposure
to extreme heat.

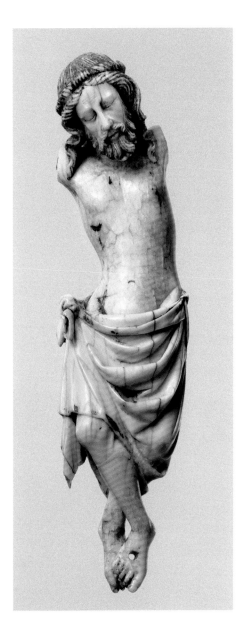

The Crucified Christ
Northern Europe, ca. 1300
Walrus ivory with traces of paint and gilding,
7½ @ 2⅛ @ 1⅜ in. (19.2 @ 5.3 @ 3.5 cm)
The Cloisters Collection, 2005 (2005.274)

Extraordinary in its monumental character and
sensitive rendering of the human body, this
statuette is one of the finest extant Gothic ivory
carvings of the crucified Christ. While hundreds
of Gothic ivory diptychs and triptychs and
more than fifty small sculptures of the Virgin

and Child survive, relatively few statuettes of
the crucified Christ remain, though many must
also have been made. Stylistically this piece
accords well with works produced in Paris about
1300 during the reign of King Philip the Fair
(1285–1314). The use of walrus ivory, however,
suggests that the sculpture was carved by a
Parisian artist (or one who had trained in the
French capital) active in England, Scandinavia,
or Cologne, where valuable elephant ivory was
less easily obtained. The arms, made separately,
have been lost.

Head of an Apostle
Alsace, probably Strasbourg (modern France),
ca. 1280–1300
Sandstone, H. 11⅞ in. (30 cm)
The Cloisters Collection, 2004 (2004.453)

This bearded head is carved from a single
block of pink, fine-grained sandstone of a type
often found in Alsace, in present-day France.
Overall it is in good condition with few signs
of weathering; on the back a vertical patch of
unfinished surface runs from the crown of
the head to the neck, suggesting that it came
from a statue that had been placed against a
wall or a niche in the interior of a church or
sheltered by a canopy on the exterior. Without
surviving attributes, the identity of the figure
remains unknown; most likely it represents
an apostle or saint. Although the head's gentle
facial features and voluminous hair and beard
recall an expressive figural style populating the
west facade of Reims Cathedral and the south
transept of the cathedral of Notre-Dame in Paris
in the 1250s and 1260s, its purposeful gaze and
slightly parted lips bear special resemblance
to a number of figures on the central portal of
the west facade of Strasbourg Cathedral, whose
construction began about 1275–77.

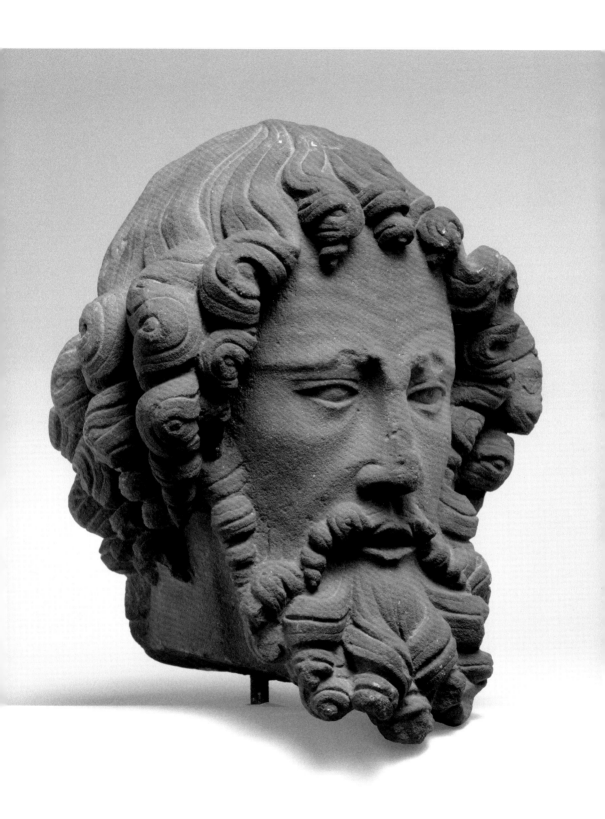

Cloister

France, Midi-Pyrénées (Haute-Pyrénées),
late 13th or early 14th century
With elements from the Franciscan monastery
at Tarbes and other nearby monuments
Marble, 54 ft. 3 in. @ 49 ft. (16.6 @ 14.9 m)
The Cloisters Collection, 1925 (25.120.531–.1052)

Reconstructed with twenty-one double capitals
surmounting slender columns, the L-shaped
arcade of this cloister screens the delightful
herb garden of the Museum. The decorations of
the capitals fall loosely into two groups: those
with bulbous leaves forming prominent volutes
at the corners (sometimes in two registers),
and those with large, flattened foliage hugging
the body of the capitals (below). Traditionally
thought to have come from a Cistercian
monastery in Bonnefont-en-Comminges near
Toulouse, at least nine of the double capitals (six
installed here, one in the Trie Cloister, and two

in storage) are now known to have come from a
late thirteenth-century Franciscan monastery in
Tarbes that was demolished in 1907–8. Stylistic
analyses of the remaining sculptures support
the long-held belief that they came from other
monuments in this region.

Not copied after any specific model, the layout of the cloister garden approximates that of a
medieval herb garden, with raised beds bordered
by bricks and wattle fences. Grouped and labeled
according to their medieval usage (e.g., medicinal, culinary, magic, household), all of the plants
grown in the garden are species documented
in medieval sources, such as the ninth-century
Capitulare de villis vel curtis imperialibus (Directive
for the Administration of Imperial Courts). Of
particular interest are the plants used by medieval artists, including those providing pigments
for manuscript painting and textile dyeing.

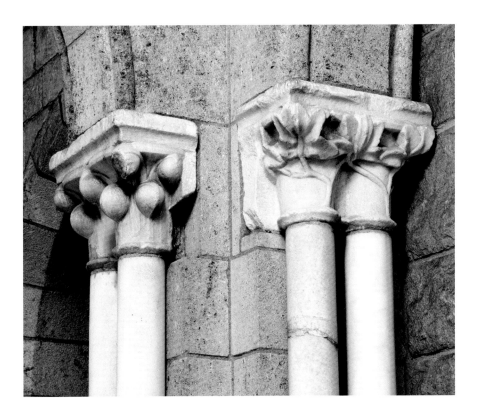

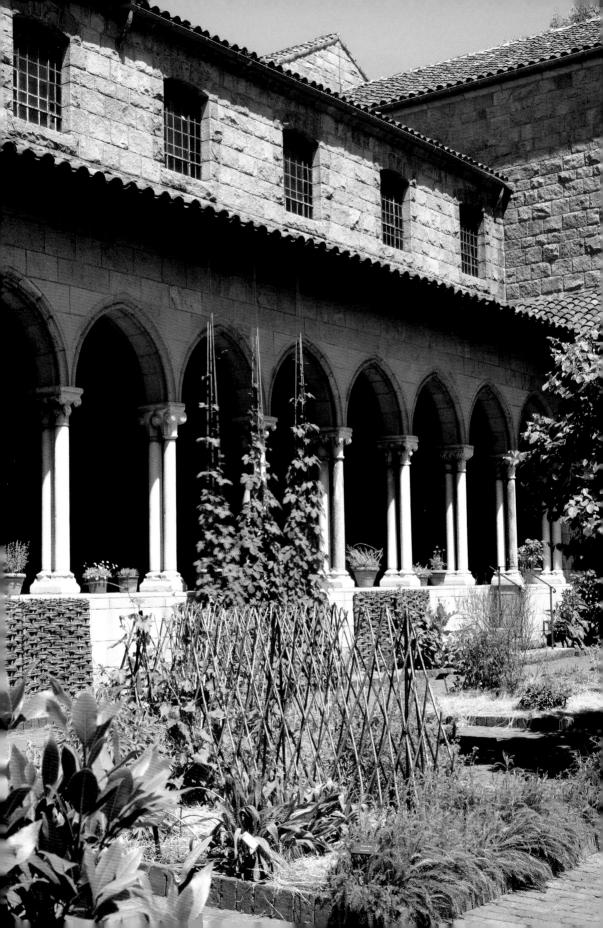

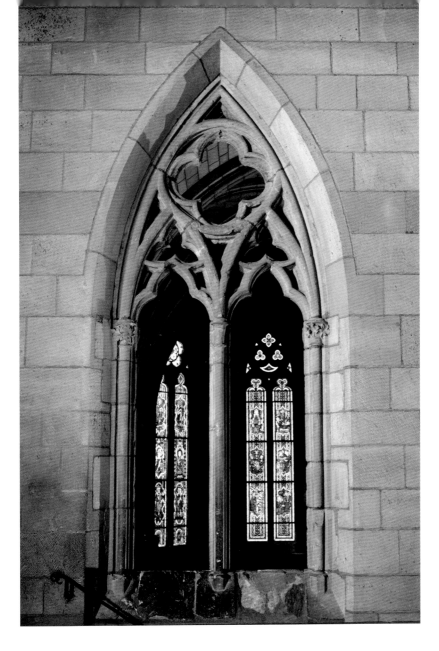

Double-Lancet Window

France, Poitou-Charentes (Vienne), ca. 1275–1300
From a church in La Tricherie, near Châtellerault
Limestone, 13 ft. 6 in. @ 7 ft. ⅝ in. (411.5 @ 214.9 cm)
The Cloisters Collection, 1934 (34.20.1)

This limestone window from La Tricherie, a small village near Châtellerault (between Tours and Poitiers), is constructed in a style typical of the late thirteenth century. The overall opening is organized into two identical lancets topped by a circle (oculus), which circumscribes a quatrefoil—a basic scheme that first appeared in window designs in the late twelfth century. In this version new elements have been introduced, such as trefoils composed of pointed, rather than rounded, leaf forms. The desire to create a diaphanous effect is evident in the piercing of the remaining surfaces between traceries, which leaves no solid fields in the skeletal structure. Small capitals decorate the vertical members (mullions) of the inscribed lancets. On the interior face the capitals are carved with broad, flattened leaves; on the exterior face the outer two are transformed into whimsical male and female heads.

Grisaille Lancet

France, probably Normandy, 1270–80
Pot-metal and colorless glass with vitreous paint,
94 @ 23¾ in. (238.8 @ 60.2 cm)
The Cloisters Collection, 2010 (2010.253.1–.4)

Designed with some of the most intricate and
complex patterns found in thirteenth-century
windows, these four panels of colorless grisaille
glass are organized by a latticework pattern in
dark blue glass, its intersections accentuated
alternately with painted bosses in dark red and
small red squares. Each boss is circumscribed
by two additional rings in grisaille; traversed
and interconnected by stems, together they
create an overall carpet effect of circular motifs.
Each red square marks the center of a pointed
quatrefoil pattern that fills the void between
the circular motifs. The composition is made
richer still with painted scrolling foliate motifs
and hairline hatching throughout. The ivylike
leaves entwined within the circular motifs are
almost identical to those on the grisaille panels
from the chapel of the Château de Bouvreuil in
Rouen (69.236.2–.9), now on display in the Early
Gothic Hall. Other characteristics comparable
to examples from Fécamp and Sées suggest that
these panels were produced in Normandy during
the third quarter of the thirteenth century.

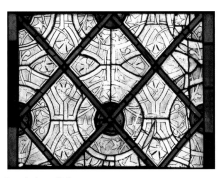

Detail of grisaille lancet

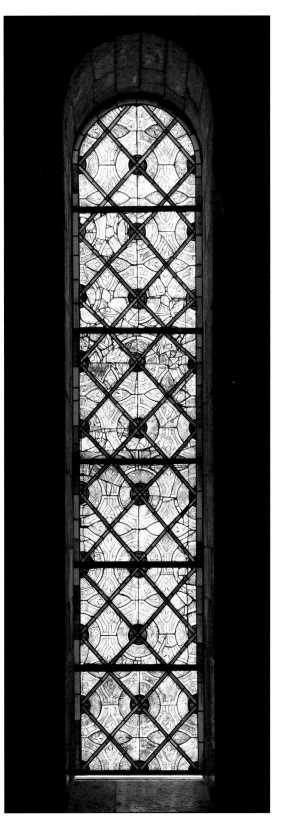

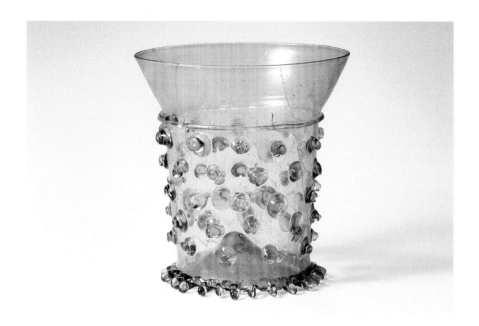

Beaker

Germany or Switzerland, late 13th–early 14th century
Free-blown colorless glass with applied decoration,
3⅝ @ 3¼ in. (9.1 @ 8.4 cm)
The Cloisters Collection, 2010 (2010.521)

By the thirteenth century, glass beakers with
prunted decoration were among the most commonly found types of drinking vessels in many
areas of Europe, though few have survived with
the delicate, thin-wall glass of which this beaker
is made. The cylindrical body is decorated with
five rows of prunts—blobs of molten glass
applied to the vessel and quickly turned and
pulled with a pontil to create the snail-like nubs.
A thin trail of glass circumscribes the juncture
between the body and the flaring neck, while
another, thicker trail of glass—crimped at
intervals—serves as the foot of the vessel. The
base of the beaker has a high kick, a conical dent
protruding into the vessel itself, which might
have been intended to prevent the piece from
breaking during the cooling process.

In contrast to glass that has a green tint,
caused by the presence of iron oxide in its raw
materials, here the addition of manganese oxide
has counteracted the effects of the iron and
resulted in the colorless glass frequently found
in southern Germany, Switzerland, and northern and central Italy.

Tomb Effigy of Jean d'Alluye

France, Loire valley (Indre-et-Loire), mid-13th century
From the Cistercian abbey of La Clarté-Dieu, north of Tours
Limestone, 83½ @ 34½ @ 13¾ in. (212.1 @ 87.6 @ 34.9 cm)
The Cloisters Collection, 1925 (25.120.201)

The effigy of Jean d'Alluye shows the knight
in full armor, including the surcoat he wears
over a long-sleeved mail shirt. His sword hangs
from a belt and is partially obscured by a large
shield. The arms and armor depicted are typical
thirteenth-century chivalric accoutrements, as
is his footrest in the form of a lion, a symbol of
bravery and valor. The youthful features of the
recumbent effigy, a type known as a gisant, are
probably idealized portrayals of a knight in his
prime rather than a representation of his actual
age at death. Jean assumed the title of seigneur
of Châteaux and Saint-Christophe in 1209 and
returned from a visit to the Holy Land with a
fragment of the True Cross. He died before
July 1248.

The tomb was once in the Cistercian abbey
of La Clarté-Dieu, founded in 1239/40 on a
property over which Jean had seigneurial rights.
Following the French Revolution, the abbey was
destroyed, and the effigy—alleged to have served
as a footbridge over a stream—eventually found
its way into the nearby Château Hodebert. It was
purchased in 1910 by George Grey Barnard.

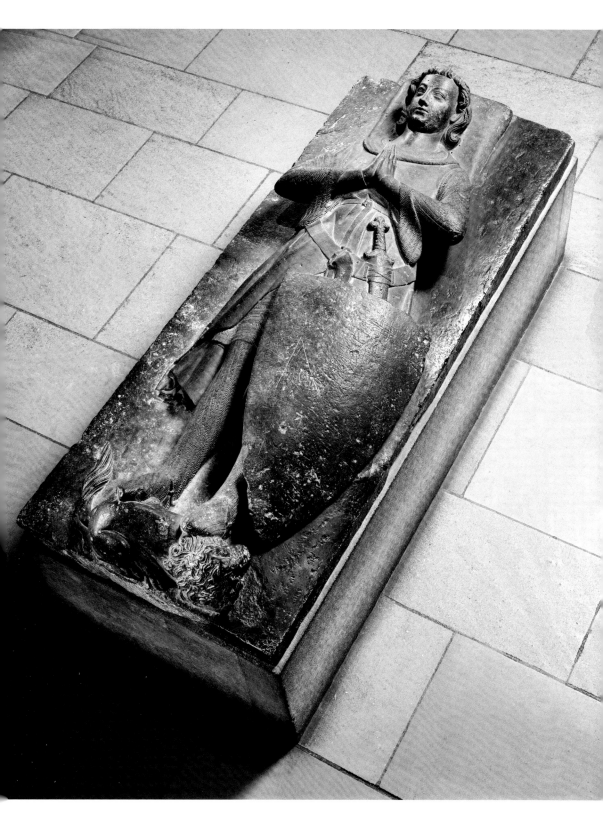

Tomb of Ermengol VII, Count of Urgell

Catalonia (Lleida), ca. 1300–1350
From the Premonstratensian monastery of Santa Maria
de Bellpuig de les Avellanes, Spain
Limestone with traces of paint, 89 @ 79½ @ 35 in.
(226.1 @ 201.9 @ 88.9 cm)
The Cloisters Collection, 1928 (28.95a–i)

This elaborate structure, supported by three
stone lions, is the sepulchral monument
traditionally associated with Ermengol VII,
count of Urgell. The various styles and
disparate dimensions of the individual parts
of the tomb suggest that it was assembled
from elements originally intended for several
different monuments. The effigy itself shows
the count resting his head on two tasseled
cushions, with his eyes closed and his hands
crossed above a sheathed sword. A group of
mourners, now damaged, is carved into the
same slab, just behind the effigy. Below is a
carved panel showing Christ in Majesty, at

center, accompanied by the Twelve Apostles,
all standing under traceried arches. A separate
relief above the effigy shows a funeral rite, with
three celebrants, at center, standing beneath
pointed arches. At the top, on a much smaller
rectangular panel, are angels transporting a
soul to heaven.

According to tradition, the monastery of
Santa Maria de Bellpuig de les Avellanes was
founded by Ermengol VII and his wife, doña
Dulcia. Ermengol died in 1184, but not until
about 1300 were plans made by Ermengol X
to construct a chapel as the family necropolis.
Little progress had been made at the time
of the latter's death in 1314, and the chapel
was not completed until the eighteenth century. The original appearance and intended
placement of the tombs can thus no longer be
ascertained, but their refined execution ranks
them among the outstanding examples of
Catalan Gothic sculpture.

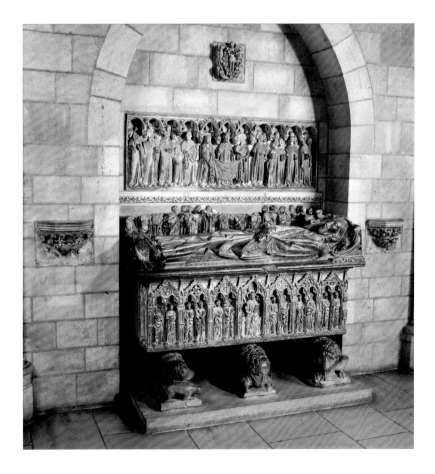

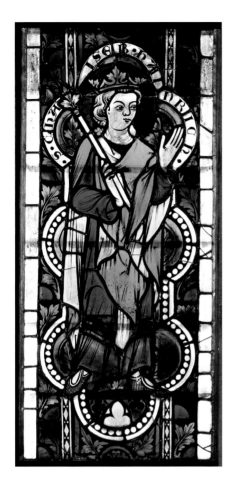
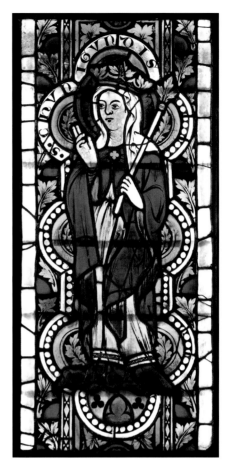

Stained Glass with Emperor Henry II and Queen Kunigunde

Austria, Carinthia (Lavanttal), 1340–50
From the choir and north chapel windows of the church of Saint Leonhard at Bad St. Leonhard im Lavanttal, near Klagenfurt
Pot-metal glass, white glass, and vitreous paint, 39 @ 17¾ in. (99.1 @ 45.1 cm); 38½ @ 17½ in. (97.8 @ 44.5 cm)
The Cloisters Collection, 1965 (65.96.3, .4)

The church of Saint Leonhard was constructed in the early decades of the fourteenth century, with some of its choir and chapel windows in place by 1350. The program of the choir windows included scenes from the life of Christ as well as images of the Twelve Apostles and locally venerated saints. Twenty-three panels from six different windows at Saint Leonhard are now installed in three lancet windows in the Gothic Chapel. The center window contains narrative scenes, while more static, iconic images occupy the two flanking windows. Some of the figures are framed within so-called keyhole medallions: polylobed variations on the traditional circles used as framing devices in France a century earlier. The background is composed largely of foliate motifs and schematic architectural members, providing a colorful, intricate contrast to the heavyset figures often admired for their simple, childlike features.

Standing at the bottom register of the left window are two crowned figures, identified in an inscription as Holy Roman Emperor Henry II (r. 1014–24) and his queen, Kunigunde. They are the patron saints of Heinrich and Kunigunde Kropf, who paid for a window in the choir of the church. Panels with depictions of the Kropfs are still in the church today. It is believed that the glass at Saint Leonhard was made by an itinerant workshop from Judenburg, where the Kropfs lived.

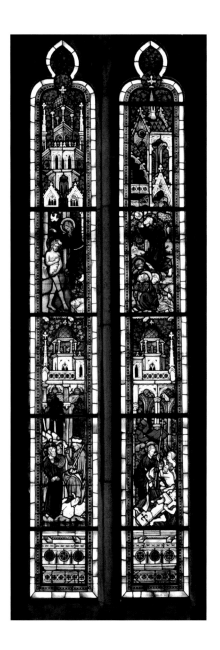

Stained Glass with the Baptism of Christ and the Agony in the Garden

Austria, Lower Austria, ca. 1390
From the choir of the castle chapel at
Ebreichsdorf, south of Vienna
Pot-metal glass, colorless glass, vitreous paint,
and silver stain, 11 ft. 8¾ in. @ 12⅛ in.
(357.2 @ 30.8 cm) each lancet
The Cloisters Collection, 1986 (1986.285.4, .5)

Seven scenes from the private chapel of the
Ebreichsdorf castle are installed in the Gothic
Chapel. Representing episodes from the life of
Christ—the Annunciation, Adoration of the
Magi, Presentation in the Temple, Baptism,
Agony in the Garden, Trial before Pilate, and
Harrowing of Hell—they constitute almost
all of the surviving panels from the original
stained-glass program. The scenes are organized
into vertical groups of four rectangular panels,
arranged two over two; the lower panels in each
group are narrative, while the upper panels represent architectural canopies. Most of the narrative panels contain a single scene, as is the case
with the Annunciation, which was originally
paired with a Visitation (now in Vienna). Others,
however, combine to form a unified episode,
such as the Adoration of the Magi.

The glazing program of the chapel has been
attributed to a "ducal workshop" favored by the
local nobility and best known for its use of rich
colors, fanciful architectural forms, and elegant
figural styles. In the Baptism panel (detail opposite, left), the figures of Christ, John the Baptist,
and the dove, representing the Holy Spirit, are
positioned to create an upward thrust that lends
movement and drama to the overall effect.

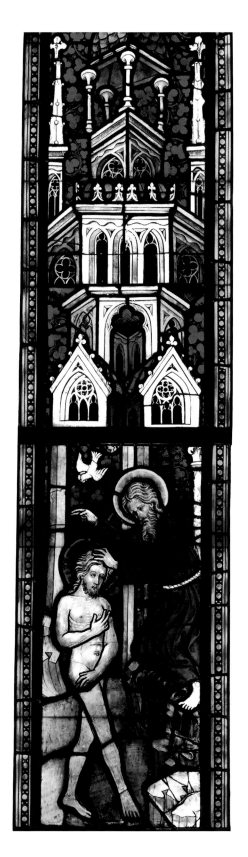
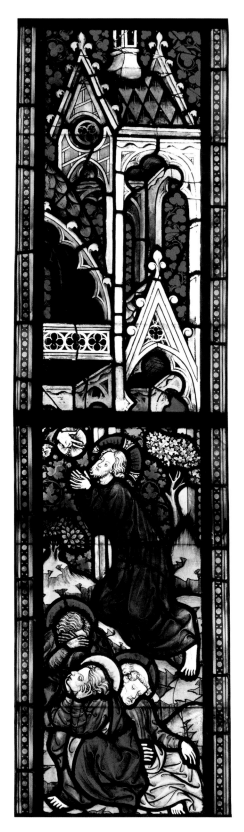

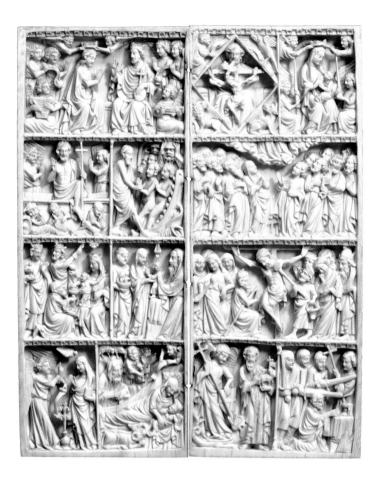

Diptych with Scenes of the Life of Christ and the Virgin, Saint Michael, John the Baptist, Thomas Becket, and the Trinity

Germany, Lower Rhineland, Cologne, ca. 1350
Elephant ivory, 10 @ 8⅜ in. (25.5 @ 21.1 cm)
The Cloisters Collection, 1970 (1970.324.8a, b)

This large, intricately carved diptych is distinct from the many surviving fourteenth-century French diptychs. Stylistically, it can be compared to a number of German sculptures, especially the marble reliefs from the high altar of Cologne Cathedral dating before 1322. The diptych also incorporates a number of scenes that, in terms of iconography, are unusual to ivory carving. The sequence begins at lower left, with two standard episodes from the life of Christ: the Annunciation and the Nativity with the Annun-

ciation to the Shepherds. This routine narrative is interrupted at lower right by scenes of saints, which are rarely depicted in ivory carving. Saint Michael Triumphant over the Dragon and Saint John the Baptist with the Sacrificial Lamb appear to the left of the Martyrdom of Saint Thomas Becket. The second and third registers continue with well-known images: the Adoration of the Magi and the Presentation of Christ in the Temple, with the Crucifixion to the right, and the Resurrection of Christ and Descent into Limbo, with the Ascension to the right. Atypical scenes return in the upper register: the Coronation of the Virgin, at upper left; the Trinity surrounded by symbols of the Four Evangelists, to the right of center; and, in the upper right corner, the Virgin nursing the Christ Child as she is crowned by angels.

Pair of Altar Angels

France, Artois (Pas-de-Calais), ca. 1275–1300
Oak with traces of paint, H. 29½ in. (75 cm); 29 in. (73.7 cm)
The Cloisters Collection, 1952 (52.33.1, .2)

We know from illuminated manuscripts that angels such as these in all likelihood were originally placed on freestanding colonnettes around an altar in groups of four or six. The colonnettes would have been linked by rods supporting curtains. Our examples are carved in the round and are now missing their wings, which were attached in sockets behind the shoulders. Their hands, also missing, would have held candles, censers, or the Instruments of the Passion. Like most sculpture of the period, the angels were almost surely once painted and gilded. They were probably carved in the late thirteenth century, but they exhibit the enduring popularity of the style of the exterior sculpture of Reims Cathedral, particularly in their smiling faces and curling hairstyle, which dates to about the middle of the century.

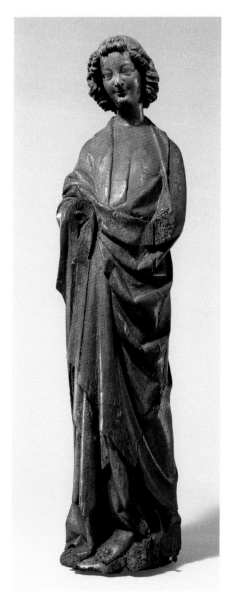
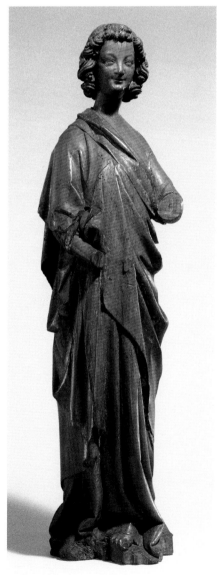

Standing Virgin and Child

France, Île-de-France, possibly Paris, 1340–50
Limestone, paint, gilding, and glass, H. 68 in. (172.7 cm)
The Cloisters Collection, 1937 (37.159)

This monumental image of the Virgin and
Child is carved in the style of Parisian sculptures from about 1340. For example, a silver-
gilt statuette given to the abbey of Saint-Denis
in 1339 by Jeanne d'Evreux, widowed queen
of Charles IV (now in the Musée du Louvre,
Paris), has essentially the same composition.
In both groups the Virgin's mantle is pulled
across her hips and falls over her right arm. In
The Cloisters' sculpture the Christ Child play-
fully reaches for the Virgin's veil, while in the
Louvre statuette he reaches for her chin. The
Cloisters' piece also retains most of its original
paint and gilding and appears today much as
it would have in the fourteenth century.

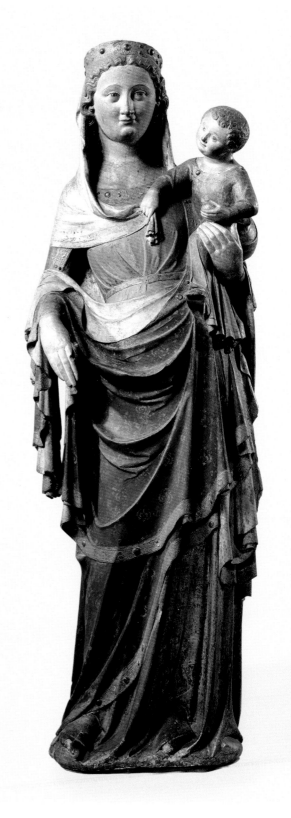

Mirror Case with Scenes of the Attack on the Castle of Love

France, Île-de-France, Paris, ca. 1320–40
Elephant ivory, DIAM. 5½ in. (14.1 cm)
The Cloisters Collection, 2003 (2003.131.1)

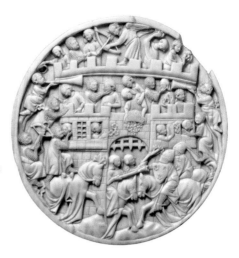

Among the most appealing products of the prolific Parisian ivory-carving workshops were mirror cases, combs, caskets, and other precious objects decorated with secular scenes. In this complex circular relief, twenty-eight figures and five horses occupy the battlements, windows, and grounds before a castle. At the top is the crowned and winged figure of the god of Love bending down as he prepares to launch an arrow from his bow. The castle is defended by a force of ladies armed with roses, which they hurl at the attacking knights (one of whom, at lower left, wields a crossbow). Some of the women greet the knights with welcoming gestures and smiles; in the upper left, a lady offers a crown to one of the two trumpeters flanking the castle and heralding the playful joust about to occur before the portcullis. Two armed and helmeted knights, their shields decorated with roses, ride in from the right to face their female opponents. To the left of the castle entrance is a third knight, who has lost his shield and removed his helmet. He stands on his horse to embrace a lady in a window.

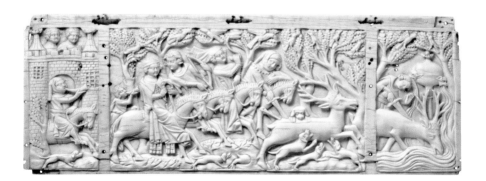

Panel with Hunting Scenes

France, Île-de-France, Paris, ca. 1350
Elephant ivory, 4⅜ @ 12⅛ in. (11 @ 30.8 cm)
The Cloisters Collection, 2003 (2003.131.2)

Three scenes from a stag hunt are deeply carved into this exceptionally large rectangular plaque, the only surviving panel from an ivory casket with a hinged lid. (The other panels are known from an eighteenth-century engraving.) The narrative flows from left to right, beginning with an attendant on horseback. Accompanied by a hound, he emerges from the castle gate blowing his horn as two ladies look down on him from the ramparts above. The hunt takes place in a dense woods. The party comprises two men and two women on horseback; one woman is feeding a falcon, and the other pursues a bird with a lure. One of the hunters has released an arrow from his bow that has struck the stag, while the other hunter drives his sword into the beast, already tormented by the hounds. The hunt continues on the right with the stag drinking from a fountain as the hunter again stabs the animal with his blade.

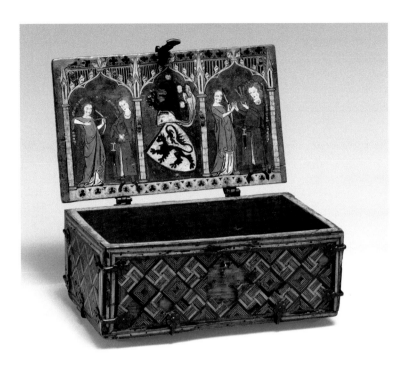

Coffret (*Minnekästchen*)

Germany, Upper Rhineland, 1325–50
Oak, inlay, and tempera; wrought-iron mounts,
4¾ @ 10¾ @ 6½ in. (12.1 @ 27.3 @ 16.5 cm)
Rogers Fund and The Cloisters Collection, by
exchange, 1950 (50.141)

Depicted inside the lid of this coffret, on the
left, is Frau Minne, the mythical goddess of
courtly love in medieval German literature,
aiming an arrow at a young man. At right, he
surrenders his heart, which has been pierced
by three arrows, to the lady. The German
inscriptions can be translated as: "Gracious
lady, I have surrendered" and "Lady send me
solace, my heart has been wounded." Like the
French ivory carving representing the Attack
on the Castle of Love (p. 97), this painted
coffret embodies the notion of courtly love that
envisioned romance as playful warfare between
suitor and beloved. The coat of arms on the
box has not been firmly established but may be
that of the Berstett family of Alsace, Baden, and
Austria. The term *Minnekästchen* (*Kästchen* is
German for small chest or coffret) was coined
in the nineteenth century to refer to German
objects of this type.

Support Figure of a Seated Cleric or Friar

France, Champagne-Ardenne (Marne), Reims(?), ca. 1280
Copper alloy with mercury gilding, 2⅝ @ 1⅜ @ 1¾ in.
(6.7 @ 3.4 @ 4.3 cm)
The Cloisters Collection, 1991 (1991.252)

The pose of this statuette of a cleric or friar,
echoing ancient figures of Atlas, and the
indentation cast into its back tell us that it was
originally intended as a support for a larger

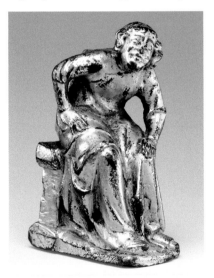

object. Like the carved pair of altar angels in The Cloisters' collection (p. 95), the style of this cast figure derives ultimately from the seminal sculpture of thirteenth-century Reims Cathedral—in this case from the console figures on the west facade and nave exterior. No thirteenth-century shrine survives intact with support figures like this one, but some are described in medieval inventories and there are examples from the later Middle Ages. Furthermore, a number of the scenes depicted in the Hours of Jeanne d'Evreux (below) are set in architectural frameworks supported by similar bent figures.

──────────────────

The Hours of Jeanne d'Evreux, Queen of France

Jean Pucelle (active 1319–34)
France, Île-de-France, Paris, ca. 1324–28
Grisaille, tempera, and ink on vellum,
3½ @ 2⅝ in. (8.9 @ 6.7 cm) each leaf
The Cloisters Collection, 1954 (54.1.2)

This tiny devotional prayer book was painted by Jean Pucelle, one of the greatest artists of the fourteenth century, for Jeanne d'Evreux, third wife of King Charles IV (r. 1322–28). The queen would have used it at regular intervals throughout the day in imitation of the prayer cycles observed by monks and nuns. Although the manuscript lacks some of the ostentation we might associate with a royal book, such as large scale and lavish use of color and gold, in terms of the quality and subtlety of its decoration it ranks among the great masterworks of medieval manuscript illumination. The predominance of gray enabled the painter to render the figures in a remarkably sculptural way. Here, we see the manuscript opened to an image of Jesus carrying the Cross on his way to the Crucifixion (fol. 61v, left). The architectural frame is supported by two seated figures quite similar to the cast-bronze support figure of a cleric or friar, also in the collection (opposite). On the facing page is a depiction of the Annunciation to the Shepherds (fol. 62r). Characteristic of this inventive artist's work, the illustrations on this page extend beyond the frame to surround the miniature scene with angels and shepherds in the margins.

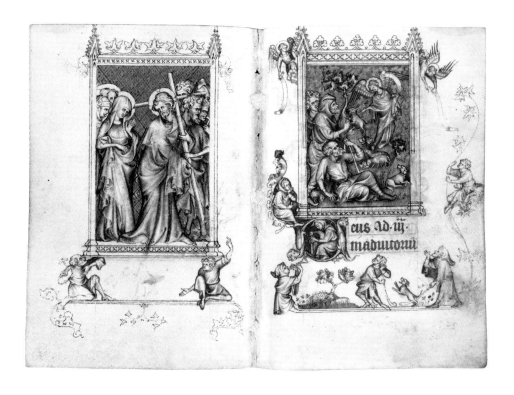

Reliquary Shrine

Attributed to Jean de Touyl (d. 1349/50)
France, Île-de-France, Paris, ca. 1320–40
From the convent of the Poor Clares at Buda, Hungary
Silver gilt, translucent enamel, and paint,
10 @ 16 @ 3¾ in. (25.4 @ 40.6 @ 9.5 cm) open
The Cloisters Collection, 1962 (62.96)

In the form of a polyptych, this reliquary has folding wings that can be closed over the central portion. In the center of the arcaded canopy is the Enthroned Virgin about to nurse the Christ Child; flanking her are angels displaying relics. The wings of the polyptych are decorated in translucent enamel, a technique that evokes stained glass—highly appropriate given the architectural form of the shrine. Scenes from the life of the Virgin and the infancy of Christ appear below music-making angels on the insides of the wings, while additional angels, four female saints, and figures of the apostles decorate the exterior. Although the reliquary belonged to the convent of the Poor Clares in Budapest, the style of the goldsmith work and enamel is purely Parisian and can be associated with the goldsmith Jean de Touyl. It is possible the shrine was purchased in Paris for or by Queen Elizabeth of Hungary, who founded the convent in 1334.

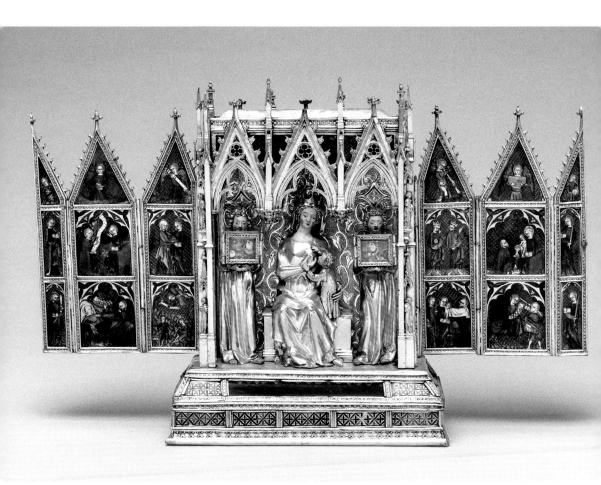

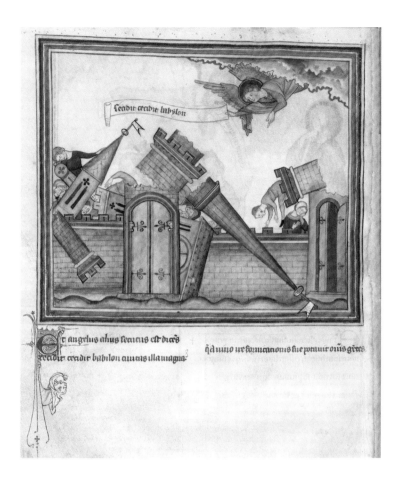

The Cloisters Apocalypse

France, Normandy, ca. 1330
Paint, gold, silver, and brown ink on vellum,
12⅛ @ 9 in. (30.8 @ 22.9 cm) each leaf
The Cloisters Collection, 1968 (68.174)

The Apocalypse, or the book of Revelation (Greek *apokalupsis*, meaning "revelation" or "unveiling"), is the last book of the New Testament. Written by John on the island of Patmos toward the end of the first century, it opens with letters to the seven churches in Asia, followed by a series of visions describing calamitous destructions toward the end of time, while promising the faithful the splendor of the Heavenly Jerusalem. There are seventy-two decorated miniatures in this manuscript; their composition and narrative seem to share a common source with two other Apocalypse manuscripts made in northern France (now in London and Paris). A number of heraldic shields included in the manuscript, as well as its stylistic resemblance to another early fourteenth-century manuscript and to stained glass produced in Normandy, suggest its place of origin to be in or near Coutances in western Normandy.

A horrific scene depicting the Fall of Babylon unfolds on folio 26 verso (Revelation 14:8; detail above): crenellated towers and soaring spires topple from their bases, city gates are dislodged, and buildings collapse onto one another. Inhabitants are thrown like toys among the falling debris. Above the chaotic city an angel unfurls a scroll that exclaims, "That great Babylon is fallen, is fallen" (*Cecidit, cecidit Babylon*). The destruction of Babylon is one of a series of eschatological prophecies in which the unrepentant are punished and the damned meet their inevitable fate.

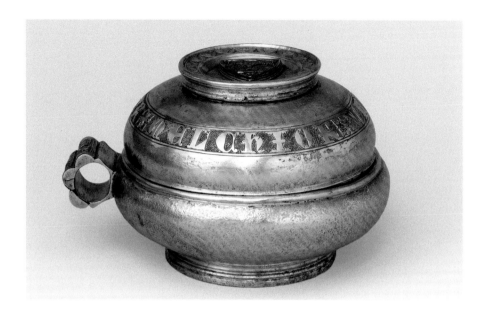

Double Cup

Germany or Bohemia, possibly Prague, 1330–60
Silver, silver gilt, and opaque enamel,
H. 4¼ in. (10.6 cm); DIAM. 4⅞ in. (12.4 cm)
The Cloisters Collection, 1983 (1983.125a, b)

In the fourteenth century, the Epiphany, or Three Kings' Day, was frequently celebrated with special toasts, and decorative cups like this one were often given as gifts in emulation of the biblical Magi. This double cup comprises two vessels stacked rim to rim. Around the exterior of the upper vessel, which served as a second cup as well as a lid, is an inscription with the names of the Three Magi—Caspar (Gaspar), Melchior, and Waltazar (Balthasar). The interior of the lower cup bears an enamel image of a helmet surmounted by three conical hats of the type Jews were forced to wear (below, left). Inside the foot of the upper cup are three similar hats, conjoined at their tips at the center of a heraldic escutcheon (below, right). The presence of the Jewish hats does not necessarily indicate that the cup's owners were Jews, since Gentiles and Jewish converts used similar emblems or devices.

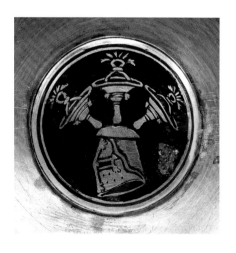

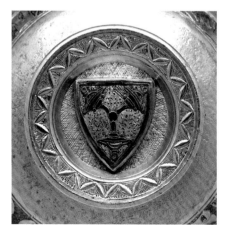

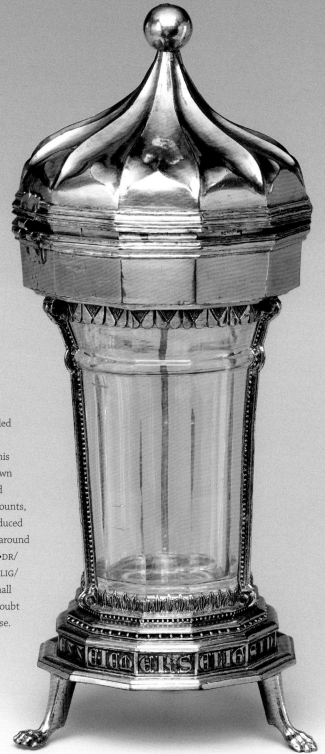

Covered Beaker

Vessel: Italy, Veneto, Venice, 1325–50
Mounts: Austria, Vienna, 1340–60
Silver gilt, rock crystal, and translucent enamels,
H. 8¼ in. (21 cm); DIAM. 3⅜ in. (8.6 cm)
The Cloisters Collection, 1989 (1989.293)

Hard-stone vessels such as this twelve-sided
rock crystal example are among the most
treasured products of the Middle Ages. This
beaker was likely produced in Venice, known
as an important center for the cutting and
polishing of rock crystal. The silver-gilt mounts,
however, compare closely with pieces produced
in Vienna. The silver is inscribed in verse around
the base in a German dialect: WER/HIE•V•DR/
INCE/ET•W/INDE/R•MV/EZZ/E•IEM/ER•S/ELIG/
SIN (He who drinks wine from me, ever shall
happy be). That exhortation leaves little doubt
that this vessel was intended for secular use.

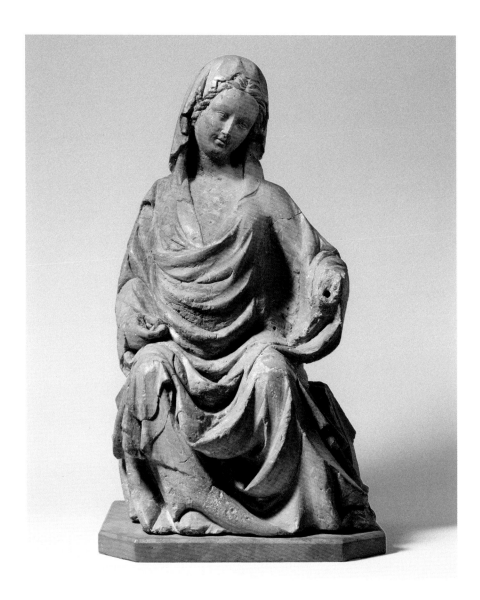

Enthroned Virgin

Goro di Gregorio (documented 1311–33)
Italy, Tuscany, first half of 14th century
Terracotta, 17⅝ @ 10 @ 9½ in. (44.8 @ 25.4 @ 24.1 cm)
The Cloisters Collection and Rogers Fund, 1998 (1998.214)

This work is a rare surviving example of medieval sculpture in terracotta—no other Italian
examples from the period exist today. The
sketchiness of the modeling and the omission
of the figure of the Christ Child, among other

details, suggest that the sculpture was most
likely created as a workshop model rather than
as a finished piece. It has been proposed that the
terracotta was made as a goldsmith's model for
a Virgin and Child group intended for the center
of an altarpiece. The graceful pose of the Virgin,
the rhythmic folds of drapery, and the delicate
treatment of her face are consistent with the
French-inspired style seen in Tuscany from the
first half of the fourteenth century.

Relief with Saint Peter Martyr and Three Donors

Giovanni di Balduccio (active 1318–49)
Italy, Lombardy, ca. 1340
From the church of Sant'Eustorgio, Milan
Marble, 31½ @ 33⅞ @ 5¾ in. (80 @ 86 @ 14.5 cm)
The Cloisters Collection, 2001 (2001.221)

With quiet monumentality, this panel depicts the standing, bearded Saint Peter Martyr wearing Dominican garb. The head wound, the saint's primary attribute, is clearly visible, along with a (restored) palm of martyrdom in his right hand. His cloak, which he holds open with outstretched arms, frames three praying donor figures; he places his hands on the heads of the oldest and youngest of them. The relief is carved in a white, fine-grained marble set into a frame of slightly coarser, grayer marble.

The sculpture is one of three surviving panels from a tomb originally in the Milanese church of Sant'Eustorgio. The damaged center panel (Castello Sforzesco, Milan) depicts the Enthroned Virgin and Child between two angels. The relief originally on the viewer's left (still in Sant'Eustorgio) shows Saint John the Baptist with four kneeling donors in a composition that mirrors the Museum's panel, which must have been on the right. Details such as the molding beneath the ledge supporting the figures and the buttons on the undersides of the sleeves suggest that the reliefs were meant to be seen from below, and thus were presumably positioned above eye level. The artist, Giovanni di Balduccio, was trained in Pisa and is noted for having brought the innovations of Tuscan sculptors to northern Italy.

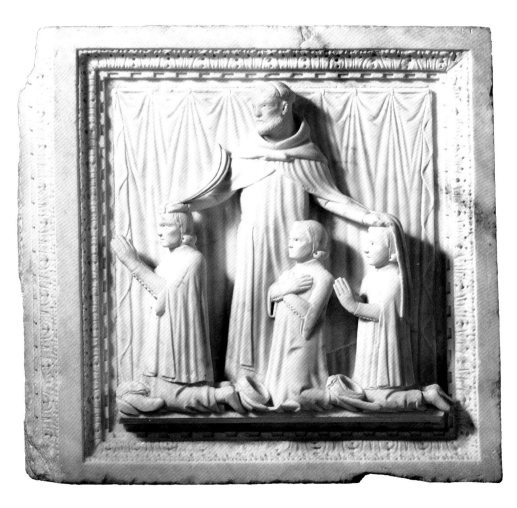

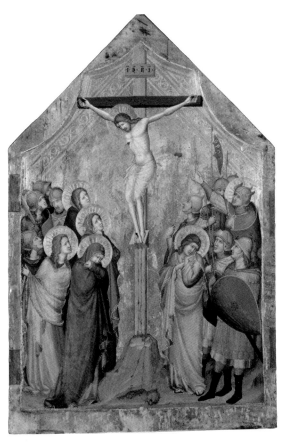
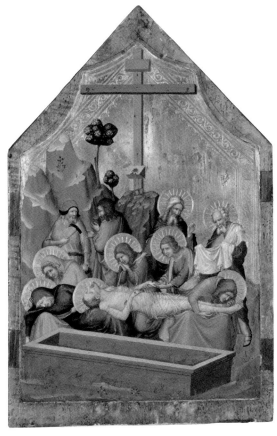

The Crucifixion and the Lamentation

Master of the Codex of Saint George (active ca. 1325–50)
Italy, active in France (Avignon), ca. 1340–45
Tempera and gold leaf on wood panel
Whole: 18 @ 11¾ in. (45.7 @ 29.8 cm) each
Painted surface: 15⅝ @ 10⅝ in. (39.7 @ 27 cm) each
The Cloisters Collection, 1961 (61.200.1, .2)

The grieving faces and bold gestures on these exquisitely painted panels, highlighted against a stark gold ground, dramatically convey the emotion of the Passion of Christ. The panels are among the few surviving works by the so-called Master of the Codex of Saint George, who is named for a missal he illuminated now in the Biblioteca Apostolica Vaticana, Vatican City. Although trained in Florence, the Master of the Codex of Saint George spent much of his career in Avignon, home of the papal court from 1309 to 1377, where he assimilated characteristics of Sienese and French painting of the period.

These panels were once thought to constitute a complete devotional diptych, but careful examination has shown that they were originally part of a folding polyptych probably composed of six panels organized in an accordion-like fashion, with the pairs of panels closing over one another face-to-face. The cycle likely began with the Annunciation and the Nativity (both missing), continued with the two Cloisters panels, and concluded with the Resurrection and the Coronation of the Virgin (both Museo Nazionale del Bargello, Florence).

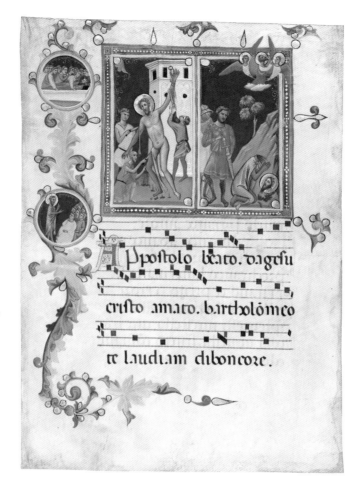

Leaf from a *Laudario* with the Martyrdom of Saint Bartholomew

Pacino di Bonaguida
(active 1303–ca. 1340)
Italy, Florence, ca. 1340
From a *laudario* created
for Sant'Agnese, Florence
Tempera, gold, and ink
on parchment
Overall 18½ @ 13¾ in.
(47 @ 35 cm)
The Cloisters Collection,
2006 (2006.250)

Framed as a diptych, this depiction of the martyrdom of Saint Bartholomew was painted with graphic realism and expressiveness by Pacino di Bonaguida, a prominent member of the Florentine painters' guild. On the left, with his left arm chained to a tower, Bartholomew endures being flayed; on the right, the beheaded martyr kneels on the ground praying, his own skin tied around his neck and his haloed head lying nearby. Three four-line staves with musical notation appear below the illumination, set to the text in contemporary Italian: "Appostolo beato da gesu cristo amato. Bartholomeo te laudiam di bon core" (Blessed Apostle, beloved by Jesus Christ, Bartholomew, we praise you with good heart). Two roundels to the left show Bartholomew preaching in India (bottom), and his body lowered into a tomb (top).

Intended for the feast day of Saint Bartholomew on August 24, this leaf is the 109th page of a *laudario*—a collection of devotional songs of praise (*laude*)—commissioned by the confraternity of Saint Agnes in Florence. The tradition of commissioning *laude* by *laudesi* (singing societies) was especially influenced by the teaching of Saint Francis, resulting in hundreds of songs praising Christ, the Virgin Mary, and many saints with passion and devotion.

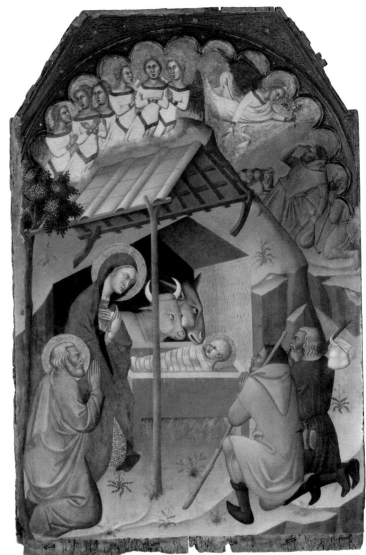

The Adoration of the Shepherds

Bartolo di Fredi
(active by 1353–d. 1410)
Italy, Tuscany, Siena, 1374
Probably from the Dominican
convent of SS. Annunziata in
San Gimignano
Tempera, gold, and gesso
on wood
Whole: 69⅛ @ 45⅛ in.
(175.6 @ 114.6 cm)
Painted surface: 63¼ @ 45⅛ in.
(160.7 @ 114.6 cm)
The Cloisters Collection, 1925
(25.120.288)

In all likelihood this panel was originally the center element of a large altarpiece in the convent of SS. Annunziata in San Gimignano. It is described here by an early nineteenth-century writer: "In a crumbling chapel . . . a Nativity of our Lord Jesus Christ. On either side are the Four Evangelists; above is the Virgin Annunciate, the Coronation [of the Virgin], the Baptism of the Saviour; and in the predella Saint John the Evangelist with two other saints. Beneath is written Bartholus M[agistr]o Fredi. 1374." Although neither particularly innovative nor especially refined,

Bartolo di Fredi, the artist who signed and dated the altarpiece, was nevertheless a highly successful Sienese painter of frescoes and panels. The appeal of his work is evident in the wealth of details in this narrative scene. A choir of angels sings above the manger—occupied by the Holy Family, the ox and the ass, and two adoring shepherds—as the Annunciation to the Shepherds appears at the upper right. In addition to its well-preserved paint surface, the panel retains much of the decorative gilt gesso (*pastiglia*) at the top.

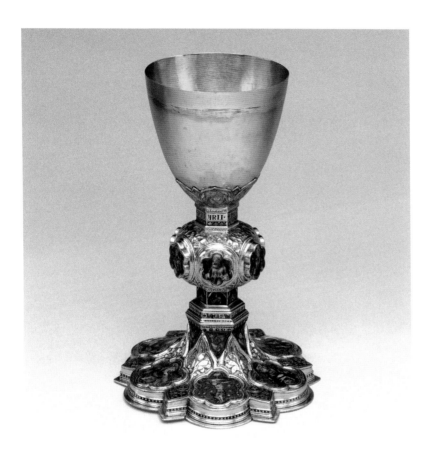

Chalice

Italy, Tuscany, Siena, ca. 1341–42
Silver gilt and translucent enamel,
H. 8½ in. (21.7 cm); DIAM. 5⅞ in. (14.9 cm)
The Cloisters Collection, 1988 (1988.67)

This richly decorated chalice is representative
of the finest achievements of Sienese goldsmiths. On the foot are six enamel plaques: an
image of Jesus on the Cross flanked by representations of the Virgin and Saint John the Evangelist, and depictions of Saint Louis of Toulouse,
John the Baptist, and Saint Anthony of Padua.
On the knop are Saints Michael, Francis, an

unidentified female saint (possibly Mary
Magdalen), Catherine of Alexandria, and
Elizabeth of Hungary. The Latin inscription
above the knop links the chalice with a noted
Franciscan leader and a member of an important
papal tribunal: + FRA/T(R)IS P/ETRIPENIT/ ENTI/
ARII + /DOMI/NI PA/PE (of Brother Peter Peni-
tentiary of the Lord Pope). Continuing below
the knop, the inscription reads: + LOCI/SAS/
SIFERATI/NON VEN/DATVR/NEC DI/STRATVR
(of the place of Sassoferrato neither sell nor
destroy). The silver cup is an early replacement.

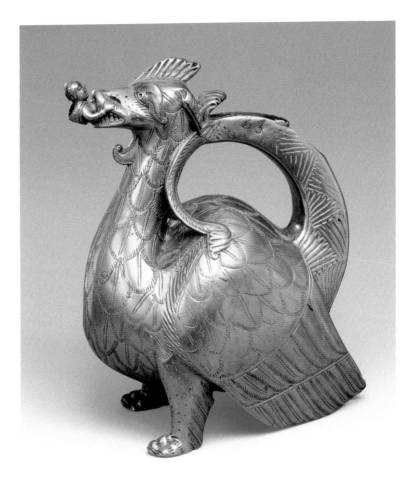

Aquamanile in the Form of a Dragon

North Germany, ca. 1200
Copper alloy, 8¾ @ 7¼ in.
(22.2 @ 18.4 cm)
The Cloisters Collection,
1947 (47.101.51)

Aquamanilia, which are water vessels used for washing hands, served both liturgical and secular purposes. Those made in the shape of an animal are among the most distinctive products of medieval craftsmen. The most commonly seen zoomorphic aquamanilia are lions, but dragons, griffins, and many other forms were also produced (see opposite and pp. 112–13).

This striking vessel represents a dragon, which is supported by its legs in front and on the tips of its wings behind, with a tail that curls up into a handle. It was filled through an opening in the tail, now missing its hinged cover. Water was poured out through the spout formed by the hooded or cowled figure held between the dragon's teeth. In addition to its visual power, this aquamanile is distinguished by fine casting, visible in the carefully chased dragon's scales and other surface details.

Aquamanile in the Form of a Ram

England, North Yorkshire, probably Scarborough,
ca. 1250–1350
Glazed earthenware, 9⅜ @ 11½ @ 5¼ in.
(23.9 @ 29.2 @ 13.3 cm)
The Cloisters Collection, 2007 (2007.142)

Pottery aquamanilia like this one were inspired
by the more prestigious metal versions (see
opposite and pp. 112–13). Because of the
fragility of earthenware, though, they are
significantly rarer. This ram has considerable
charm, and even with the loss of its horns
and much of its dark green glaze, it is among
the finest and most intact pottery examples
to survive from the Middle Ages. The main
body of the vessel was skillfully thrown on a
potter's wheel before the addition of the feet,
handle, and head. A funnel-shaped opening that
served to fill the aquamanile with water projects
vertically from the shoulders; the opening in
the mouth served as a spout. The work can
be dated to about 1250 to 1350 (confirmed by
thermoluminescence analysis), and stylistic
comparisons with excavated earthenware vessels
suggest that it was made in the prolific kilns of
Scarborough on the east coast of England.

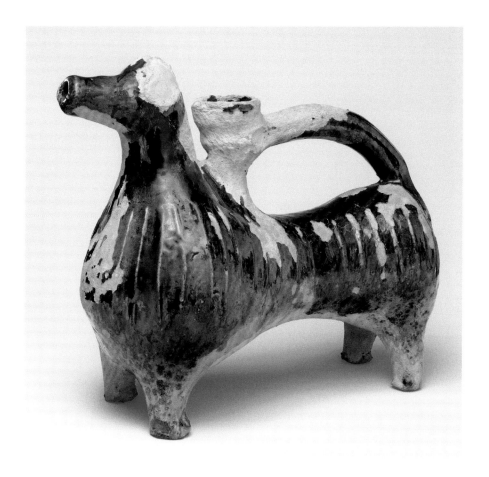

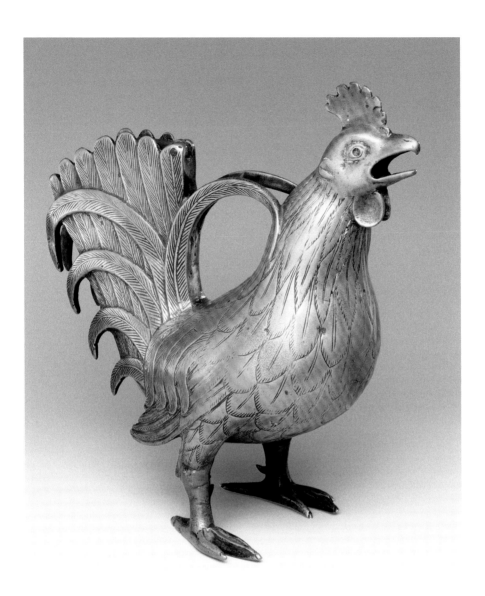

Aquamanile in the Form of a Cock

Germany, Lower Saxony, 13th century
Copper alloy, 10 @ 3½ in. (25.4 @ 9 cm)
The Cloisters Collection, 1989 (1989.292)

A carefully observed, naturalistic sculpture in the round, this vessel, like the slightly earlier dragon aquamanile (p. 110), was cast using the lost-wax process. Surface details were then skillfully engraved in the cold metal. The ewer was filled through a covered hole hidden between the rows of tail feathers, and water was poured out through the bird's open beak. Although the cock is not without religious significance (most notably in the story of Saint Peter's denial of Jesus), it is also possible that this aquamanile served a secular function. The cock was a popular character in such twelfth-century literature as the tale of Renart the Fox and is perhaps best known today from Chanticleer, the rooster in Chaucer's fourteenth-century "The Nun's Priest's Tale."

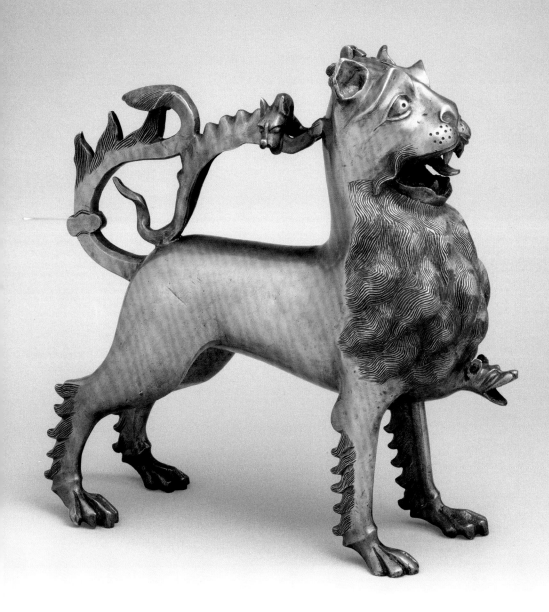

Aquamanile in the Form of a Lion

Germany, Franconia, Nuremberg, ca. 1400
Copper alloy, 13⅛ @ 4¾ in. (33.3 @ 12.1 cm)
The Cloisters Collection, 1994 (1994.244)

This lion aquamanile is certainly one of the
Museum's most magnificent examples of
this type of utilitarian object. The animal's
energized stance, with its chest pushed forward
and its tongue extended, instantly conveys a
sense of great pride and power. There is the
familiar covered opening at the top of the lion's
head for filling the vessel with water, but unlike
the earlier examples we have seen (pp. 110–12),
the lion has a spout attached to its chest.
Comparison with other aquamanilia suggests
that this one was cast in the free imperial city
of Nuremberg, a leading artistic center from
the middle of the fourteenth century until the
sixteenth century.

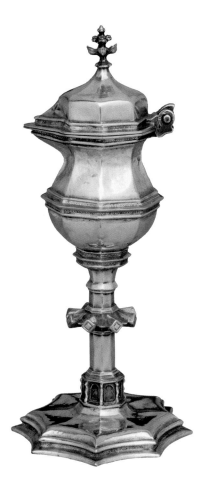

Altar Cruet

Central Europe, mid-14th century
Silver and silver gilt. H. 8¾ in. (22.2 cm);
DIAM. 4 in. (10.2 cm)
The Cloisters Collection, 1986 (1986.284)

Altar cruets were used to mix water with wine
for Holy Communion and were thus usually
made in pairs. Although frequently crafted
in silver throughout the Middle Ages, cruets,
because they held the water and wine *before*
consecration, were not required to be made
of precious metals. For the same reason, the
shape and decoration of the cruet were less
standardized than those of the chalice and
paten. This mid-fourteenth-century example
is notable for its strong profile and restrained
decoration. The form is characteristic of the
silver production of a broad area of central
Europe, making it difficult to determine a
precise place of manufacture.

Brooch

Germany, Saxony or South Germany, 1340–60
Gold and freshwater pearl, 1¼ @ ⅞ @ 1½ in.
(3.2 @ 2.2 @ 3.8 cm) closed
The Cloisters Collection, 1986 (1986.386)

In terms of its function, decoration, and
inscription, this intimate piece of jewelry
conveys the chivalric ideal of love. Made in the
shape of the letter *E*, the brooch has a hinged
cover that allowed it to function as a locket. The
cover bears the figure of a man holding arrows
aimed at his heart, while the interior inscription
(in a Saxon dialect?) reads: • V/REWELININ •
VRME DEI + HRZE • LEVE•/ NSTE • MOIS IC IN
•/•SIN (Fair lady, may I always remain close
to your heart).

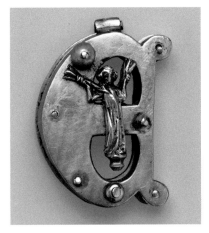

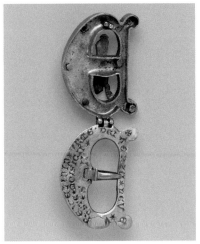

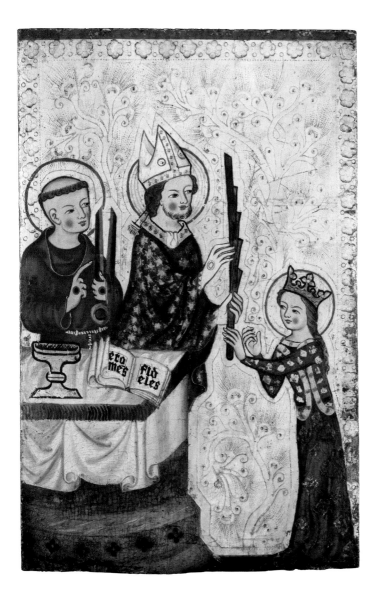

The Bishop of Assisi Giving a Palm to Saint Clare

Germany, Franconia, ca. 1360
Probably from the convent of the
Poor Clares at Nuremberg
Tempera and gold on oak panel,
13¼ @ 8¾ in. (33.5 @ 22 cm)
The Cloisters Collection, 1984 (1984.343)

On Palm Sunday 1212, the bishop of Assisi presented a palm to Clare, the daughter of a nobleman and an early follower of Saint Francis. She is seen in this charming panel wearing richly decorated garments, but soon after the event depicted here she renounced her life of luxury and entered the Franciscan order. Her entry into monastic life was the first step toward the creation of the sister order known as the Poor Clares, which Pope Innocent III permitted to live on alms alone, with no property at all.

The Cloisters' panel is one of several with scenes from the saint's life to survive from altarpieces probably created for the convent of the Poor Clares in Nuremberg. The crown on Clare's head is an allusion to her eventual coronation in heaven. Standing behind the bishop is the tonsured figure of Saint Francis holding a pair of scissors, with which Clare's hair was shorn.

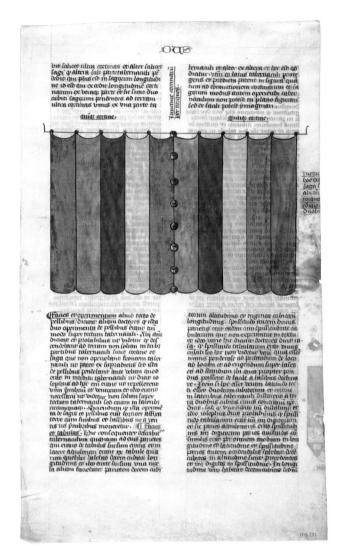

Curtains of the Tabernacle

One of six illustrated leaves from
the *Postilla Litteralis* (Literal
Commentary) of Nicholas of Lyra
France, Île-de-France, Paris,
ca. 1360–80
Opaque watercolor, iron-gall ink,
and gold on vellum, 16½ @ 9¾ in.
(41.9 @ 24.8 cm)
The Cloisters Collection, 2011
(2011.20.1)

One of the most influential university texts
of the Middle Ages, the *Postilla Litteralis*
provided an extended commentary on the
entire Christian Bible. Its author, the Franciscan
Nicholas of Lyra (ca. 1270–1349), who taught
at the University of Paris, was particularly
interested in architecture and included numerous
bold diagrams of biblical structures to clarify his
explanations. His text frequently asks the reader
to consult the accompanying illustrations. This
leaf accompanies a discussion of the Tabernacle
from the book of Exodus (26:1–14). It shows
hanging from a delicate rod the ten panels of the
curtain ordered by God to be made of violet and
purple, and scarlet twice-dyed, and fine, twisted
linen. The small circles of gold leaf running
across the top and down the center represent
fastening loops.

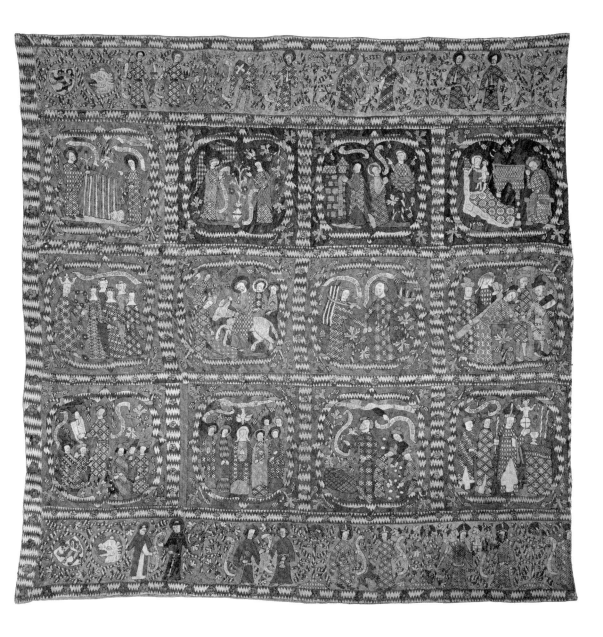

Embroidered Hanging

Germany, Lower Saxony, late 14th century
Silk on linen with painted inscriptions and
faces, 63 @ 62½ in. (160 @ 158.8 cm)
Gift of Mrs. W. Murray Crane, 1969 (69.106)

This large but fragmentary embroidery, with
charming, doll-like figures, is characteristic of
work produced in the region of Lower Saxony,
probably by nuns. Moving from left to right,
the scenes are arranged horizontally in pairs,
with each New Testament episode prefigured
by one or more from the Old Testament. In
the top row: the Flowering of Aaron's Rod and
Gideon's Fleece; the Annunciation; the Closed
Gate of Ezekiel and the Burning Bush; and the
Nativity. In the second row: David Acclaimed;
the Entry into Jerusalem; the Sacrifice of Isaac;
and Jesus Carrying the Cross. In the third row:
Moses Receiving the Law; the Pentecost; Moses
Striking the Rock, with the Gathering of Manna,
at right; and Christ Appearing in the Bread of
the Consecration.

Bust of the Virgin

Bohemia, Prague, ca. 1390–95
Terracotta with paint, 12¾ @ 8⅞ @ 5⅜ in.
(32.5 @ 22.4 @ 13.8 cm)
The Cloisters Collection, 2005 (2005.393)

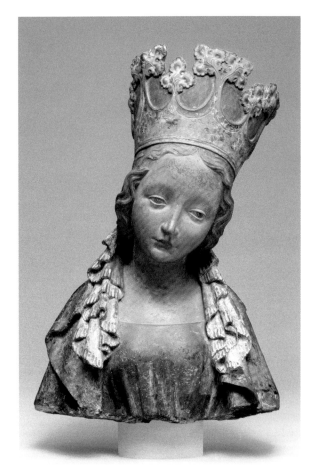

Medieval terracotta sculpture is rare, and this
bust is the only known surviving work from
Bohemia. This exquisite portrayal of the Virgin
is a quintessential example of a type of sculpture
known since the late fourteenth century as the
"Beautiful Madonna" (*Die schöne Madonna*). The
Virgin's delicate, pensive features are framed by
her wavy hair and cascading veil; her eyes are
cast downward, probably looking at her son, now
lost (see opposite). On her gently tilted head
sits a crown decorated with prominent finials of
ridged leaves, a motif found often in Bohemia
at the time. This piece would have been part of
a full-length statue of the Virgin holding the
Christ Child, most likely intended for a church
interior. Large-scale terracotta figures were
frequently created in two or three sections to
ensure that the clay would dry evenly and could
then be transported safely. The bust would have
been the top section of the complete figure,
whose final assemblage required mortar joints
disguised under traces of paint still visible today.

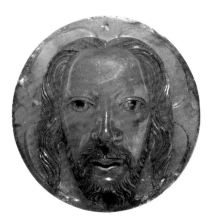

Medallion with the Face of Christ

Lands of the Teutonic Knights (modern Poland),
ca. 1380–1400
Baltic amber with traces of paint, 3¼ @ 1¼ in. (8.2 @ 3.3 cm)
The Cloisters Collection, 2011 (2011.503)

Images of the face of Christ, known as the Vera
Icon or the Holy Face, became increasingly
popular in private devotional use from the
thirteenth century on. This luminous medallion,
however, is one of only three known medieval
examples in translucent amber, a honey-colored,
fossilized pine resin. While the style of the
carving can be compared to works produced
in Bohemia toward the end of the fourteenth
century, trade in Baltic amber was controlled
by the neighboring territory of the Teutonic
Knights, and it is likely that the carving was
produced there, in what is present-day Poland.
Royal and princely inventory references reveal
that amber was highly prized; these records and
the two other surviving medallions (in London
and Munich) suggest that the Museum's
example was likely originally encased in a frame
of precious material, either silver or ivory.

Pietà (*Vesperbild*)

Bohemia, possibly Prague, ca. 1400
Limestone, 15 @ 15⅜ @ 5½ in. (38.1 @ 39.1 @ 14 cm)
The Cloisters Collection, 2001 (2001.78)

Although the term usually used by English speakers to refer to this image is Pietà, Italian for "pity," the German word used since the Middle Ages is *Vesperbild*, literally "evening image." As such, *Vesperbild* refers to the moment in the Passion narrative when Christ's body was removed from the Cross, in the late afternoon; it is also a reference to the office of Vespers on Good Friday. Interestingly, the specific scene the word describes—after the body is removed from the Cross but before the Entombment— is not mentioned in the Gospels. Nonetheless, the image was increasingly popular in private devotional practice during the late Middle Ages. As made apparent in this finely carved, small sculpture, the *Vesperbild* was intended to evoke empathy in the viewer as it confronted him or her with the intense suffering of the now dead Christ and his grieving mother. The sculpture is a moving example of the *Schöne Stil*, or "Beautiful Style," popular in central Europe at the end of the fourteenth century. Prague was a key center for works in this style, and it is likely that the sculpture was carved there.

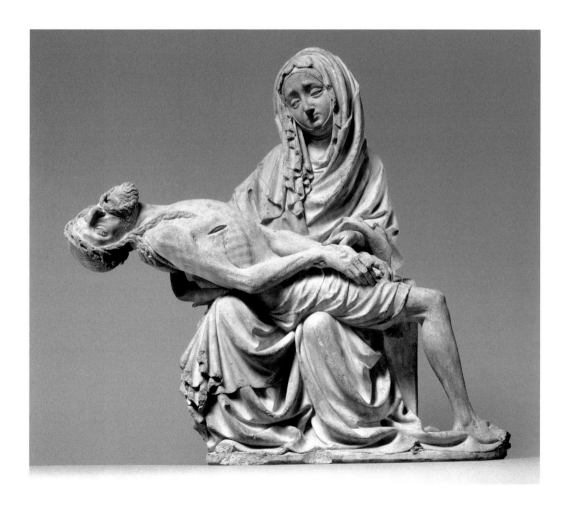

Credenza

Italy, 1440–50
Walnut and intarsia, 58 @ 125 @ 25 in.
(147.3 @ 317.5 @ 63.5 cm)
The Cloisters Collection, 1953 (53.95)

Originally a functioning sideboard intended
for the preparation and serving of food, the
credenza evolved in the late Middle Ages into
a display for expensive plates and other vessels
and was thus often draped in luxurious fabrics.
Whereas most medieval furniture has suffered
from use and climate over the centuries, this
credenza is unusually well preserved. It has been
attributed to the brothers Lorenzo (1425–1477)
and Cristoforo Canozi (ca. 1426–1491) from
Lendinara, in northern Italy, and associated with
their early style. The piece is decorated with a
total of eight panels. The top two-thirds of each
panel contains a circular form resembling a rose
window, with a row of intricate lancets below;
square fields, each covered with rectilinear patterns in intarsia, occupy the bottom thirds of
the panels. The six panels that form the front
face are divided into three pairs of doors, each
opening into a two-shelf interior where dishes
could be stored.

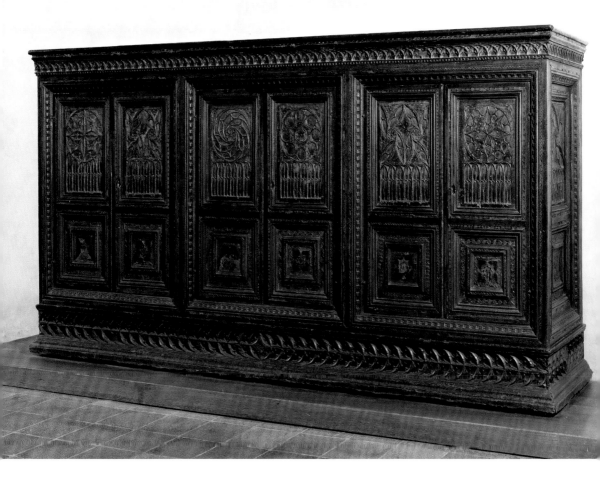

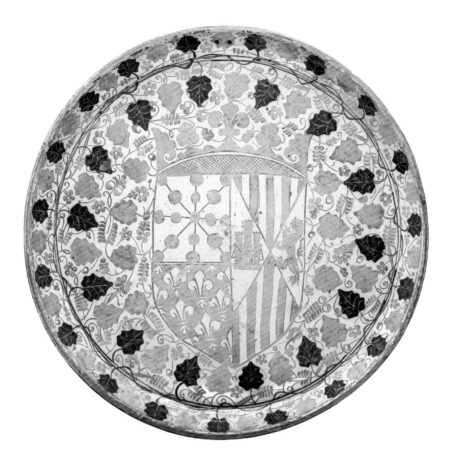

Plate with the Arms of Blanche of Navarre
Spain, Valencia, Manises, 1427–38
Tin-glazed and lustered earthenware,
DIAM. 15¾ in. (40 cm)
The Cloisters Collection, 1956 (56.171.148)

The prolific workshops of Manises, near the city of Valencia, made colorfully decorated tin-glazed earthenware vessels in many shapes. Such wares were widely appreciated across Europe, but Italians appear to have been the biggest customers for them. This plate, which bears the prominent arms of Queen Blanche of Navarre (1391–1441) and her husband, John II of Aragon, was probably part of a larger service. In a letter of 1454, for example, Maria of Castile, consort of Alfonso V of Aragon, ordered just such a service, including dishes for meat, washing basins, porringers, broth bowls, pitchers, vases, and other objects to be "lustered inside and out." During the fifteenth century, Italian maiolica workshops gradually began to surpass Spanish ones in terms of quality and sheer numbers.

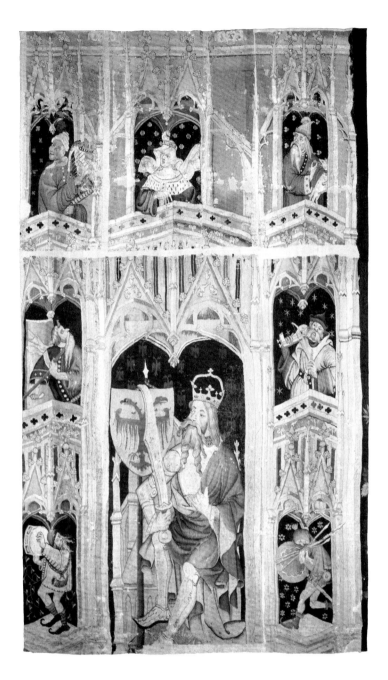

Julius Caesar and Attendants, from the Nine Heroes Tapestries

South Netherlands, 1400–1410
Wool warp and wefts, 13 ft. 9½ in. @ 91 in. (420.4 @ 231.1 cm)
Gift of John D. Rockefeller Jr., 1947 (47.101.3)

The subject of the Nine Heroes first appears about 1312 in a romance by the poet Jacques de Longuyon called *Les Voeux du paon* (The Vows of the Peacock). The nine worthies in Longuyon's tale were considered to embody both wisdom and valor, the consummation of chivalric ideals. Of the nine, three are classical (Hector of Troy, Alexander the Great, and Julius Caesar), three are Hebrew (Joshua, David, and Judas Maccabaeus, who led the Jews against the Syrians), and three are Christian (Arthur, Charlemagne, and Godfrey of Bouillon, who recaptured Jerusalem during the First Crusade).

Although fragmentary, The Cloisters' Nine Heroes constitute one of the very few extant tapestry sets from the turn of the fifteenth century. They were originally three large horizontal hangings, each with a trio of protagonists sitting across its width beneath vaulted spaces. Architectural elements such as crenellation and tracery windows functioned as compartmentalizing devices and helped create convincing spatial depth. The group was later cut down and used as curtains, and now just five heroes from this remarkable set remain: Julius Caesar (opposite), Hector, David, Joshua, and Arthur. Many of the details included in the tapestries are meant to enhance our understanding of the heroes depicted. Julius Caesar, for example, is surrounded by musicians and courtiers, some of whom appear to be African or Asian—perhaps an allusion to his military campaigns outside Europe. Arthur, on the other hand, is portrayed as a Christian ruler, accompanied, fittingly, by a group of clergymen of different ranks. The small attendants in secondary spaces are comparable to similarly marginalized and equally elusive figures often found in contemporary stained glass and manuscript paintings.

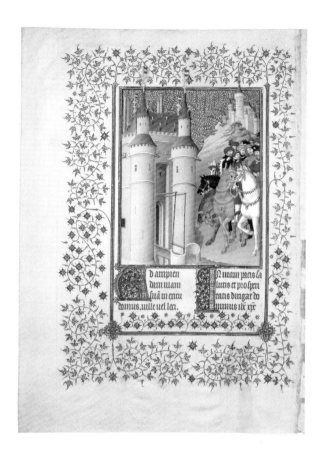

The Belles Heures of Jean de France, Duc de Berry

The Limbourg Brothers (active by 1399–1416)
France, Paris, 1405–1408/9
Ink, tempera, and gold leaf on vellum,
9⅜ @ 6⅝ in. (23.8 @ 16.8 cm)
The Cloisters Collection, 1954 (54.1.1)

Jean de France, duc de Berry (1340–1416), was the son, brother, and uncle of three different French kings, but it is as an art patron, collector, and connoisseur that he is guaranteed a prestigious place in the history of France. Books, in particular, were the duke's guiding passion, and

his books of hours were among the most richly embellished of all his illuminated manuscripts. The Belles Heures, described in the duke's inventory as "very well and richly illustrated," has 172 miniatures, including 94 full-page scenes like this one, in sumptuous colors and gold leaf. This page (fol. 223v), which illustrates a prayer for safe journey, shows the duke on a white horse followed by his entourage as he rides toward an impressive, turreted castle.

The artists who painted the Belles Heures, the Limbourg brothers, were originally from the South Netherlands (county of Gelders) and first trained as goldsmiths, a fact evident in the refined details of the manuscript. Among the greatest artists of their time, they were especially adept at narrative scenes and carefully observed depictions of the natural world. Although the Limbourg brothers created other important works for the duke, the Belles Heures was the only manuscript they completed for him.

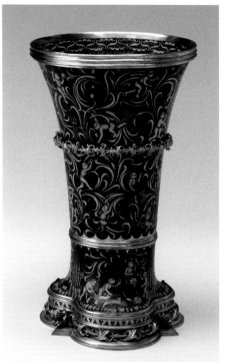
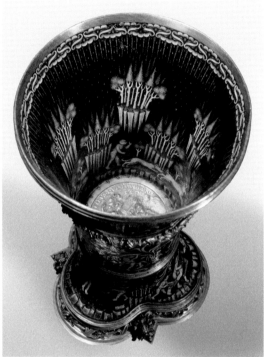

Beaker with Apes

South Netherlands, probably the
Burgundian territories, ca. 1430–40
Silver, silver gilt, and painted enamel,
H. 7⅞ in. (20 cm); DIAM. 4⅝ in. (11.7 cm)
The Cloisters Collection, 1952 (52.50)

The exterior of this cup depicts a sleeping ped-
dler being robbed by apes, a popular tale in
the late Middle Ages. In all, thirty-five of the
mischievous creatures cavort amid the cup's
scrolling foliage. Two more can be seen on the
interior, which is embellished with an elaborate
scene of a stag hunt. The apes are equipped
with hunting horn and bow and arrow and are

accompanied by hounds as they pursue two
stags in a forested setting. A sixteenth-century
gold medallion forms the bottom of the beaker.

Such a precious vessel, ornamented with
great sophistication, was most likely commissioned by the Burgundian court. It is decorated
in what was then the relatively new and exacting
technique of painted enamel. In that process,
before the enamel is fired it is freely applied
to the surface without wire strips (cloisons) or
shallow depressions (as in champlevé enamel)
to hold the colors in place. Here the artist has
mastered an especially difficult biconical shape,
which is adorned inside and outside in grisaille.

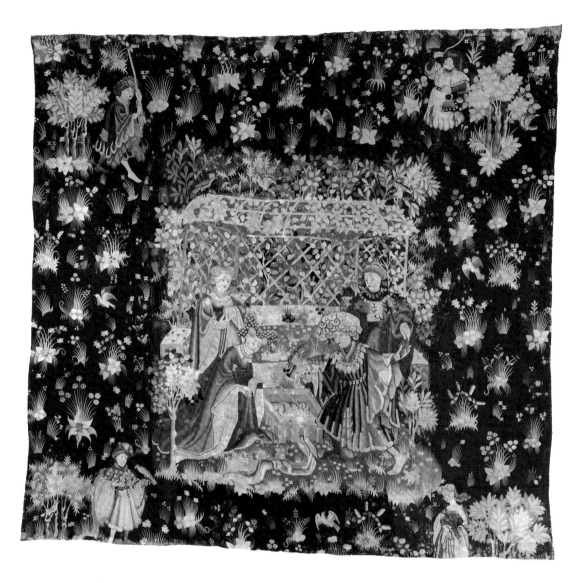

The Falcon's Bath

South Netherlands, ca. 1400–1415
Wool warp and wefts, 11 ft. 3⅞ @ 11 ft. 9 in. (345 @ 358 cm)
The Cloisters Collection, 2011 (2011.93)

Like the Nine Heroes series at The Cloisters, most tapestries surviving from the early fifteenth century are in poor condition or extensively restored. This recently discovered example depicting courtly figures training a falcon, however, is in remarkably good condition with bright colors. At the center of the tapestry, four luxuriously dressed figures are gathered in front of a rose trellis and a flowering turf bench. The lady and the gentleman in the foreground, attended by courtiers behind them, are encouraging the falcon to bathe in the basin of water between them. Surrounding the scene is a millefleurs ground, with four additional figures shown training falcons in the corners. The appearance of falconry in tapestries and other media makes it clear that hunting game birds with hawks was a favorite activity of the highest levels of late medieval society, and one of the few in which ladies could participate.

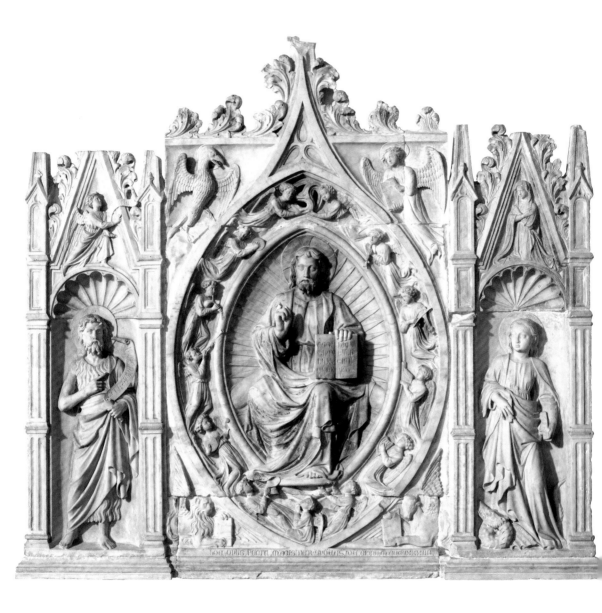

Altarpiece with Christ, Saint John the Baptist, and Saint Margaret

Andrea da Giona (active ca. 1434–46)
Italy, Liguria, 1434
From the church of San Giovanni Battista at Savona
Marble, 72 @ 80 @ 5 in. (182.9 @ 203.2 @ 12.7 cm)
The Cloisters Collection, 1962 (62.128a–i)

This marble retable, or altarpiece, is a rarity because it is signed and dated at the bottom of the center panel: HOC OPUS FECIT MAGISTER AND[R]EAS DA GIONA, MCCCCXXXIIII (made by Master Andrea da Giona, 1434). The retable itself comes from Savona, west of Genoa (in today's Liguria), but the sculptor, Master Andrea, was from the town of Giona in the Ticino, which in the fifteenth century was part of Lombardy. Here Master Andrea, like some of his fellow Lombard sculptors, has clearly assimilated aspects of Venetian art in his style—for example, the foliate decoration at top. Also, while he has retained such Gothic decorative elements as the pointed arches, other details, including the contrapposto posture of Saint Margaret and the scalloped niche above her, reveal his familiarity with the emerging Renaissance style.

At the center of the relief is Christ enthroned in majesty in a mandorla and surrounded by music-making angels. Symbols of the Four Evangelists fill the spandrels. Christ is flanked on the left by Saint John the Baptist, in a hair shirt, and on the right by Saint Margaret, with a dragon by her feet. The figures of the two saints are surmounted by the Archangel Gabriel (at left) and the Annunciate Virgin (at right), both framed by gables.

———————————————

Fragment of a Tapestry Hanging

Switzerland, Upper Rhineland, Basel, ca. 1420–30
Linen warp with wool weft, 29½ @ 33⅜ in. (74.9 @ 85.4 cm)
The Cloisters Collection, 1990 (1990.211)

With a thick mane covering its neck and upper body and a scaly hindquarter, the fantastical beast on this tapestry fragment is a composite creature similar to those illustrated in medieval bestiaries. It wears a collar hung with bells, attached to which is a spiral-striped cord leash held by a person whose left hand is still visible. Such animals were often depicted alongside courtly couples, shown leading or subduing them, and they are frequently associated in inscriptions on surviving tapestries with themes of love or unspoiled nature.

This fragment comes from a large hanging that was cut into three pieces, one of which is now kept in the Benedictine monastery at Muri-Gries near Bolzano, at the foot of the Alps. It was woven in the early fifteenth century by one of the earliest-known workshops in Basel. These domestic pieces, also called *Rücklaken,* were typically modest in size and often suspended from a molding or frieze high on a wall. The bold colors of the fierce, virile animals made such hangings popular items in late medieval homes.

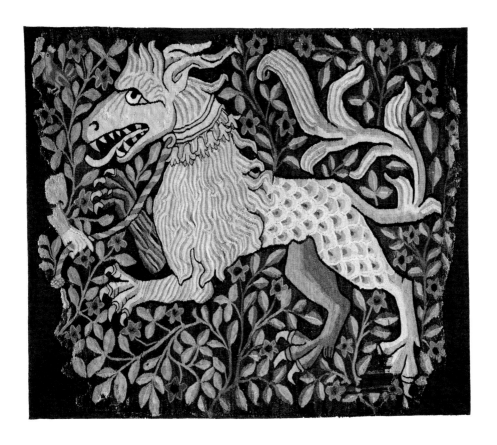

Altar Frontal with Man of Sorrows and Saints

Germany, Franconia, Nuremberg, ca. 1465
Linen warp with wool and silk wefts,
35¼ @ 65½ in. (89.5 @ 166.4 cm)
The Cloisters Collection, 1991 (1991.156)

This altar frontal, or "antependium," is a superb example of tapestries made in Nuremberg. Christ, represented as the Man of Sorrows, stands at the center, his hands raised to reveal his wounds. John the Baptist and the Virgin stand at his right, while John the Evangelist and Saint Jerome are at his left. The group appears amid a stylized meadow abloom with flowers, set against a pomegranate-patterned background. The varying shades of red, the highly expressive depiction of the Crown of Thorns, and Christ's lacerated body covered with blood combine to make this a particularly moving work. The antependium might have been one of seven donated by Margarete Toppler to the church of Saint Lawrence in Nuremberg after the death of her husband, Martin Pessler, in 1463. The coats of arms of both families appear at the bottom of the two vertical borders of climbing foliate scrolls.

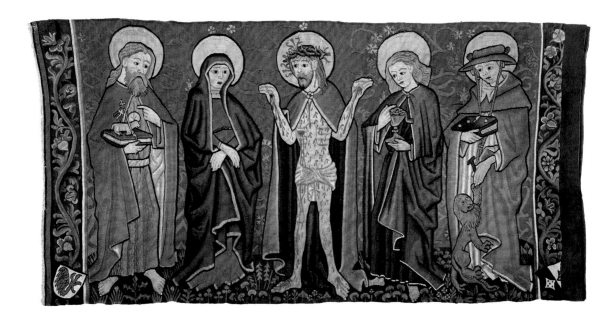

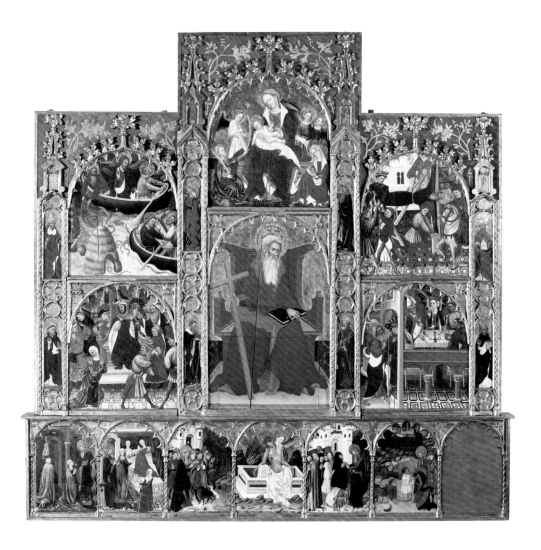

Altarpiece with Scenes from the Life of Saint Andrew

Attributed to the Master of Roussillon
Catalonia, ca. 1420–30
Said to come from a church at Perpignan
in Roussillon, France
Tempera and gilding on panel,
10 ft. 3¼ in. @ 10 ft. 3⅝ in. (313.1 @ 314 cm)
Rogers Fund, 1906 (06.1211.1–.9)

Physically imposing but delicately painted, this large altarpiece, which retains much of its original frame, is notable for the skillful use of color, careful design, and rich narrative content—for example, the various species of fish in the scene at upper left. The uppermost image, above the bearded figure of the apostle Saint Andrew in the center, is of the Enthroned Virgin and Child with Saint Catherine of Alexandria, Mary Magdalen, and angels. The other panels illustrate various episodes of Andrew's life taken from the thirteenth-century *Golden Legend*. The upper left panel depicts the calling of Saint Andrew, with the punishment of a wicked mother, below. In the upper right is his crucifixion, and below that he is seen saving a bishop from the devil disguised as a fair woman. At bottom, five additional scenes (the sixth is lost) flank a central image of Christ as the Man of Sorrows. From left to right, these are: Saint Andrew and the woman who prayed to Diana on behalf of her sister; a woman bringing the saint to her sister; Andrew driving away devils in the form of dogs; Andrew raising a dead youth; and Andrew bringing drowned men to life.

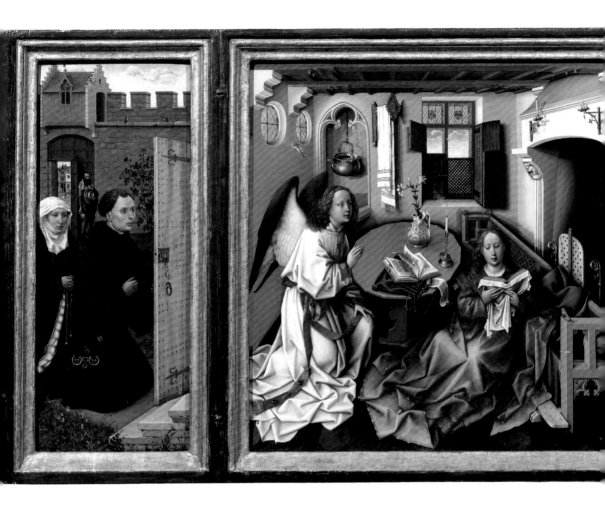

Annunciation Triptych (Merode Altarpiece)

Workshop of Robert Campin (ca. 1375–1444)

South Netherlands, Tournai (modern Belgium), ca. 1427–32

Oil on oak, center panel: 25¼ @ 24⅞ in. (64.1 @ 63.2 cm);
each wing: 25⅜ @ 10¾ in. (64.5 @ 27.3 cm)

The Cloisters Collection, 1956 (56.70a–c)

One of the best-known works of art at The
Cloisters, this masterful triptych is notable for
the superb quality of its execution, its fine state
of preservation, and the innovative treatment
of the subject matter. In the center panel, the
Annunciation to the Virgin takes place in a
carefully detailed domestic interior rather than
in the usual church setting. The Archangel
Gabriel arrives in the room followed by a tiny
image of the Christ Child borne on rays of light
and carrying a cross. Their entrance appears
to have extinguished the candle burning on

the table, but the Virgin, her eyes downcast
on devotional reading, seems unaware of her
heavenly guests. The right wing of the triptych is
devoted to Saint Joseph, who is rarely accorded
such prominence in medieval art. The carpenter
Joseph is shown at work in his shop, with an
unfinished mousetrap on the workbench and
a completed one on the window ledge. This
detail might allude to Saint Augustine's analogy
that the Cross was the Devil's mousetrap and
the crucified Christ his bait. The left wing was
probably painted by an assistant in Campin's
workshop, perhaps a young Rogier van der
Weyden. It depicts the donor with his wife
witnessing the center scene through a door;
a messenger, echoing Gabriel, stands in the
background. Heraldic emblems on the stained-
glass panels behind the Virgin have helped

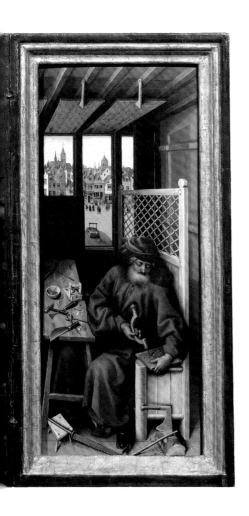

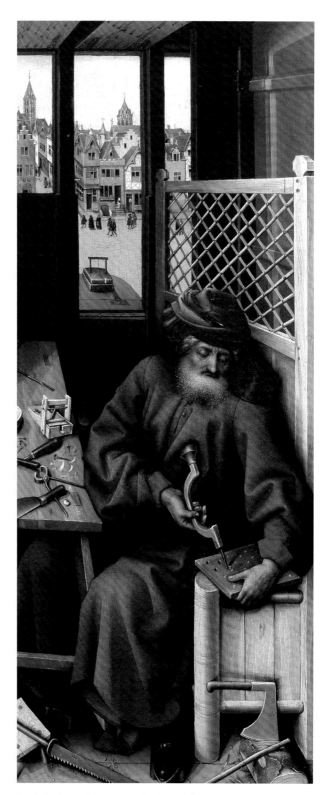

identify the kneeling male donor as Peter Engelbrecht, who probably commissioned the piece for his home.

The triptych is a masterpiece of what at that time was the relatively new medium of oil, which was replacing tempera (color pigments mixed with egg yolks) as the preferred material for painting panels. Just as significant (and typical of northern European art of the period) is the careful attention to detail, evident in the meticulous depictions of strands of hair, folds of drapery, and the cityscape seen through Joseph's window. The representation of three-dimensional space on a two-dimensional surface is achieved with foreshortening; for example, in the way the ceiling beams in the center panel recede into the background to create a convincing sense of spatial depth.

Detail of right panel, showing Joseph in his workshop

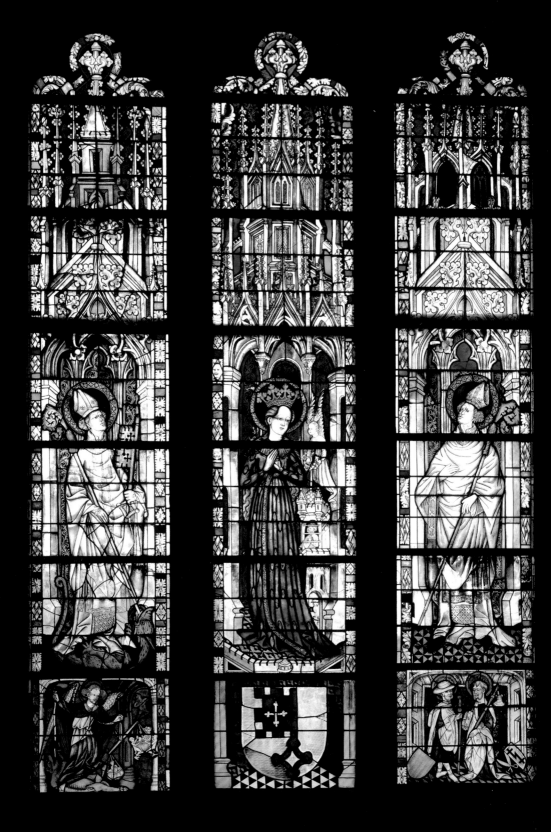

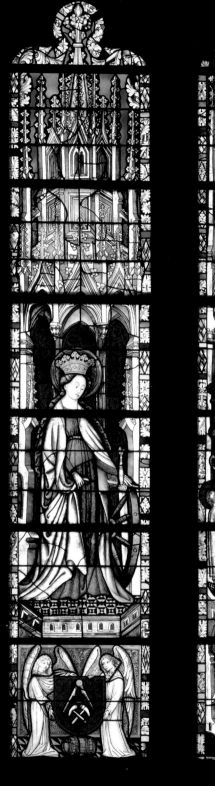
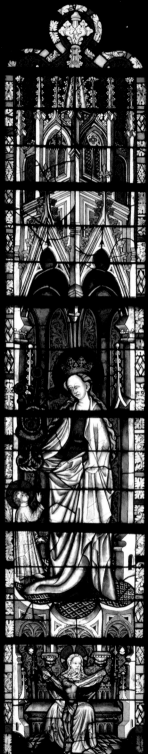
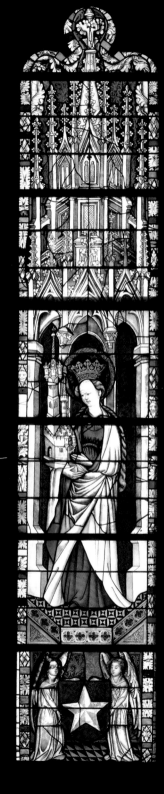

The Virgin Mary and Five Standing Saints Above Predella Panels

Germany, Middle Rhine valley, 1440–46
From the north nave of the former Carmelite church
at Boppard-am-Rhein in Rheinland-Pfalz (Rhein-
Hunsrück-Kreis), near Koblenz
Pot-metal glass, white glass, vitreous paint, and
silver stain, 148½ @ 28¼ in. (337.2 @ 71.8 cm) each
The Cloisters Collection, 1937 (37.52.1–.6)

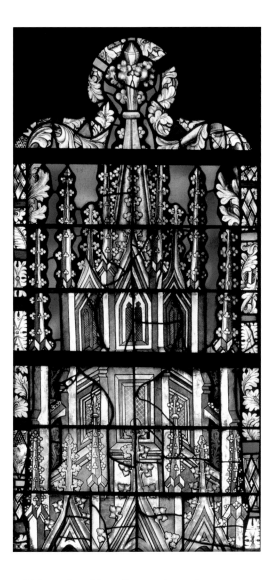

The Carmelite church at Boppard-am-Rhein
was once the home of an extensive program of
stained glass. The six windows from the church
now installed at The Cloisters (pp. 132–33) were
originally arranged on two levels, three over
three, to form a single unit on the north wall
of the north nave, whose construction began
in 1439. The three virgin saints occupied the
lower level, each carrying attributes associated
with her legend: Catherine with the wheel and
the sword; Dorothea with the Christ Child
and a basket of roses (opposite, right); and
Barbara holding a miniature tower. The three
other figures constituted the upper tier: Saint
Servatius holding a key and subduing a dragon
(opposite, left); the Virgin Mary in a corn robe;
and Saint Lambert, the bishop of Liège. Each
of the six figures stands beneath an elaborate
architectural canopy (above) and is anchored
at the bottom by a small panel containing a
subject related to the larger panel above. The
Archangel Michael, for example, who is depicted
weighing souls and trampling on a dragon, is a
visual mirror of Saint Servatius; so are the three
roses springing from Dorothea's basket, which
correspond to the Trinity below. The figural
style is elegant and gentle, particularly for the
female saints, who have high foreheads, delicate
features, and slender bodies under their robes.
In addition, the generous use of white glass in
the ensemble adds considerable radiance to the
primarily red and blue palette. These six lancets
constitute the only window from Boppard to
have survived in its entirety.

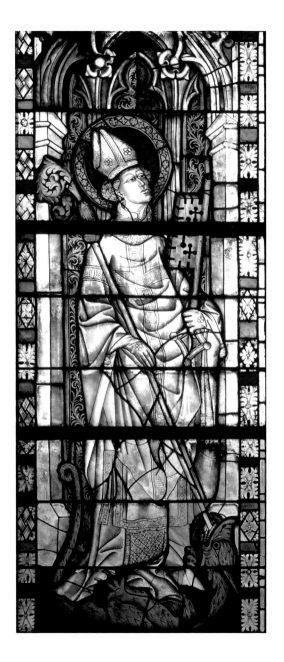
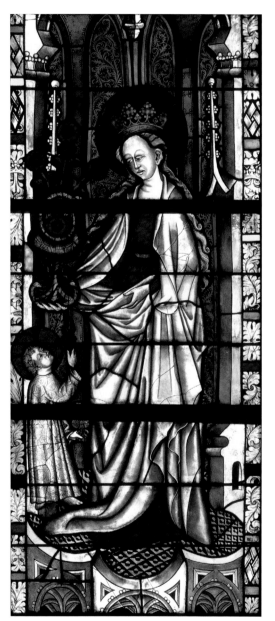

135

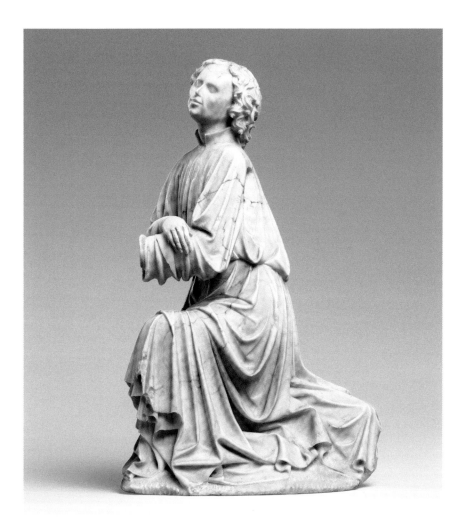

Kneeling Angel

South Netherlands or Rhineland, ca. 1430–40
Alabaster, 14½ @ 3¾ @ 8¾ in. (36.8 @ 9.5 @ 22.2 cm)
The Cloisters Collection, 1965 (65.215.3)

This elegant angel was originally part of a group
of statuettes depicting either the Annunciation
to the Virgin or Christ as the Man of Sorrows;
if the latter, the angel's crossed hands may have
held Instruments of the Passion. The angel's
refined features, the loose curls of long hair,
and the fluid treatment of the folds in the thin
drapery recall a group of alabaster sculptures
from a retable with the Crucifixion and the

Twelve Apostles formerly in Santa Maria
delle Grazie, Rimini-Covignano (now in the
Städtische Galerie Liebieghaus, Frankfurt). The
anonymous artists responsible for the ensemble
probably worked in the South Netherlands
or the Rhineland, but, as the Rimini altar
suggests, they appear to have produced many
sculptures in alabaster for export. The personal
style of the Rimini Master is closely linked to
the widespread, so-called International Gothic
style of about 1400, seen in this and many
other alabaster statuettes of the first half of the
fifteenth century.

Paschal Candlestick

Spain, Castilla-León, ca. 1450–1500
Wood with paint and gilding,
77 @ 17¼ in. (195.6 @ 43.8 cm)
Fletcher Fund, 1944 (44.63.1a, b)

Paschal candlesticks figure prominently in
the liturgy of the Easter vigil as part of the
celebration of the Resurrection. In a practice
that dates to the early church, the congregation gathers around the candlestick while
the deacon inserts grains of incense into five
holes in the wax of the candle arranged in a
cruciform pattern. The ceremony, known as
Lumen Christi, concludes with the lighting
of the paschal candle, which is raised above
the congregants—in the case of this example,
more than six feet above them. The decoration of the hexagonal candlestick is organized
in three tiers. The upper register is devoted to
the Hebrew Bible: Adam and Eve, the Expul-
sion of Adam and Eve (depicted on two faces),
and the prophets Jeremiah, Ezekiel, and
Zachariah. The second register depicts Saint
Benedict and five Franciscan saints: Francis,
Bernardine, Anthony of Padua, Louis of Toulouse, and Clare. Six of the apostles appear at
the bottom: Saints Bartholomew, Thomas,
Barnabas, John, Philip, and Matthias.

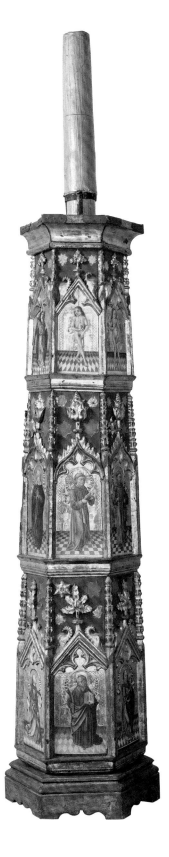

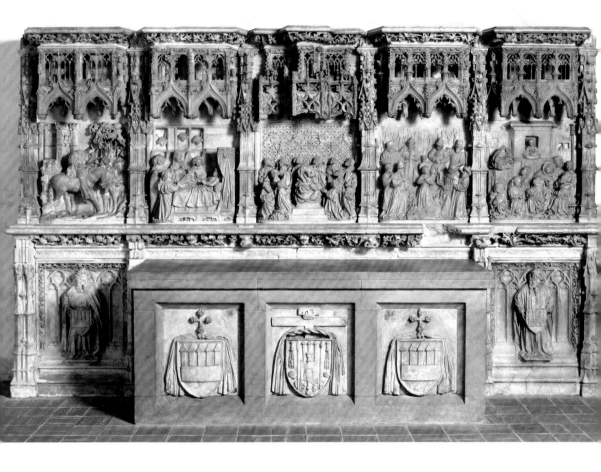

Altar Predella and Socle of Archbishop Don Dalmau de Mur y Cervelló

Franci Gomar (active 1443–ca. 1493)
Spain, Aragon (Saragossa), ca. 1456–58
From the chapel of the archbishop's palace at Saragossa
Alabaster with traces of paint and gilding, 8 ft. 11 in. @
15 ft. 3 in. @ 26¼ in. (271.8 @ 464.8 @ 66.7 cm)
Gift of J. Pierpont Morgan, 1909 (09.146)
Rogers Fund, 1914 (14.101.1, .2)
Gift of Emile Pares, 1916 (16.79)

Extending across five bays on two levels, this massive structure was commissioned by don Dalmau de Mur y Cervelló, archbishop of Saragossa from 1434 to 1458/59, for an altar in the chapel of the archiepiscopal palace. The upper level (intended as the predella for the altarpiece or retable) contains five scenes:

Saint Martin of Tours dividing his cloak with a beggar and Christ appearing to him in a dream (left panels); the Descent of the Holy Spirit (center panel); and Saint Thecla listening to the preaching of Paul (far right panel) and, after her conversion, being saved by divine intervention from burning fire (second panel from right). Each of the two outer panels on the lower level (or socle) shows a bearded figure carrying the coat of arms of the archbishop. The central shield on the reconstructed altar, festooned against a cross, depicts the Arma Christi (the instruments associated with the Crucifixion).

The structure is made of alabaster, a soft yet compact stone with a translucent glow. The workability of the material allowed the

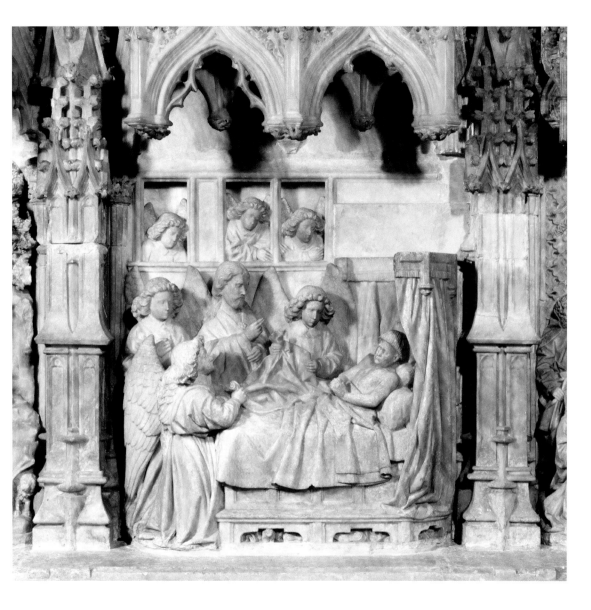

sculptor, Francí Gomar, to create exquisite details. Only a few traces of the original painting and gilding remain. According to a 1458 contract, the painter Tomás Giner (active 1458–80) was commissioned to paint and gild panels intended to stand above the predella. The unusual combination of painted altarpieces with a stone predella may have been a necessary measure to speed completion of the ensemble before the archbishop's death.

Detail of predella panel, showing Christ appearing in a dream to Saint Martin of Tours

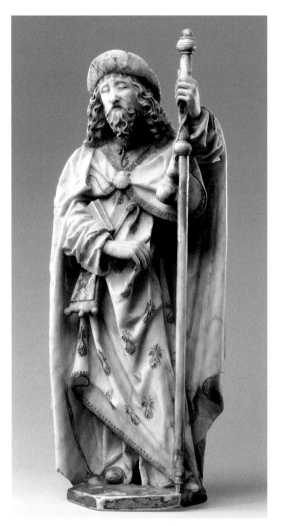
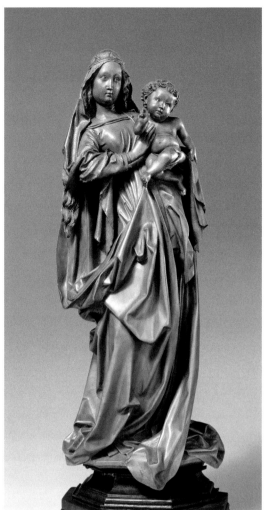

Saint James the Greater

Gil de Siloe (active 1475–1505)
Spain, Castilla-León (Burgos), 1489–93
From the tomb of Juan II of Castile and Isabel of Portugal
in the Cartuja de Miraflores, outside Burgos
Alabaster, gold, and paint, H. 18⅛ in. (45.9 cm)
The Cloisters Collection, 1969 (69.88)

This statuette of the apostle Saint James the
Greater, patron saint of Spain, was originally
part of the tomb of Juan II of Castile and Isabel
of Portugal. The monument, which still stands
in the church of the royal Carthusian monastery
of Miraflores outside Burgos, was commissioned
in 1486 by Isabel of Castile, daughter of the
king and queen, and was carved by the master
sculptor Gil de Siloe and his workshop. Lifesize

effigies of the royal couple rest on a star-
shaped platform, where they are surrounded by
statuettes of the Four Evangelists. Originally
these were accompanied by the Twelve Apostles.
Saint James, who once stood at the queen's left,
is seen here with a pilgrim's staff, water gourd,
and cockleshells adorning his hat, cloak, and
bag—attributes that evoke the dress of the
pilgrims who traveled across northern Spain
to reach his shrine at Santiago de Compostela,
where his body lay.

During the late Middle Ages alabaster was
frequently used for the decoration of tombs and
altars. The soft stone is easily cut and polished,
but it is also slightly soluble in water and
therefore not suitable for outdoor sculpture.

Standing Virgin and Child

Attributed to Niclaus Gerhaert von
Leyden (active 1460–73?)
Austria, probably Vienna, ca. 1470
Boxwood, H. 13¼ in. (33.6 cm)
Purchase, The Cloisters Collection and Lila
Acheson Wallace Gift, 1996 (1996.14)

Like elephant ivory, boxwood is a dense, fine-
grained material ideally suited to carving on a
small scale. This Virgin and Child (opposite,
right), a sculptural tour de force, conveys a sense
of monumentality that far exceeds its small size.
The group is masterfully conceived in the round,
with extraordinary drapery that falls and loops
around the Virgin in front as her veil and the
long curls of her hair carry the visual flow to the
back. The cross-legged, active figure of the
Child echoes the motion of the Virgin's mantle.

The artist, Niclaus Gerhaert von Leyden,
who was probably of Netherlandish origin,
became the most important German sculptor
of his generation. One can see in the statuette
many of the distinguishing characteristics of
Gerhaert's monumental works—the lively sense
of movement, the complex treatment of the
figure in space, and the richness of the textured
surface. Gerhaert is best known for his work in
Strasbourg, but this statuette likely dates to the
end of his life, when he worked in Vienna.

Saint Barbara

Alsace, probably Strasbourg (modern France), ca. 1490
Lindenwood with paint, H. 50¼ in. (127.6 cm)
The Cloisters Collection, 1955 (55.166)

Saint Barbara, the daughter of a wealthy pagan
of the third century, stands here in an elegant
and complex formal pose. Leaning slightly to
her left, she subtly tilts her head in the other
direction; her arms are crossed, left over right.
In her left hand she holds an open book, and in
the right one she grasps the hem of her voluminous mantle. The figure retains much of its
original painted and gilded decoration, including
the richly gilded foliate pattern in low relief on
the mantle's interior. The sculpture can be associated with three other figures of saints, now

dispersed, that once flanked the Virgin and Child
in a large altarpiece from the church of Saint
Mauritius in Kippenheim, in the Upper Rhine
valley. Strasbourg and other centers in that area
were home to a number of innovative sculptors
working in wood, beginning with the masterful
Niclaus Gerhaert von Leyden (see entry above).

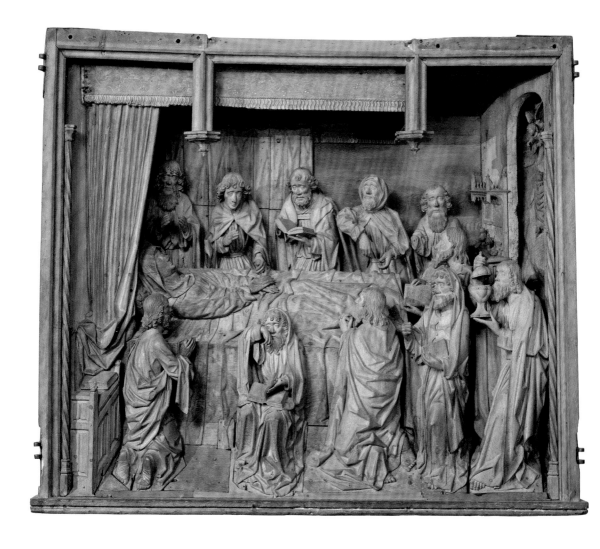

The Death of the Virgin (The Dormition)

Workshop of Tilman Heysacker
Germany, Lower Rhineland, Cologne, late 15th century
Oak, 63 @ 73¾ @ 17¼ in. (160 @ 187.3 @ 43.8 cm)
The Cloisters Collection, 1973 (1973.348)

This shrine was originally painted and had two wings decorated in low relief with scenes of the Birth of the Virgin and the Adoration of the Magi (both now in the Rijksmuseum Twenthe, Enschede, Netherlands). The center image, seen here, represents the Death, or Dormition, of the Virgin, which is set in a domestic interior. Saint Peter stands at the back holding a book as he officiates at the sacrament of extreme unction.

He is accompanied by ten other apostles. Through a doorway at far right we glimpse a depiction of a legend, recorded in the thirteenth century, in which Saint Thomas does not reach the Virgin before her death and is convinced of her Assumption only after her belt is dropped into his hands by an angel. Many of the other iconographic and stylistic elements of the shrine are derived from Netherlandish painting. This affinity is not surprising given that Tilman Heysacker, the carver whose workshop made this piece, was active in the late fifteenth century in Cologne, a city that enjoyed close ties with the Netherlands.

Triptych with the Passion of Christ

South Germany, ca. 1475–85
Mother-of-pearl, gilt-wood frame, silk backing, and tooled leather covering, 8⅜ @ 9½ @ ⅞ in. (21.2 @ 24 @ 2.2 cm)
The Cloisters Collection, 2006 (2006.249)

Of small scale but with a commanding presence, this gilt-wood devotional triptych mounted with a series of mother-of-pearl plaques in openwork relief is a great rarity. It appears to be the only such triptych decorated with this lustrous and highly prized material to survive intact. The format and arrangement of the plaques suggest a South German origin, perhaps Augsburg, where the sole other recorded example,

illustrated in the early sixteenth-century catalogue of objects belonging to Cardinal Albrecht von Brandenburg, is said to have been made. Curiously, the narrative sequence of the Passion scenes on both triptychs begins with the plaque second from the top on the left wing and reads clockwise, with the final scene, the Crucifixion, in the center. Like goldsmiths, masters of the adjunct art of mother-of-pearl carving relied directly or indirectly on prints and model books for their compositions. These plaques would seem to be loosely based on the small Passion engravings of the fifteenth-century German printmaker Master E.S.

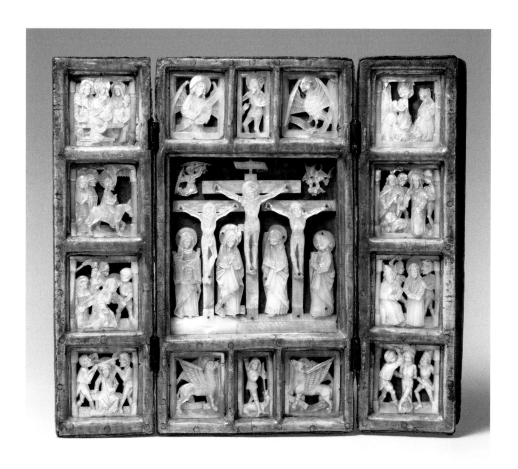

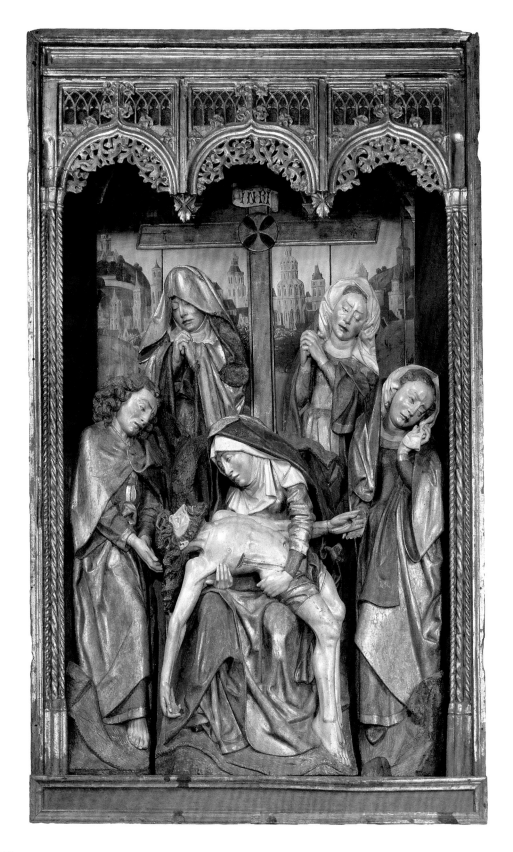

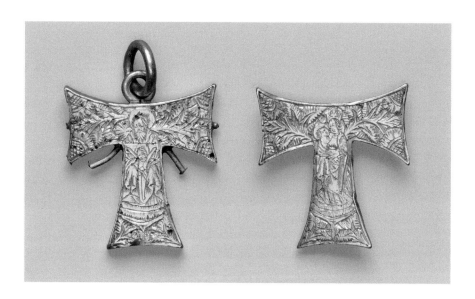

The Lamentation
Spain, Castilla-La Mancha (Guadalajara), ca. 1480
From the Benedictine monastery at Sopetrán
Walnut, paint, and gilding, 83 @ 48½ @ 13½ in.
(211 @ 123 @ 34.3 cm)
The Cloisters Collection, 1955 (55.85)

The highly emotional, wrenching expressions
on the faces of the standing figures in this
shrine are heavily influenced by the work
of the South Netherlandish painter Rogier
van der Weyden (ca. 1399–1464). Indeed, it is
possible the Spanish workshop that created
this panel included at least one Netherlandish
artist, or perhaps the workshop had access to a
sketchbook that included elements taken from
Rogier's paintings. The shrine was originally the
center section of an altarpiece from the ruined
Benedictine monastery of Sopetrán, northeast
of Madrid. The two panels with four painted
scenes that formed the wings of the retable are
now in the Prado, Madrid.

Tau Cross
England, Lincolnshire, ca. 1485
Found in a field at Winteringham
Cast and engraved gold, 1⅜ @ 1⅛ @ ⅛ in.
(3.5 @ 2.9 @ 0.3 cm)
The Cloisters Collection, 1990 (1990.283a, b)

A depiction of the Trinity is delicately engraved
on the front of this pendant cross, which is
actually a shallow capsule. An image of the
Virgin and Child decorates the back. The stems
that extend from beneath the arms of the cross
at an angle originally held pearls; at the bottom
edge there is a hole that once held a bell. The tau,
or T-shaped cross, was associated with the Order
of Saint Anthony Abbot. In the fifteenth century
the disease called Saint Anthony's fire—a toxic
condition caused by the consumption of spoiled
rye—was widespread, and the order founded
many so-called Antonine hospitals. The capsule
most likely held an herbal compound used in
treating the burning heat that was a primary
symptom of the disease.

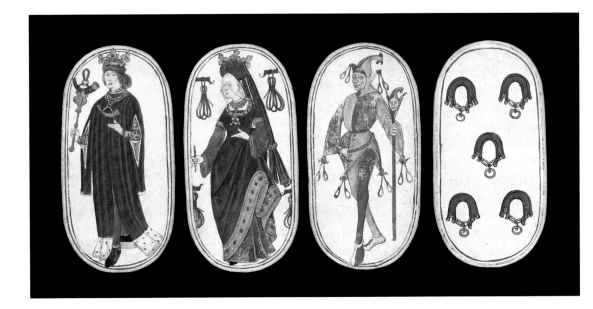

Set of Fifty-Two Playing Cards

South Netherlands, Burgundian territories,
ca. 1470–80
Ink, tempera, and metal foil on pasteboard,
5⅜ @ 2¾ in. (13.7 @ 7 cm) each card
The Cloisters Collection, 1983 (1983.515.1–.52)

The outstanding condition of these painted
playing cards, the only known complete set to
survive from the Middle Ages, suggests that
they were never used. Each of the four suits is
represented by number cards from one to ten
and by a knave, queen, and king. Created before
the standardization of the suits as we know
them today, the set relies on symbols drawn
from hunting paraphernalia: dog collars and
horns (both red), and nooses and tethers (blue).
The figures on the cards are dressed in elaborate
costumes characteristic of the Burgundian court.
Regrettably, we know little about how medieval
card games were played.

Armorial Bearings and Badges
of John, Lord Dynham

South Netherlands, 1488–1501
Wool warp and wefts with a few silk wefts,
12 ft. 8 in. @ 12 ft. 1 in. (386.1 @ 368.3 cm)
The Cloisters Collection, 1960 (60.127.1)

Although fragmentary, this large tapestry contains heraldic motifs with enough detail to allow
us a glimpse into the life of John, Lord Dynham
of Devonshire (1433–1501). Lord Dynham's personal badge (topcastle and broken mast) appears
twelve times on the hanging, indicative of his
long naval career under five English kings. But
the hanging is dominated by his full achievement of arms, with his personal shield circumscribed by a blue garter, supported by a pair of
stags, and surmounted by an ermine standing
between two candles. The elaborate design
marks the crowning moment of Lord Dynham's
life—when he was elected to the Order of the

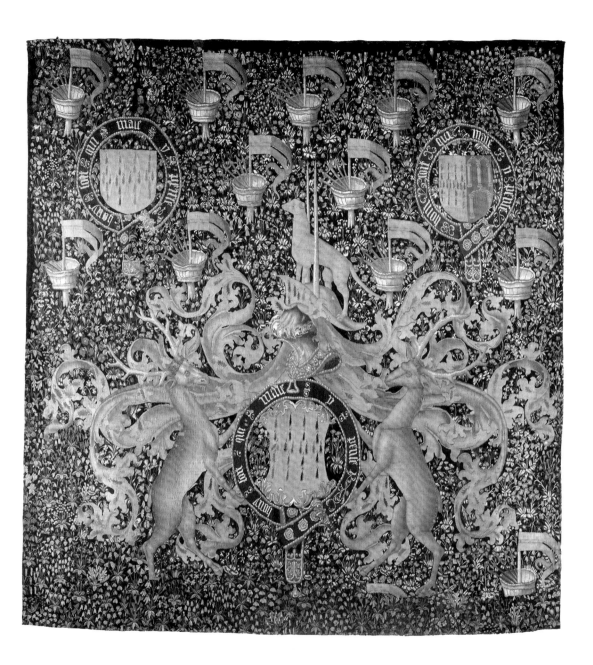

Garter in 1487/88—and in all probability the hanging was commissioned to celebrate this occasion. Quite a few tapestries from the second half of the fifteenth century employ this kind of millefleurs background interspersed with heraldic motifs, suggesting that the basic formula had become somewhat standardized. It is likely that clients would commission an artist to design an armorial device that would later be incorporated in such a tapestry.

Fragment of a Chasuble

England, late 15th century
Silk, metallic threads on linen and velvet,
28¾ @ 14¼ in. (73 @ 36 cm)
The Cloisters Collection, 1982 (1982.432)

A chasuble is an ecclesiastical vestment that
is shaped like a sleeveless mantle and worn by
the celebrant of the Mass. It is often made of
luxurious fabrics such as silk and velvet and
embellished with gold threads, precious stones,
and other valuable materials. These splendid
vestments reaffirm and enhance the prestige of
the clergymen as well as the solemnity of the
service. This chasuble fragment is decorated
with two cherubim, each standing atop a wheel
radiant with light, four fleurs-de-lis, and four
thistles. The design and the shape of the fragment suggest that it formed the lower-right
quadrant of the chasuble. The embellishments
were embroidered in silk and silver-gilt threads
and then appliquéd onto velvet. The vestment
was made in England, whose workshops were
known for producing some of the best embroideries, especially from the thirteenth to the fifteenth century. Indeed, the term *opus anglicanum*
(English work), which became synonymous with
English embroideries, appears more than one
hundred times in the Vatican inventory of 1295.

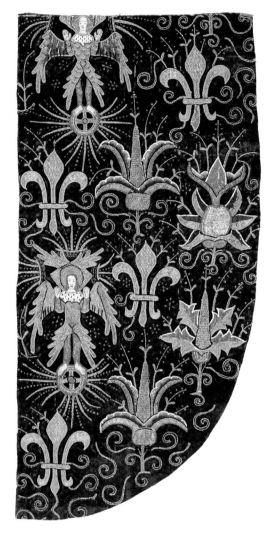

Seated Bishop

Tilman Riemenschneider (1460–1531)
Germany, Franconia (Lower Franconia),
Würzburg, ca. 1495–1500
Lindenwood, 35½ @ 14 @ 5⅞ in. (90.2 @ 35.6 @ 14.9 cm)
The Cloisters Collection, 1970 (1970.137.1)

Tilman Riemenschneider was one of the
finest and most successful sculptors of the late
Middle Ages. This well-conceived image of a
venerable but unidentified bishop is representative of the carver's early work. With its seated,
S-shaped pose and finely carved details, it can be
compared to the evangelist figures of Riemenschneider's Münnerstadt altarpiece of 1492–94

(Staatliche Museen zu Berlin, Skulpturensammlung). There are no indications of painted
decoration on the sculpture other than black in
the irises and red on the lips. In fact, many of
the figure's carefully realized details, such as the
facial wrinkles and the fringe on the bishop's
cope, would be obscured by the layer of gesso
applied beneath a paint. Riemenschneider was
an innovator in the use of lightly stained sculpture, so it is likely that the bishop is an example
of this aspect of his work. The fine grain of lindenwood, or limewood, made it well suited for
this purpose.

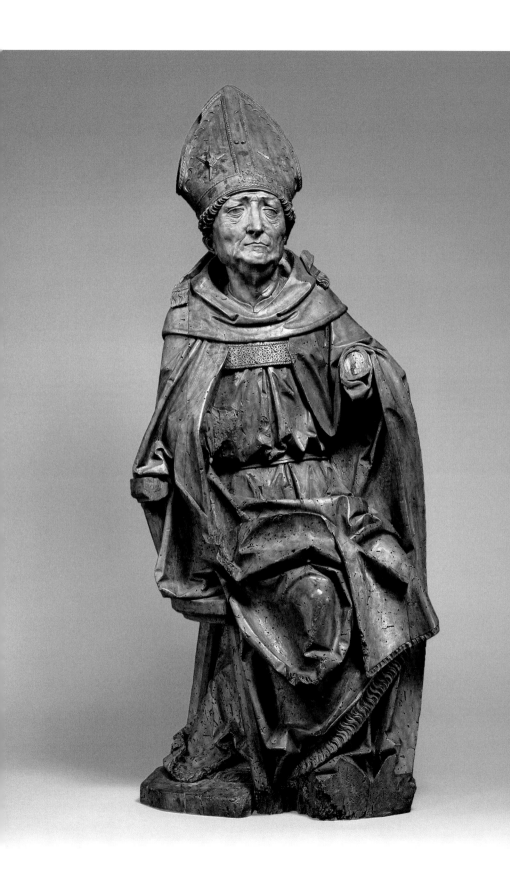

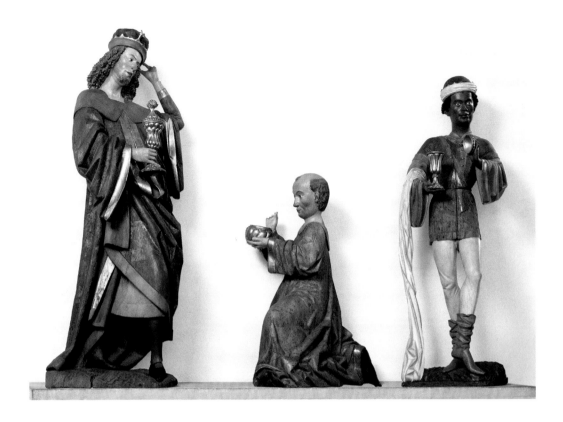

Three Kings from an Adoration Group

Germany, Swabia, before 1489
From the high altar of the Cistercian abbey at
Lichtenthal, near Baden-Baden, in Baden-Württemberg
Poplar, paint, and gilding, H. left to right: 64½ in.
(163.8 cm); 40 in. (101.6 cm); 61½ in. (156.2 cm)
The Cloisters Collection, 1952 (52.83.1–.3)

Ever since the Holy Roman Emperor Frederick
Barbarossa acquired their relics for Cologne in
1164, the Three Kings, or Magi, have enjoyed
great popularity in the art of northern Europe.
By the late Middle Ages they were believed to
have descended from the sons of Noah and
were thus often represented as three distinct
races: European, Asian, and African. These three
almost lifesize statues, decorated with extensive
painting and gilding, were once part of an

altarpiece depicting the Adoration of the Magi.
Two of the sculptures, the crowned Balthasar
and the kneeling Melchior, would have stood
on either side of the seated Virgin and Child
group, which remains in the Cistercian convent
at Lichtenthal. Together they form a descending
diagonal balanced by the dancerlike Gaspar on
the far right. In animated and playful poses,
they bring to the Christ Child gifts of gold,
frankincense, and myrrh.

The Lichtenthal altarpiece was originally
flanked by two wings painted with scenes from
the life of the Virgin. The date 1489 appears on
one of the painted scenes along with the name
Margarethe, the abbess of Lichtenthal who
commissioned this impressive ensemble seven
years before her death.

Saint Anthony Abbot

Attributed to Niclaus of Haguenau (ca. 1445–1538)
Alsace, Strasbourg (modern France), ca. 1500
Walnut, H. 44¾ in. (113.7 cm)
The Cloisters Collection, 1988 (1988.159)

This is an especially dramatic representation
of Saint Anthony Abbot, the third-century
founder of monasticism who, according to
legend, overcame the temptation of demons in
the Egyptian desert. He wears the traditional
garb of monks and carries a tau (T-shaped)
cross that is now largely lost. The sculpture
depicts the violent interaction between the
satanic creature tearing at the saint's garment
and the calm, victorious Anthony trampling
the devil and thrusting the shaft of his cross
into its mouth.

Unlike wood carvings made for altarpieces
in this period, this sculpture is carved fully
in the round, suggesting that it was meant to
be installed against a column in a church and
approached from different directions. It was
probably venerated in one of the Antonine
order's foundations, such as those at Isenheim
or Strasbourg. In terms of style, the sculpture
is in keeping with the work of Niclaus of
Haguenau, one of the leading carvers of
the region in about 1500.

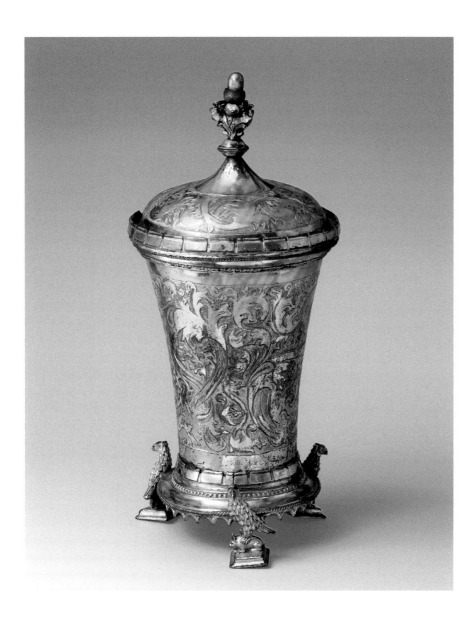

Covered Beaker

Attributed to the workshop of Sebastian
Lindenast the Elder
Germany, Franconia, Nuremberg, ca. 1490–1500
Copper gilt, H. 9⅛ in. (23 cm); DIAM. 3¾ in. (9.5 cm)
The Cloisters Collection, 1994 (1994.270a, b)

During the Middle Ages, silversmiths in
Nuremberg and other cities were generally
prohibited from working in copper gilt in order
to protect the lucrative market for precious

wares. By imperial privilege, however, the
Lindenast family was permitted to use copper,
and this finely made vessel is probably from the
workshop of Sebastian Lindenast the Elder. It is
not marked, as it likely would be if it had been
made in silver, but it is stylistically consistent
with the work of Nuremberg silversmiths. In
addition to its attractive profile and crisply
engraved, lively design, the beaker is notable
for its well-preserved gilded surface.

Covered Chalice

Spain, Castilla-La Mancha, Toledo, late 15th century
Silver gilt with rubies, sapphires, diamonds, and crystals,
H. 17¼ in. (43.7 cm); DIAM. 7¾ in. (19.7 cm)
The Cloisters Collection, 1958 (58.39a, b)

With its elaborate ornament drawn from late
Gothic architecture, the rare openwork cover
on this Spanish chalice nearly overwhelms
the form of the vessel itself. The exterior of
the bowl is engraved in Gothic letters with the
Latin text of the Hail Mary—AVE MARIA GRACIA
PLENA DOMINUS [TECUM]—the greeting of
the Archangel Gabriel to the Virgin Mary
when he announced the forthcoming birth of
Jesus. The six facets of the knop and the cover
are embellished with pointed arches beneath
which appear busts of Christ, the Virgin and
Child, and saints. On the lobes of the foot
are representations of the Crucifixion, the
Instruments of the Passion, the Virgin and
Child, and the Lamentation. Both the base
and the cover bear the mark used by goldsmiths
in Toledo during the fifteenth century.

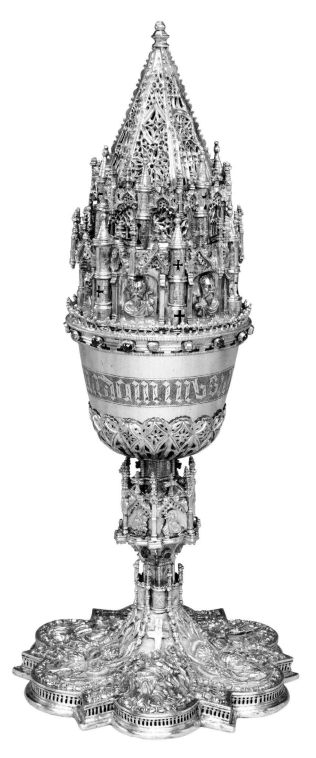

Triptych with Scenes from the Passion of Christ

Possibly Master Pertoldus (Berthold Schauer?)
Austria, Salzburg, 1494
From the Benedictine abbey of Saint Peter at Salzburg
Silver, silver gilt, mother-of-pearl, bone, and cold enamel,
27⅜ @ 9⅞ @ 7¼ in. (69.5 @ 25.1 @ 18.4 cm) open
Gift of Ruth and Leopold Blumka, 1969 (69.226)

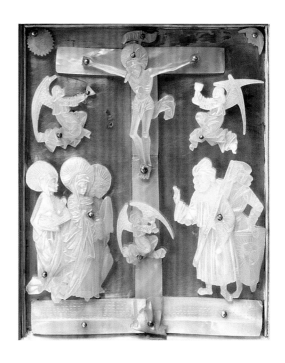

This triptych is remarkable for its completeness
as well as for the high quality of its execution.
At the center of the shrine is the Crucifixion,
with Jesus before Pilate on the bottom panel
of the left wing, and the Bearing of the Cross
above. On the right wing, the Agony in the
Garden is at top, with the Entombment below.
Above the center section are three medallions
(the one on the left is a modern replacement)
representing, from left to right: Saint Catherine,
the Virgin and Child, and Saint George and the
Dragon. The Annunciation appears on the large
medallion below the Crucifixion. In addition
to these carved appliqués and the silver figure
of Christ at the top, the triptych is embellished
with skillful engravings. Saints Andrew,
Benedict, and Catherine are portrayed on the
base, while the Last Supper is depicted on the
reverse of the central shrine, flanked by the
Flagellation and the Arrest of Christ (left), and
the Crown of Thorns and the Resurrection of
Christ (right).

The inscription above the Crucifixion—
RUDBERTI ABBATIS PERSTO EGO IUSSO SUO
(I stand by order of Abbot Rupert)—links
the triptych to Abbot Rupert Keutzl of the
Benedictine abbey of Saint Peter at Salzburg.
The date 1494 appears three times on the object.
Documents record a triptych made about this
date by the goldsmith Pertoldus, but we cannot
be certain that that work is the same as The
Cloisters' triptych.

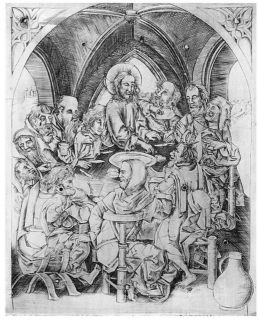

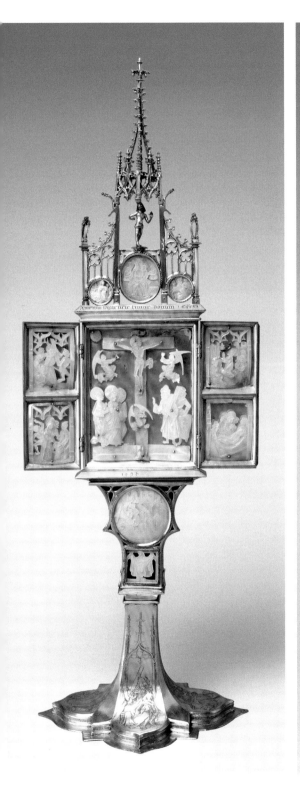

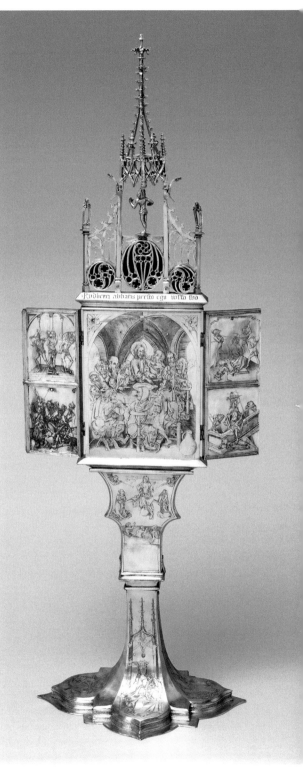

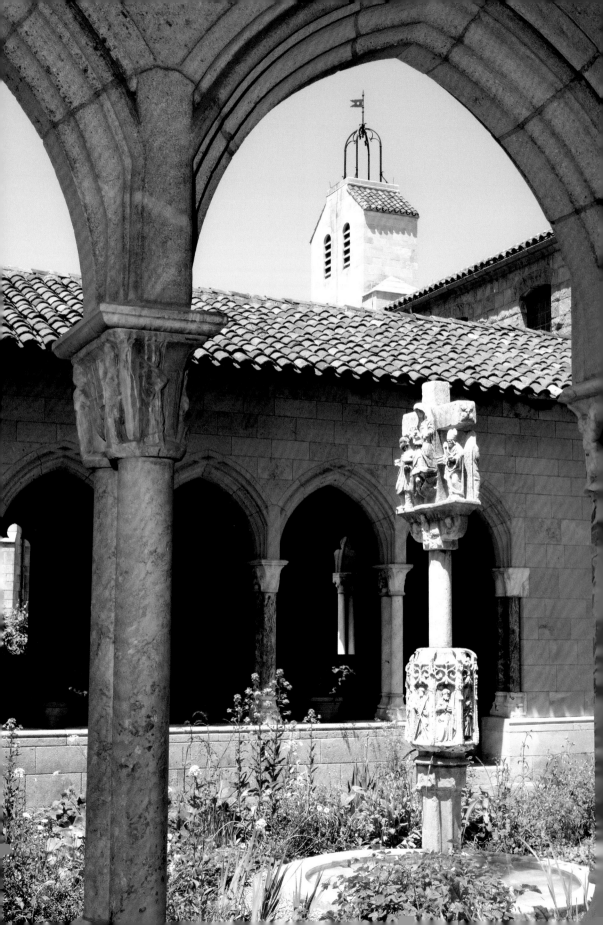

Cloister from Trie-sur-Baïse

France, Midi-Pyrénées (Hautes-Pyrénées), late 15th century
From monuments at Trie-sur-Baïse, Larreule, and Saint-
Sever-de-Rustan, near Tarbes
Marble, 35 ft. 8 in. @ 47 ft. 2½ in. (10.9 @ 14.4 m)
The Cloisters Collection, 1925 (25.120.135–.971)

The capitals from the cloister of the Carmelite monastery of Trie-sur-Baïse, near Toulouse, are decorated with scenes from the Old and New Testaments and the lives of the saints. The use of white marble for the capitals and colored marble for the shafts indicates that this was a prestigious commission. Since the original arrangement of the capitals is unknown, they are displayed sequentially, corresponding to their unfolding narratives. Many coats of arms are found on them (below); those of Catherine de Foix, queen of Navarre, and her husband, Jean d'Albret, who married in 1484, help establish the earliest possible date for the construction of the cloister. After the Huguenots destroyed all of the monastic buildings except for the church in 1571, some of the Trie capitals were sold to the Benedictine monastery of Saint-Sever-de-Rustan

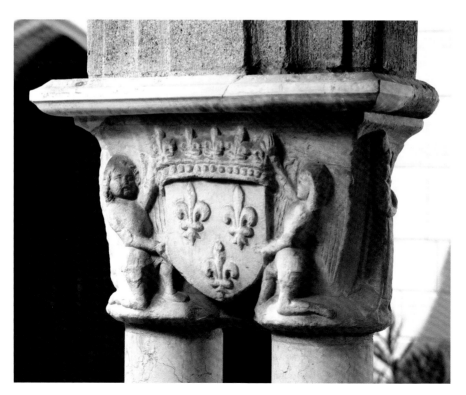

Detail of capital, showing the French royal coat of arms

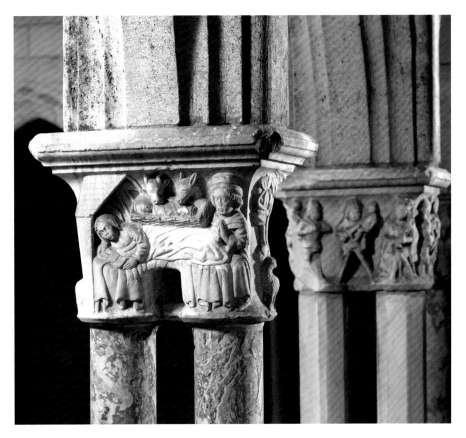

Detail of capitals, with the Nativity in the foreground

for the rebuilding of its own cloister. Twenty-eight of them changed hands again between 1889 and 1890, when they were sold to the city of Tarbes. Of the eighty-one capitals known to have been at Trie, eighteen are now at The Cloisters.

The flowery meadow familiar from so many medieval works of art is re-created in the Trie Cloister garden, where a multitude of plants blooms in different seasons on a ground bordered with periwinkles. The fragrant display is accompanied by the sound of running water from the central fountain, which is composed of late medieval and modern elements. Together with the bees, butterflies, and chirping birds, the plantings transform this delightful enclosure into a vivid display of the flora and fauna seen in tapestries of the Middle Ages.

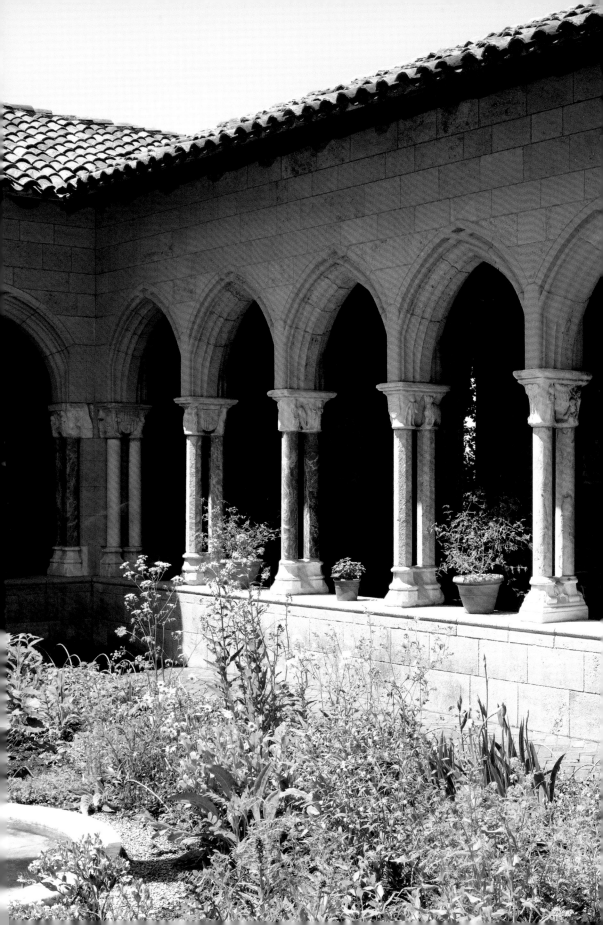

Doorway and Staircase Enclosure

France, Picardy (Somme), late 15th or
early 16th century
From 29, rue de la Tannerie, Abbeville
Oak, 14 ft. 10 in. @ 68½ in. @ 9 ft. 9½ in.
(452.1 @ 174 @ 298.5 cm)
Frederick C. Hewitt Fund, 1913 (13.138.1)

Intricately carved, this wood doorway and staircase enclosure come from a house in Abbeville,
in northern France. Although long known as the
"House of Francis I," the timber-framed, two-
story home was probably built for an affluent
tanner. The doorway opened into a passage connecting the street and the inner courtyard, while
the adjacent enclosure provided entrance to a

spiral staircase. Statuettes protected by delicate
canopies originally stood on the carved pedestals.
The openwork tracery at top exemplifies the complex and sophisticated design of the Flamboyant
style. Below, the rectangular panels are carved
with variations on a main motif, consisting of a
central vertical stem with bifurcated terminals
scrolling into a curving V at either end. A cord
is knotted or tied to the stem, which in turn is
flanked by a pair of interlacing arcs.

Before the doorway and enclosure were sold
in 1907, the house had been used as a livery stable
and a tavern (below). The area where the house
once stood was completely destroyed during
World War II, leaving no trace of the old block.

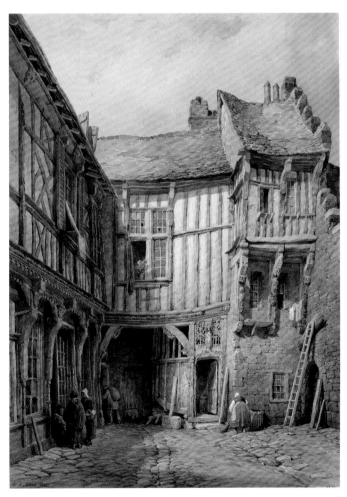

Lewis John Wood (1813–1901). *Courtyard of the "House of Francis I," no. 29, rue de la Tannerie,
Abbeville.* Watercolor on paper, 19⅛ @ 13⅝ in. (48.6 @ 34.6 cm). Rogers Fund, 1943 (43.92)

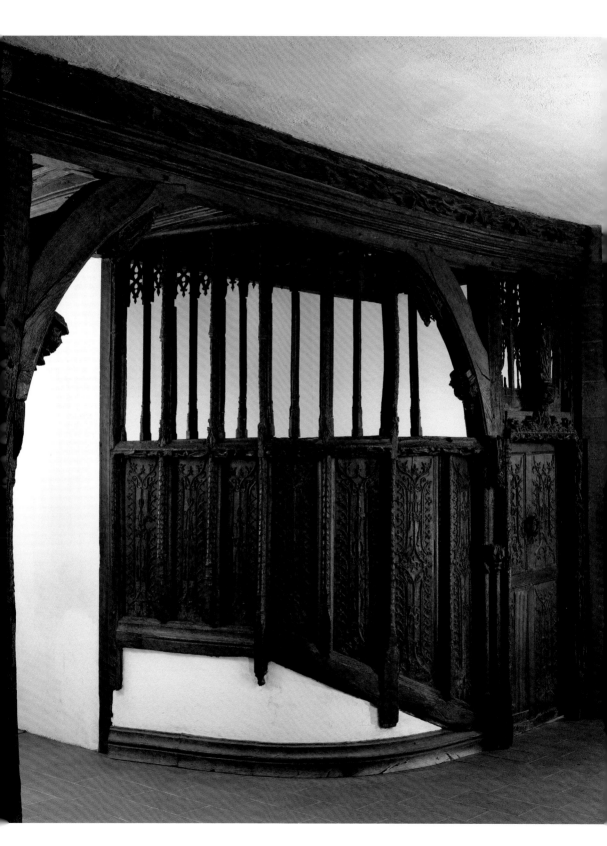

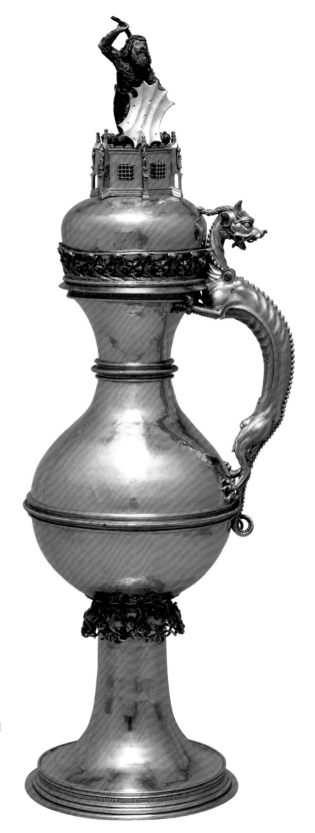

One of a Pair of Ewers

Germany, Franconia, probably Nuremberg, ca. 1500
Silver gilt, enamel, and paint, H. 25 in. (63.5 cm)
The Cloisters Collection, 1953 (53.20.2)

The lid of this large silver ewer bears the
figure of a bearded "wild man" carrying a club
over his shoulder. The mythical wild man, his
body covered with a coat of green hair, was a
popular figure in the art and literature of the
late Middle Ages. He was associated not only
with wildness but great strength, too. The
beautifully formed handle thus represents a
powerful dragon that, apparently, has been
tamed by the wild man. The ewer and its
mate, also at The Cloisters (53.20.1), have been
associated with ewers described in inventories
of the Order of Teutonic Knights, one of the
military and religious orders of knighthood
established during the Crusades and a powerful
force in late medieval Germany. The coat of
arms originally fixed to the shield held by the
wild man might have been that of Hartmann
von Stockheim, Master of the Order of
Teutonic Knights from 1499 to 1510/13.

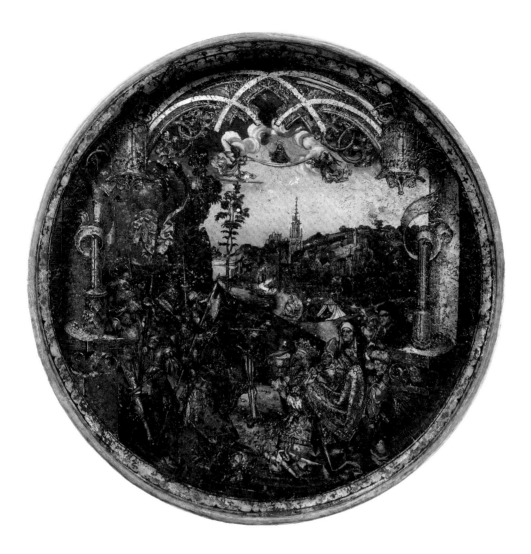

Paten with Abraham and Melchizedek

Hans Wertinger (d. 1533)
South Germany, 1498
Free-blown glass with paint and metallic foils,
14½ @ 1⅝ in. (36.9 @ 4.2 cm)
The Cloisters Collection, 2008 (2008.278)

The complex technique of applying pigments, colored glazes, and metallic foils to the surface of this large glass vessel—in the reverse order of panel painting—is unprecedented at this early date. At the center of the plate, the patriarch Abraham, fresh from victory in battle, meets the king and high priest Melchizedek, who at once gives Abraham bread and wine, blesses him, and takes a tenth of his loot. Because Melchizedek is dressed as a bishop and his offering takes the form of a chalice and paten, the scene has been interpreted as a model of sacrifice and redemption. This suggests that the glass dish served as a paten, or plate for the bread consecrated in Holy Communion. At the top of each lantern that flanks the openwork frame, a lion holds a staff with a pennant and supports a shield: the shield on the left bears the arms of the city of Freising, while the one on the right shows those of its bishopric. The S-shaped banderole at the base of the left column is inscribed "1[4]," and its counterpart on the right "9 8," indicating the date of 1498. On the basis of style, the painting is attributed to Hans Wertinger of Landshut, a town in southern Germany, which is, in fact, represented in the background.

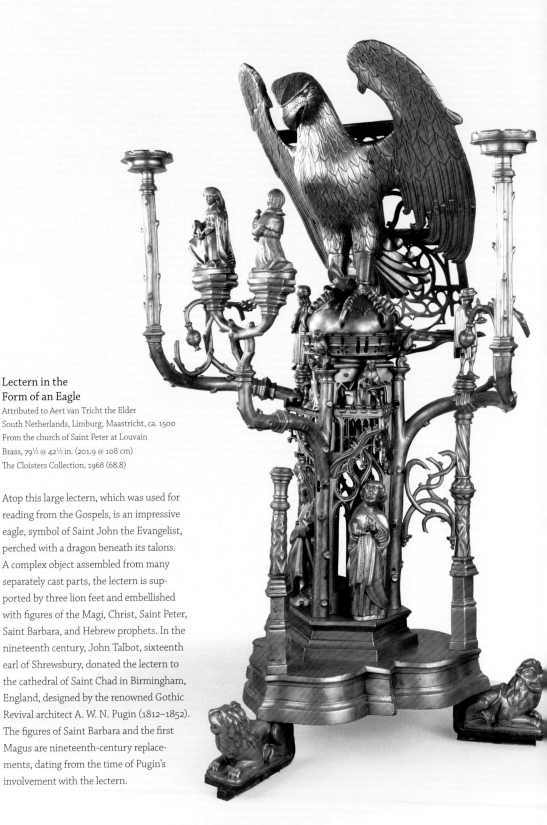

Lectern in the Form of an Eagle

Attributed to Aert van Tricht the Elder
South Netherlands, Limburg, Maastricht, ca. 1500
From the church of Saint Peter at Louvain
Brass, 79½ @ 42½ in. (201.9 @ 108 cm)
The Cloisters Collection, 1968 (68.8)

Atop this large lectern, which was used for
reading from the Gospels, is an impressive
eagle, symbol of Saint John the Evangelist,
perched with a dragon beneath its talons.
A complex object assembled from many
separately cast parts, the lectern is supported by three lion feet and embellished
with figures of the Magi, Christ, Saint Peter,
Saint Barbara, and Hebrew prophets. In the
nineteenth century, John Talbot, sixteenth
earl of Shrewsbury, donated the lectern to
the cathedral of Saint Chad in Birmingham,
England, designed by the renowned Gothic
Revival architect A. W. N. Pugin (1812–1852).
The figures of Saint Barbara and the first
Magus are nineteenth-century replacements, dating from the time of Pugin's
involvement with the lectern.

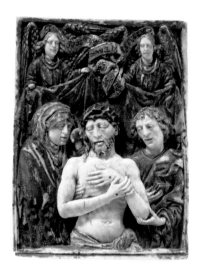

Man of Sorrows
South Germany, ca. 1500
Elephant ivory with paint and gilding,
3⅜ @ 2½ in. (8.6 @ 6.5 cm)
The Cloisters Collection, 1999 (1999.227)

After a period of prolific production from the late thirteenth century through most of the fourteenth century, European ivory carving

waned, becoming sporadic after about 1400. This finely carved plaque, which follows a composition by the influential printmaker Martin Schongauer (ca. 1430–1491), depicts the Man of Sorrows, the quintessential late medieval devotional image. The half-length figure of Christ, wearing the Crown of Thorns his tormentors placed on his head prior to his Crucifixion, appears between the mourning figures of the Virgin and Saint John the Evangelist. He is portrayed with his arms crossed over his chest, revealing the wounds on his hands. Two half-length winged angels appear above him holding a cloth behind the lower figures. This image of the suffering Christ, independent of any narrative, is intended to evoke pity and compassion in the beholder.

Scientific examination of the painted surface of the plaque has revealed that there are two layers of paint, with the second campaign following the scheme of the original. The plaque was most likely the central element in a devotional object, perhaps a triptych, that was made of silver or another metal.

Memento Mori (Dives in Hell)
North Netherlands or Lower Rhineland, ca. 1500
Boxwood, 2⅝ @ ⅞ in. (6.7 @ 2.2 cm)
Gift of Ruth Blumka, in honor of Ashton Hawkins, 1985 (1985.136)

In about 1500 workshops in northern Europe produced a number of astonishingly detailed "microcarvings" in boxwood. Traditionally such carvings have been attributed to Brabant, in the South Netherlands, but convincing new arguments suggest that they were carved in the North Netherlands or Lower Rhineland. Of these, miniature altarpieces and rosary pendants survive in the greatest numbers. This memento mori, or reminder of the inevitability of death, is more unusual. The object takes the form of a casket embellished with scenes and inscriptions referring to the parable of the rich man who refused charity to Lazarus. In the Middle Ages, that man came to be identified with the name

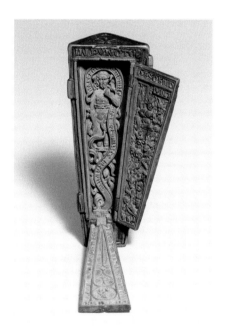

"Dives," Latin for rich, and inside the casket we see an image of Dives being tormented in hell for eternity.

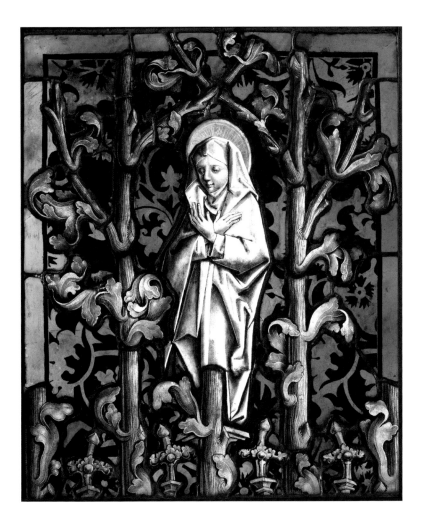

The Mater Dolorosa

Circle of Peter Hemmel von Andlau (Lautenbach Master)
Alsace, Strasbourg (modern France), ca. 1480
Made for the chapter house (formerly library) of the
cathedral of Constance
Pot-metal glass, colorless glass, silver stain, and
vitreous paint, 19⅝ @ 16⅜ in. (49.8 @ 41.6 cm)
The Cloisters Collection, 1998 (1998.215.2)

Against a deep blue background patterned
with scrolling foliate motifs stands the Virgin
Mary, her hands folded across her chest. The
soft, expressive features of the grieving Virgin
lend the panel a somber aura of serenity. She
is flanked by two trees, each with a branch
extending toward the center to form a canopy
above her head. A row of crocket finials lines
the lower border of the panel. About 1480 the
dean and chapter of the cathedral of Constance
commissioned a total of eighty-one panels of
glass for the cathedral's chapter house (formerly
library). Today, only nineteen panels survive,
including this serene portrayal of the Mother
of Sorrows. The commission was awarded to
Peter Hemmel von Andlau and his Strasbourg
Workshop-Cooperative, an association formed
just three years earlier that adhered to the
style of the master. Especially characteristic
of Hemmel's technique is the use of mattes,
in which the brush and stylus were employed
to create shades of volume. On stylistic
grounds the panels have been attributed more
specifically to the Lautenbach Master, who
documents say was either the son or son-in-law
of Peter Hemmel. The Lautenbach Master is
named after the parish church where he executed his most ambitious glazing program.

The Gathering of Manna

Workshop of Friedrich Brunner
Germany, Bavaria, Munich, 1497–99
From the cemetery church of St. Salvator
Pot-metal glass, vitreous paint, and silver stain,
19¾ @ 20⅞ in. (50 @ 53 cm)
Purchase, The Cloisters Collection and Gift of
The Hearst Foundation, by exchange, 2010 (2010.22.1)

This stained-glass panel depicts the Gathering of Manna, the breadlike substance provided by God for the Israelites on their journey from Egypt (Exodus 16:11–35). Moses, in a fur-lined robe and with his brother Aaron behind him, watches as the manna and a quail fall from the sky. Two Israelites are busy collecting the miraculous sustenance; the figure in the foreground seems overwhelmed by the weight of his catch. Both this panel and its companion, *The Storing of Manna* (2010.22.2), came from the late fifteenth-century cemetery church of St. Salvator in Munich. There they were juxtaposed with a scene of the Last Supper; manna is considered a prefiguration of the Eucharist instituted by Jesus at that occasion. Together, the panels formed part of a large window located near the altar, where the Mass would have been celebrated. Above them were depictions of Saints Martin and John the Evangelist, patron saints of the wine tavern guild that paid for the window.

The panels' bold colors and dramatic composition are representative of the well-known workshop of Friedrich Brunner, active in southern Germany at the time. Employing etching, back painting, and silver stain, the workshop showcased a number of the most sophisticated techniques attained by late medieval glass painters. In the early nineteenth century, some of the St. Salvator glass was taken to the nearby cathedral church. Other panels, including these two, were removed either by the restorer Franz Xaver Zettler in 1906 or along with other glass at the start of World War I. Never returned to St. Salvator, The Cloisters' panels consequently escaped the devastating effects of World War II and remain in remarkably good condition.

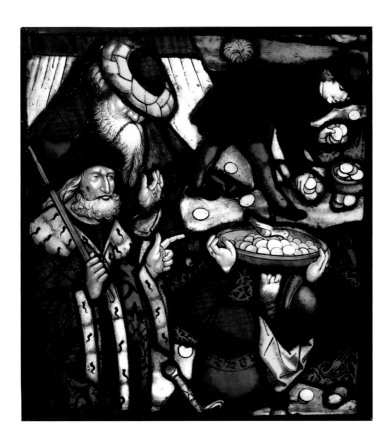

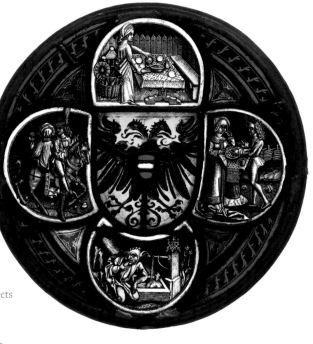

Quatrefoil Panel with Secular Scenes

Germany, Franconia, Nuremberg, 1490–1500

Pot-metal glass, white glass, vitreous paint, and silver stain, DIAM. 12¼ in. (31.1 cm)

Samuel P. Avery Memorial Fund, 1911 (11.120.2)

At the center of this roundel are the arms of the Holy Roman Empire, surrounded by four medallions that represent secular subjects associated with feasting and courtship. In the bottom medallion, for example, a fool helps himself to food, perhaps an allusion to the period preceding Lent, when carnivals, tournaments, and masquerades were held. A companion panel in The Cloisters' collection (11.120.1) depicts scenes of heralds announcing the start of tournaments, which as we see here were participated in by knights and fools alike. Such images, really parodies or mockeries of chivalric ideals, were a popular form of social satire in the late medieval period.

Roundels of this type were luxury items used to decorate windows in nonreligious buildings. The presence of the imperial arms indicates that this panel's intended destination had courtly connections. Sufficient examples have survived to attest to the popularity of quatrefoil roundels, most of which were produced in workshops in Nuremberg.

The Hunters Enter the Woods

South Netherlands, 1495–1505

Wool warp with wool, silk, silver, and gilt wefts, 12 ft. 1 in. @ 10 ft. 4 in. (368.3 @ 315 cm)

Gift of John D. Rockefeller Jr., 1937 (37.80.1)

This tapestry is one of seven hangings at The Cloisters that depict the hunt of the unicorn, a

mythical creature first mentioned by the Greek physician Ctesias in the fourth century B.C. In the Middle Ages the animal was best known for its supposed invincibility and for the therapeutic property of its horn. So strong was the belief in the horn's miraculous cures that by the twelfth century the tusks of male narwhals, a small whale native to the Arctic, came to be regarded as "unicorn horns."

The Unicorn Tapestries, as the group of seven is known, were probably designed in Paris but woven in Brussels. They are first documented in 1680, when they hung in the Paris home of François VI de La Rochefoucauld. By 1728 five of them decorated a bedroom at the family's château in Verteuil, in western France. The tapestries were looted during the French Revolution but were recovered in the 1850s; by 1856 they had been restored and rehung in the château's salon. No documentation sheds light on the early history of the tapestries, including either their commission or sequence of hanging. Striking differences in dimension and composition have prompted scholars to question whether the hangings constitute one set or are, in fact, from multiple sets. Although ostensibly showing hunting episodes leading to the capture of the unicorn, the dramatic narratives and rich botanical details of the tapestries have inspired multiple interpretations, including chivalric and Christological readings.

The Hunters Enter the Woods, like *The Unicorn in Captivity* (p. 174), is set against a millefleurs background: a field of dark green spangled with blossoming trees and flowers. Of the 101 species of plants represented in the series, 85 have been identified, including, in this hanging, the prominent cherry tree behind the hunters and the lush date palm in front of the sniffing hound. The cipher "AE" that is woven into each of the Unicorn Tapestries—and repeated here five times—alludes to their original owners, who remain unknown.

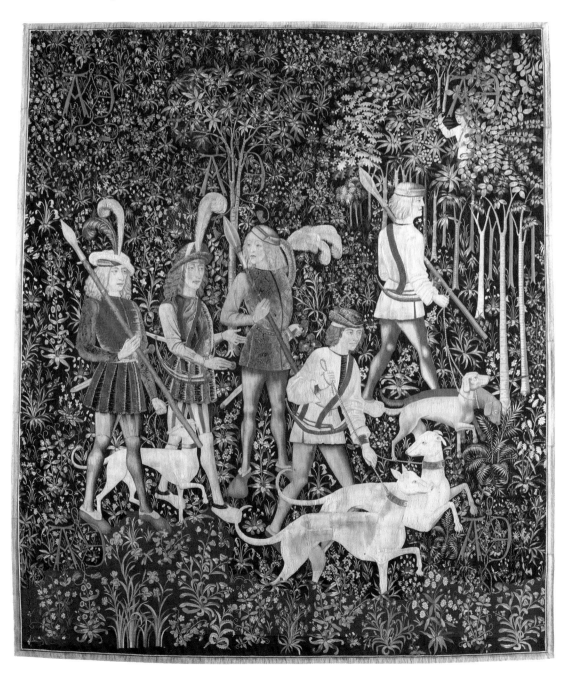

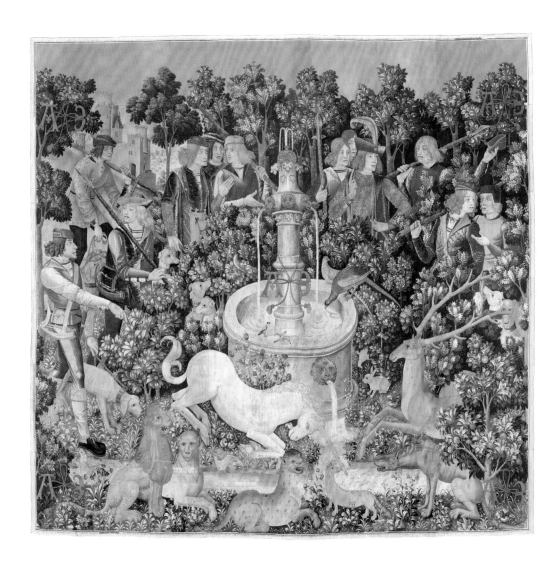

The Unicorn Is Found

South Netherlands, 1495–1505
Wool warp with wool, silk, silver, and gilt wefts,
12 ft. 1 in. @ 12 ft. 5 in. (368.3 @ 378.5 cm)
Gift of John D. Rockefeller Jr., 1937 (37.80.2)

In this tapestry the unicorn kneels before a tall
white fountain that has a pair of pheasants and
a pair of goldfinches perched on its edge. Other
animals both exotic and native to Europe lounge
about, while twelve hunters in the back of the
scene discuss the discovery of their quarry. Flora
and fauna play a significant role in the narratives
of the Unicorn Tapestries. Plants prescribed
in medieval herbals as antidotes to poisoning,
such as sage, pot marigolds, and orange, are
positioned near the stream, which is being
purified by the unicorn's magic horn. Visual cues
have led some scholars to read the tapestry as an
allegory of the Passion of Christ, including the
presence of exactly twelve hunters (the apostles)
and the prominent rosebush (martyrdom)
directly behind the unicorn.

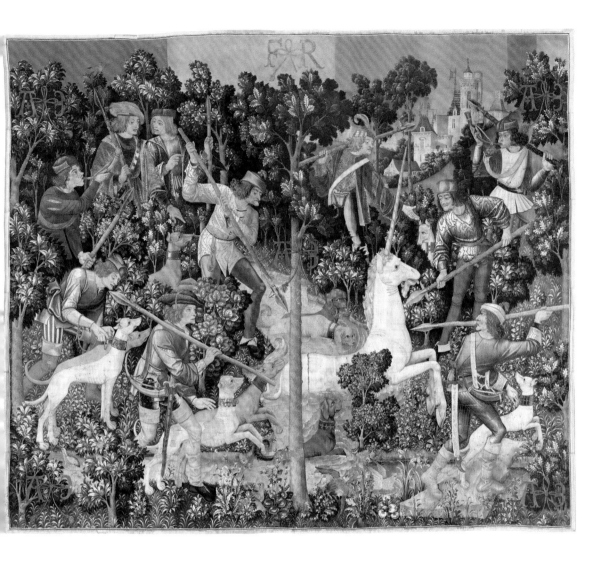

The Unicorn Is Attacked

South Netherlands, 1495–1505
Wool warp with wool, silk, silver, and gilt wefts,
12 ft. 1 in. @ 14 ft. (368.3 @ 426.7 cm)
Gift of John D. Rockefeller Jr., 1937 (37.80.3)

According to tradition, the unicorn cannot be disturbed while performing a magical act. The attack by the hunters thus presumably begins soon after the action depicted in *The Unicorn Is Found*, and the scene is one filled with chaos and commotion. The ferocity of the battle is conveyed by the converging lances aimed at the animal, the sounding of the hunting horns, and the menacing hounds. Already wounded on his back, the unicorn leaps across a stream in a desperate attempt to escape his encircling enemies.

The use of hounds to scout, chase, and eventually attack the quarry was typical practice in medieval stag hunts, and the palatial buildings in the background might be a further allusion to the hunt as a royal or aristocratic pastime. Unlike *The Hunters Enter the Woods* and *The Unicorn in Captivity*, this and the other hangings are set in realistic landscapes that enhance the drama of the hunt.

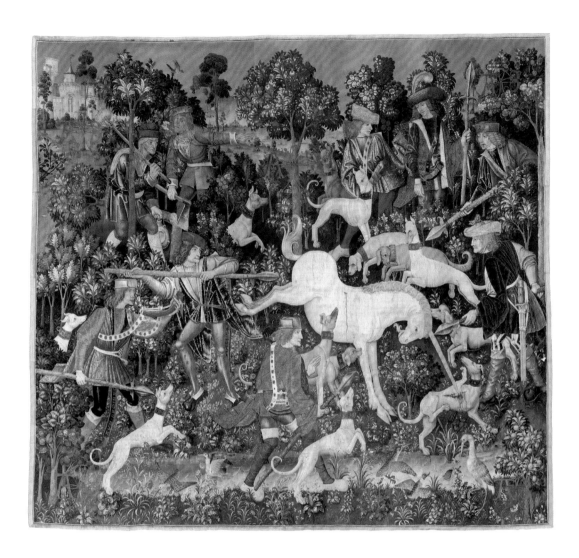

The Unicorn Defends Itself

South Netherlands, 1495–1505
Wool warp with wool, silk, silver, and gilt wefts,
12 ft. 1 in. @ 13 ft. 2 in. (368.3 @ 401.3 cm)
Gift of John D. Rockefeller Jr., 1937 (37.80.4)

Here the injured unicorn is being held at bay
by three hunters ready to pierce him with their
lances. The furious animal reacts with a grue-
some attack on a greyhound before him, almost
tearing the dog's body apart. The horn-blowing
hunter at lower left wears a scabbard with the
inscription AVE REGINA C[OELI] (Hail, Queen
of the Heavens). He is often thought to represent the Archangel Gabriel, who announced to
the Virgin Mary that she is to give birth to the
Christ Child. The huntsmen and other figures

are garbed in the fashions of about the turn of
the sixteenth century, including round-toed
shoes and fitted bodices, and their headdresses
and hairstyles also reflect contemporary tastes.
The mastery of the weavers is evident in the
convincing representation of different materials
and textures in the costumes, such as brocade,
velvet, leather, and fur.

In order to make the tapestries, plain wool
yarns (the warp) were stretched between two
beams of a large loom; a bobbin then brought
dyed and metallic threads (the wefts) over and
under the warp threads to create the design.
Chemical analyses reveal that the dye pigments
used in the Unicorn Tapestries came from such
plants as weld (yellow), madder (red), and woad

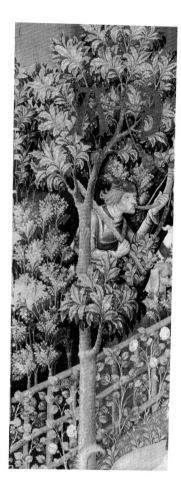

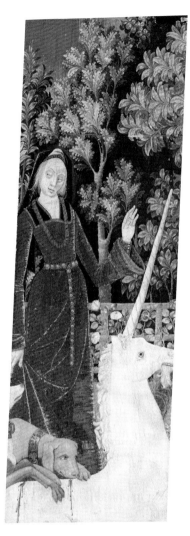

(blue), all of which are grown in the "Bonnefont" Cloister garden (pp. 84–85). With the aid of mordants, substances that help fix the dyes to fabric, these three primary colors were blended to achieve a dazzling spectrum of hues strategically highlighted by the addition of metallic threads.

The Mystic Capture of the Unicorn

South Netherlands, 1495–1505
Wool warp with wool, silk, silver, and gilt wefts, 66½ @ 25½ in. (168.9 @ 64.8 cm); 78 @ 25½ in. (198.1 @ 64.8 cm)
Gift of John D. Rockefeller Jr., 1938 (38.51.1, .2)

In these two fragments of a single tapestry, the unicorn appears to have been tamed. He seems so docile, in fact, that he is oblivious to the dog licking the wound on his back and stares lovingly at the maiden who must have subdued him. Most of her figure is missing, the result of damage incurred after the tapestries were looted in 1793. The remaining traces include the maiden's right arm, clothed in red velvet and visible between the beard and throat of the unicorn, and her fingers, seen gently caressing the bottom of the animal's mane. She sits in an enclosed garden (*hortus conclusus*), often a metaphor for the purity of a maiden. The more complete female figure may be signaling to the hunter outside the garden, who in turn sounds his horn to summon the others.

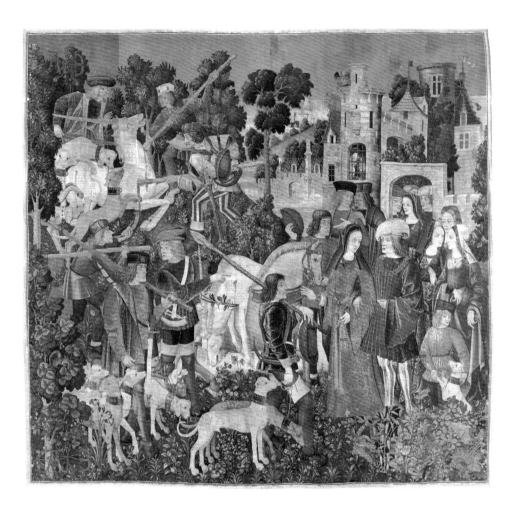

The Unicorn Is Killed and Brought to the Castle

South Netherlands, 1495–1505
Wool warp with wool, silk, silver, and gilt wefts,
12 ft. 1 in. @ 12 ft. 9 in. (368.3 @ 388.6 cm)
Gift of John D. Rockefeller Jr., 1937 (37.80.5)

Two episodes of the hunt narrative are brought together in this hanging. At left, two hunters drive their lances into the neck and chest of the unicorn, as a third delivers the coup de grâce from the back. It has been suggested that the doomed unicorn is an allegory for Christ dying on the Cross; the large holly tree (often a symbol of the Passion) rising behind his head seems to reinforce this association. In the other episode, at right, a lord and his lady receive the body of the unicorn in front of their castle. They are surrounded by their attendants, with more curious onlookers peering through windows of the turret behind them. The dead animal is slung on the back of a horse, his horn already cut off but still entangled in thorny oak branches—possibly symbolizing the Crown of Thorns. The rosary in the hand of the lady and the three other women standing behind the lord have encouraged a deeper reading of the scene, as a symbolic Deposition witnessed by the grieving Virgin Mary, John the Baptist, and the Holy Women.

The Unicorn in Captivity

South Netherlands, 1495–1505
Wool warp with wool, silk, silver, and gilt wefts,
12 ft. 1 in. @ 99 in. (368 @ 251.5 cm)
Gift of John D. Rockefeller Jr., 1937 (37.80.6)

One of the most beloved objects at The Cloisters, this tapestry shows the captured unicorn

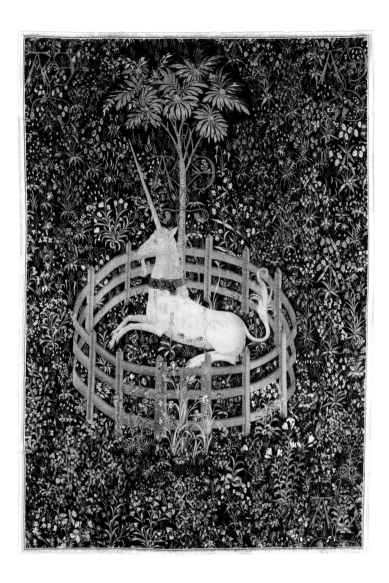

resting in a flowery meadow within the confines of a circular fence. Behind him is a pomegranate tree, some of its fruits bursting with seed. This seemingly simple design belies many layers of possible readings. According to some, the unicorn here symbolizes a happy groom now bonded by marriage (the circular fence) to his love (his collar, a form of the "chain of love"). The red drops on his back can thus be read as the juice of the pomegranate, a fruit considered a fertility symbol in the Middle Ages. Plants such as bistort (by his right knee) and the large European orchid (whose bloom is set against his body) were believed to have medicinal properties that would, respectively, help women conceive

and determine the sex of the unborn child. Not all of the plant symbolism is secular, however. Both the Madonna lily and Saint Mary's thistle make reference to the Virgin Mary, while the carnation (to the left of the irises) is thought to symbolize the Passion of Christ.

The brilliant colors, beautiful landscapes, and realistic depictions of flora and fauna in all of the Unicorn Tapestries combine to make these hangings invaluable and cherished works of art. It is the free blending of the secular and the sacred, however, that truly distinguishes this group of seven tapestries as a rich source for the study of medieval art, iconography, and lore.

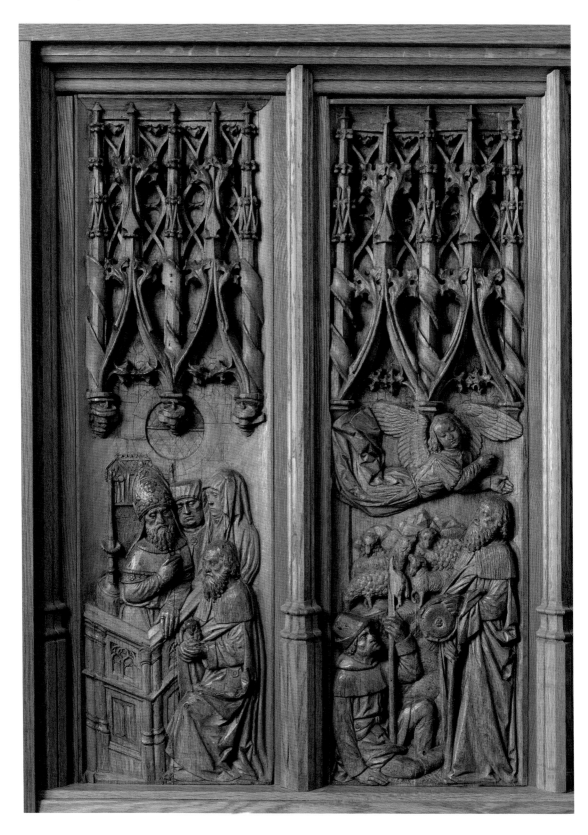

Panels with Scenes from the Life and Passion of Christ

France, Normandy (Seine-Maritime),
early 16th century
Probably from a church at Jumièges
Oak, 35½ @ 11⅜ @ 1½ in.
(90.2 @ 28.9 @ 3.8 cm) each
The Cloisters Collection, 1950 (50.147.1, .2)

Until 1950 these panels lined the Great Hall of Highcliffe Castle in southern England. Constructed in the 1830s for Lord Stuart de Rothesay, the castle was furnished in part with stonework acquired from the ruined royal abbey at Jumièges in Normandy, where the panels might also have originated. In all likelihood they once decorated the backs of choir stalls ordered in 1501 by the abbot of Jumièges.

Carved on The Cloisters' thirty-five oak panels are scenes from the lives of the Virgin and Christ, each set under an elaborate canopy of single or double arches. The exuberant lattice-work surrounding the arches provides an almost encyclopedic display of pinnacles, crockets, spirals, and other fanciful decorations. The panels shown here open the narrative sequence, with the childless Joachim and Anne standing inside the Temple, saddened by the refusal of their offering. On the next panel an angel, arching his body, appears to Joachim with the news that he and Anne will have a daughter and that she will be named Mary. As in many late medieval works, the figures are foreshortened within their inhabited surroundings, adding depth and drama to the composition.

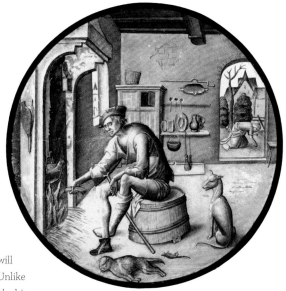

Sorgheloos (Carefree) in Poverty

North Netherlands, probably Leiden, 1510–20
Colorless glass with silver stain and vitreous
paint, DIAM. 9 in. (23 cm)
The Cloisters Collection, 1999 (1999.243)

The story of Sorgheloos ("carefree" in Dutch) is one of the best-known moral lessons of the late medieval period. Like the Prodigal Son of the Christian parable, Sorgheloos led a carefree life, spending at will until he became penniless and friendless. Unlike the Prodigal Son, however, who is received by his forgiving father, Sorgheloos is condemned to the perpetual companionship of Aermoede ("poverty"), whom we see gleaning straw in the background of this roundel. Sorgheloos, meanwhile, sits in his impoverished room before a fire, stirring a kettle of boiling herring with a sheath of straw and using a wood tub for a chair. He owns only an empty cupboard and a handful of utensils, his grinding poverty vividly illustrated by the emaciated dog, expiring cat, and dead rat.

Silver-stained roundels were commissioned largely for domestic, civic, or professional settings in northern Europe. In the Netherlands, particularly, moralizing tales taken or adapted from biblical and secular sources were extremely popular, reflecting the values of the rising middle class. They were made in great quantities, a factor of their small size and the relative ease with which they could be displayed. The final color of the silver stain depended on many variables, including the materials used and the duration of the firing, but only the finest glass painters were able to achieve the warm and luminous shades of gold unique to this type of glass.

Christ Blessing

Gerard David (ca. 1455–1523)
South Netherlands, Bruges, ca. 1500–1505
Oil on wood, 4¾ @ 3½ in. (12.1 @ 8.9 cm)
Purchase, The Cloisters Collection, Hester Diamond and
Kowitz Family Foundation Gifts, Dodge Fund, and
Malcolm Hewitt Wiener Foundation Gift, 2009 (2009.415)

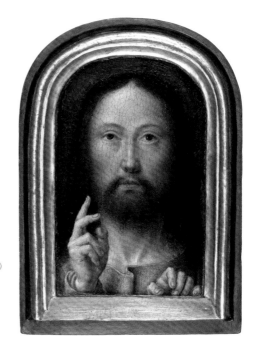

This highly spiritual and exquisitely rendered small painting is a newly discovered work by Gerard David, the leading painter of late fifteenth- and early sixteenth-century Bruges. The image of Christ Blessing was adapted from Byzantine icons brought to the region in the fifteenth century and made popular through copies by David and his predecessor Hans Memling. The panel differs from the Byzantine models in the freshness of observation evident in Christ's face and the delicate articulation of the hands, which were based on David's drawings made from life. The arresting psychological presence of all of these images was intended to intensify the meditational experience of the viewer, especially when such tiny personal icons were handheld as inspiration for the recitation of daily prayers.

Saint Michael

North Spain, Castilla-León (Burgos),
probably Burgos, ca. 1530
Wood, paint, and gilding, H. 73½ in. (186.7 cm)
The Cloisters Collection, 1953 (53.65)

Judging from Saint Michael's leaning posture and the sculpture's large scale, it seems likely that this statue was intended to be seen from below, in a manner appropriate to the archangel associated with mountains and high places. Michael, the warrior saint, is represented wearing steel plate armor, and he originally held in his right hand a lance with which he slew the winged devil beneath his feet (now missing its head). Consistent with Saint Michael's role in weighing souls at the Last Judgment, his left hand would have held a scale. No specific attribution for the sculpture has emerged, but it is generally consistent with those produced in Burgos in the early sixteenth century. This sculpture neatly evokes that period, when the elegant spirit of late Gothic art began to blend into the emerging Renaissance style.

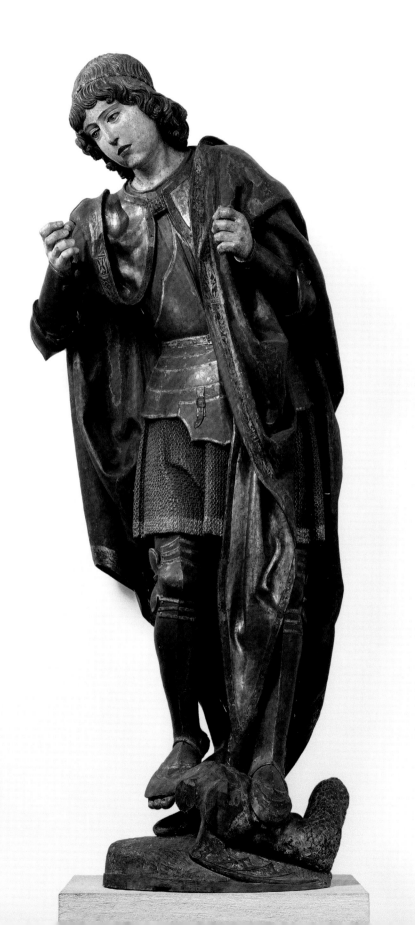

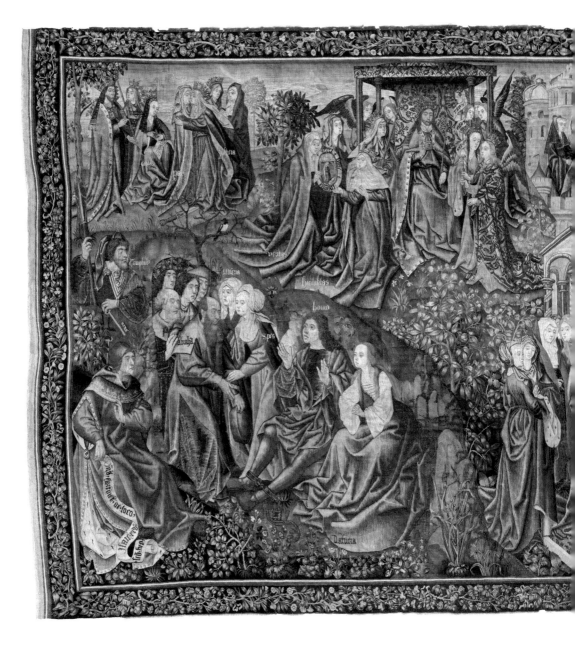

Episode from the Story of the Redemption of Man: Christ Is Born as Man's Redeemer

South Netherlands, 1500–1520

Wool warp with wool and silk wefts, 13 ft. 10¼ in. @ 26 ft. 3⅛ in. (422.3 @ 800.4 cm)

The Cloisters Collection, 1938 (38.28)

When Juan Rodriguez de Fonseca, bishop of Burgos, died in 1524, he bequeathed to the chapter of Burgos Cathedral four tapestries from a series of ten representing the Redemption of Man. This hanging, the fourth installment of the elaborate set, was divided into four pieces prior to entering The Cloisters Collection in 1938; now restored, it has been back on view since 2010. The enormous tapestry contains multiple scenes. At the center are Joseph and Mary at their wedding, set before a domed pavilion. Directly above, Joseph and Mary place a coin on a table, perhaps paying tax in Jerusalem. Flanking this scene, to the left, is Christ enthroned under a damask canopy, accompanied by angels; to the right, he appears again with Mary, God the Father,

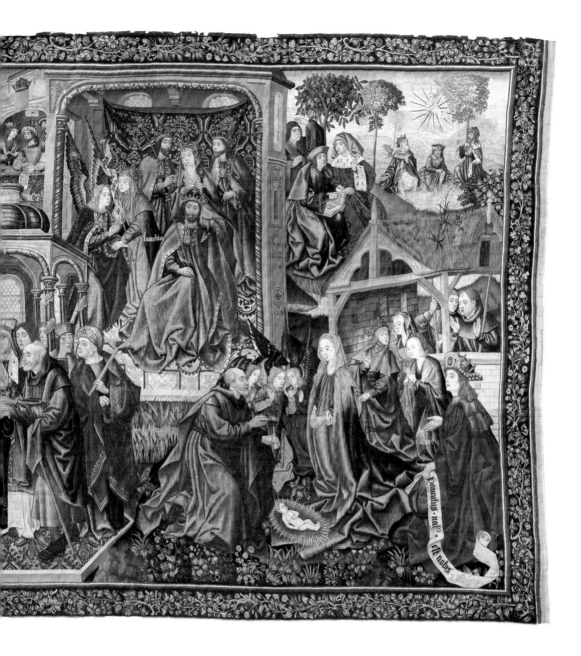

and other figures within a roofed structure. At the lower right, against a backdrop of a gabled stable, we see Joseph, Mary, and others admiring the newborn Christ Child. Elsewhere, personifications of Virtues and Vices, such as Humility and Avarice, interact with biblical as well as allegorical figures.

Altogether, more than seventy figures are organized into group scenes separated from one another by plants and waterways, some framed by architectural settings. The use of open-front architecture and the labeling of figures might have derived from staging conventions of contemporary morality plays and pageants. The superb quality of modeling, figural style, and weaving point to Brussels as the location where the series was probably produced. Details of the costumes suggest that the set was designed about the turn of the sixteenth century.

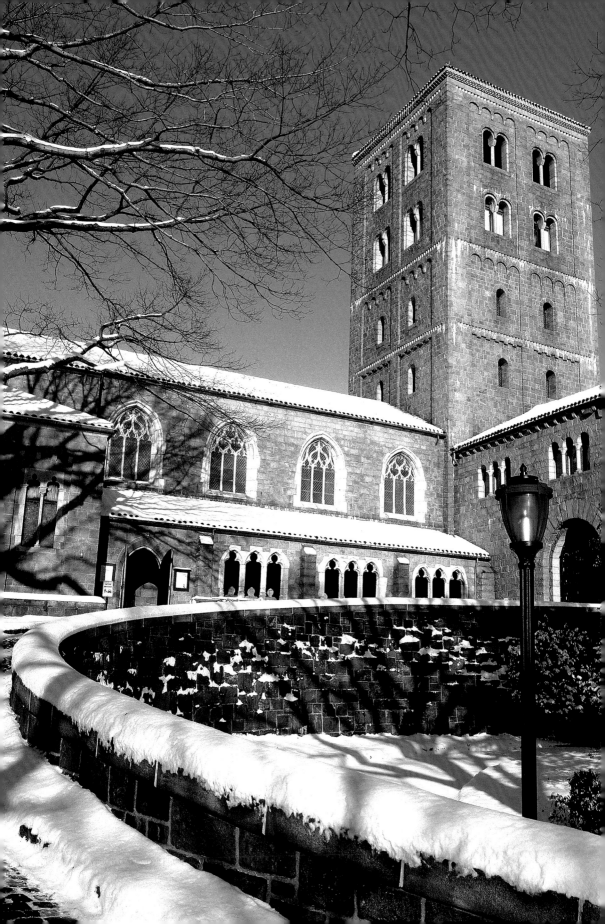

Glossary

Words appearing in *italic* type are defined elsewhere in the glossary.

A

abbot/abbess: head or superior of a *monastery.*

acanthus: Mediterranean plant whose spiky foliage has served as a decorative motif for architecture and sculpture since classical Greece.

alabaster: dense, transparent form of gypsum; used only for interior sculpture because it is slightly soluble in water.

alloy: metal composed of two or more metals (or a metal and a nonmetal) that are combined in the molten state. Bronze, for example, is primarily copper and tin.

Alsace: in the *Middle Ages,* a region of the Holy Roman Empire located west of the Rhine; today part of eastern France.

altar: table (or a fixed or portable table-like structure) used for religious ceremonies; must be consecrated before it is suitable for the celebration of the *Eucharistic sacrament,* or communion.

altar frontal: decorative cover on the front of an *altar;* also called an *antependium.*

altarpiece: decorative structure behind an *altar,* often painted or carved, sometimes consisting of several panels; also called a *retable.*

angel: spiritual being believed to be an intermediary between God and humanity. Angels are ranked in a cosmic hierarchy of nine levels and duties, such as seraphim, *cherubim,* archangels, etc.

antependium: see *altar frontal.*

Apocalypse: visions of the end of time revealed to Saint John, whose recording of it became the *book of Revelation,* the last book of the New Testament.

apostles: twelve disciples of Jesus sent out to spread his teachings.

apse: domed space, often semicircular or polygonal in shape, located usually at the east end of a church.

aquamanile: vessel, often in the form of an animal, used to pour out water for washing hands; served both liturgical and secular functions.

arcade: series of *arches,* often supported by *columns* or *pilasters.*

arch: curved frame or opening for a door or window, often composed of blocks known as *voussoirs.*

archbishop: *bishop* of the highest rank who oversees an *ecclesiastical* province. See *clergy.*

archivolt: moldings framing an *arch,* often in multiple bands.

attribute: an object or decoration known to be associated with an individual. In art, many persons represented without their names can only be identified by the attribute they hold; for example, a scallop shell (for Saint James the Greater) or a key (for Saint Peter).

B

barrel vault: stone or sometimes wooden *vault* that looks like a tunnel or a cutaway barrel.

basilisk: dragon with a serpent's tail, signifying the power to kill.

beaker: drinking vessel without a handle; usually has a wide mouth.

Benedictine order: monastic order whose followers subscribe to the Rule of Saint Benedict, which contains instructions for the structure of the community as well as how time should be spent in prayer, study, and work.

benediction: blessing or invocation of divine favor upon a person or object.

Bible: sacred Christian scripture, divided into the Old and New Testaments. The Old Testament (Hebrew Bible) includes the creation of the world and the history of the Jewish people as well as the writings of the prophets and the Psalms. The New Testament includes the *Gospels,* the *Epistles,* and the *book of Revelation.*

bishop: member of the *clergy* consecrated for the spiritual government and direction of a *diocese.* See *clergy.*

book of hours: book containing prayers to be recited at the eight *canonical hours* of the day. Meant for private use, it is often small enough to be held in one hand and its pages are frequently decorated with fine *illuminations*.

book of Revelation: see *Apocalypse, Bible.*

boss: convex, circular knob often used in decoration.

boxwood: fine-grained hardwood well suited to intricate carving.

Burgundian territories: The death of Louis II of Flanders in 1384 entitled his son-in-law Philip the Bold, duke of Burgundy and son of the French king John II, to inherit the county of Flanders. The territories ruled by the Burgundian dynasty would expand to include most of today's Belgium, Netherlands, Luxembourg, and part of northern France. With the death of Charles the Bold in 1477, the territories (but not Burgundy itself) passed to the Habsburgs through the marriage of Mary of Burgundy to Maximilian of Habsburg. See *The Netherlands.*

C

cabochon: convex, unfaceted polished gemstone.

canonical hours: stated times of day (Lauds, Prime, Terce, Sext, None, Vespers, Compline, and Matins) for prayers, the recitation of the book of Psalms, and other readings.

canonize: to declare by papal authority the sainthood of a deceased person, whose name is then placed on an officially recognized calendar, or canon, of *saints.*

capital: top of a *column* or *pilaster*. See *column.*

Carmelite order: founded in the late twelfth century on Mount Carmel in modern Israel, the order is characterized by an austere lifestyle and a particular devotion to the Virgin Mary.

Carolingian: refers to the era of Charlemagne (r. as emperor 800–814) and his successors, who reigned over territories comprising modern France, Germany, Switzerland, Austria, and Italy until the early tenth century.

casting: process of creating an object by pouring molten material into a mold and allowing it to solidify.

Catalonia: autonomous region centered in the eastern Pyrenees whose historical territories are today divided between France and Spain.

cathedral: literally, a church where the seat (cathedra) of a *bishop* is located; also the church where the bishop regularly performs the *liturgy.*

censer: container for burning incense; used in the *liturgy.*

chalice: cuplike vessel containing wine consecrated during the *Eucharistic liturgy,* or communion.

champlevé: type of *enameling* in which shallow depressions are carved into a metal base and filled with powdered glass.

chapel: place of worship, often housing its own *altar;* can refer to a space within a large building (church, castle, palace) or an individual building (typically small) without parochial functions.

chapter house: assembly room in a *monastery* where the community meets daily for religious and administrative purposes.

chasing: process of adding fine details to the surface of metal or smoothing roughness from the *casting* process.

chasuble: loose, sleeveless outer garment worn by *bishops* or *priests* during the *Mass.*

cherubim: celestial winged beings; one of the nine orders of *angels.*

choir: in architecture, a term used to describe the space typically east of the *transept* where the *clergy* and singers perform the *liturgy.*

choir screen: screen situated between the *choir* and the *nave* of a church that separates the *clergy* from the congregation.

choir stalls: seats in the *choir,* often arranged in two rows facing each other. Their hinged seats and high backs are often adorned with carvings.

Cistercian order: monastic order, founded in 1098 by Robert of Molesme at Cîteaux in Burgundy, that champions strict adherence to the Rule of Saint Benedict. With its austere spirituality and administrative efficacy, the order rapidly grew in popularity.

clergy: persons consecrated and appointed by the church to perform religious services; generally comprises the orders of *archbishop*, *bishop*, *priest*, and *deacon*.

cloister: in a *monastery,* a square or rectangular open-air courtyard surrounded by covered passageways and situated next to the monastic church; its use is limited to the monks or nuns.

coat of arms: *heraldic* design on a shield, banner, *surcoat,* etc.; also the heraldic shield and surrounding symbols. See *heraldry.*

colonnette: small *column.*

column: in architecture, a vertical member with a cylindrical, sometimes tapering, body. It stands on a base and is topped by a *capital.*

convent: in the *Middle Ages,* a word inter-changeable with the term *monastery.* In modern usage, it often refers to a community of women.

corbel: block that projects from a wall to support a roof, ceiling, or sculpture.

cornice: generally, a horizontal molding that crowns a building, often in projection.

corpus (Latin, "body"): often used to refer to the body of the crucified Christ.

credenza: legless sideboard used for storage.

crenellation: defensive parapet wall at the top of a roof with alternating open spaces (crenels) and solid blocks (merlons).

crocket (French *crochet,* "crook"): curved-leaf motif often used in architectural and sculptural decoration, especially in the later *Middle Ages.*

crosier/crozier: staff, shaped like a shepherd's crook, that is carried by *bishops* and *abbots.*

cross: composed of two intersecting bars, a symbol of Christianity evoking the Crucifixion.

crucifix: *cross* with a depiction of the crucified Christ.

cruciform: *cross*-shaped.

cruet: small container for wine or water used in the *liturgy*; often found in sets.

Crusades: military campaigns initially launched in 1095 by Pope Urban II aimed at recapturing the Church of the Holy Sepulchre in Jerusalem. Prolonged conflicts between Christians from western Europe, various Muslim powers, and, ultimately, Christians in Byzantium ensued. The crusading presence in the East ended with the fall of the city of Acre (in modern Israel) to Muslim forces in 1291.

D

deacon: member of the *clergy,* ranked below *bishop* and *priest.*

diocese: sphere of jurisdiction of a *bishop.*

diptych: pair of hinged panels, usually carved or painted. See *triptych.*

Dominican order: *Mendicant* order founded by Saint Dominic (1170–1221) in the early thirteenth century. Instead of prayers and manual labor, the Dominicans emphasize learning and preaching, which often brought them out of the seclusion of the *cloister.*

E

earthenware: low-fired pottery that is slightly porous unless glazed.

ecclesiastic: pertaining to or concerned with affairs of the church.

effigy: generally, the image of a person; in describing medieval tomb sculpture, the representation of the deceased.

embroidery: textile decorated with stitched threads.

enamel: powdered colored glass fused to a metal surface. See *champlevé.*

engraving: process of decorating a metal surface with cut or carved lines.

Epiphany: Christian feast celebrated on January 6 that commemorates Christ's appearance to the Gentiles, represented by the three *Magi,* or wise men.

Epistles: letters by early Christian writers or by the *apostle* Paul. In the context of the *Mass,* the term Epistle refers to the first scriptural passage to be read, customarily followed by the second passage, referred to as the *Gospel*.

Eucharist: central *sacrament* of the church, in which bread and wine are transformed during the *Mass* into the body and blood of Christ; also refers to the consecrated bread and wine.

Evangelists: writers of the four Christian Gospels (Matthew, Mark, Luke, and John) whose writings are believed to have been divinely inspired.

extreme unction: *sacrament* of anointing the sick who are in danger of death.

F

Flamboyant: late *Gothic* style characterized in part by the use of *tracery* patterns designed with geometric intricacies to create undulating, often flamelike forms. The style flourished from the fourteenth through the sixteenth century and was widely employed by architects as well as sculptors, painters, and furniture makers.

fleur-de-lis: stylized lily used in art and *heraldry*.

Franciscan order: *Mendicant* order founded by Saint Francis of Assisi (1181/82–1226) in the early thirteenth century that is characterized by a commitment to poverty and teaching.

fresco: painting technique in which *pigments* dissolved in water are applied to a wet plaster surface.

friar (Latin *frater,* "brother"): male member of one of the *Mendicant* orders, such as the *Franciscans* and *Dominicans*.

frieze: horizontal band, often decorated, high on a wall or the facade of a building.

G

gable: in architecture, a triangular section atop a facade that conforms to the pitched roof behind; sometimes located above window or door openings for decorative purposes.

gesso: plaster used as a ground for painting or *gilding*.

gilding: application of gold for decorative purposes.

gisant: tomb *effigy* with the deceased person represented in a recumbent position.

gold leaf: gold beaten into very thin sheets.

Gospel (Old English *gōdspel,* "good news"): term that has come to define the first four books of the New Testament (the Gospels according to Matthew, Mark, Luke, and John) and, by extension, Christ's own teachings.

Gothic: predominant style of art and architecture in western Europe from the middle of the twelfth through the fifteenth century. Gothic emerged in the region around Paris in the mid-twelfth century as an architectural style characterized by the use of pointed *arches,* flying buttresses, and *rib vaults*. The Renaissance style developed about 1400 in Florence, but Gothic persisted until the early sixteenth century in much of Europe.

granulation: technique utilized principally in jewelry-making in which tiny beads of gold or silver are soldered to a metal surface.

grisaille: painting or decoration in tones of gray.

H

halo: circle of celestial light surrounding the head; used in visual representations to indicate power, glory, or divinity.

heraldry: study or use of hereditary designs primarily appearing on the surface of a shield.

Holy Ghost or **Holy Spirit:** one of the three persons of the *Trinity,* often depicted as a dove.

host: wafer or bread consecrated and consumed at *Mass.*

Huguenots: French Protestants whose military campaigns against the Catholic Church and the monarchy, beginning in the mid-sixteenth century, came to be known as the Wars of Religion. Despite repeated persecutions, they quickly gained popularity, particularly in southwestern France.

I

iconography (Greek *eikōn,* from the verb meaning "to resemble"): study of images and, by extension, the meaning of subjects and stories in art.

illumination: use of paint, often combined with gold, in the decoration of manuscripts.

inlay: decorative technique in which an area of surface is removed and replaced by a new, usually contrasting material.

Instruments of the Passion: objects present at Christ's Crucifixion, including the Holy Cross, Lance, Nails, and Crown of Thorns; also referred to as the Arma Christi.

intarsia: *inlay* decoration, usually of wood.

ivory: dense, fine-grained white material derived from the teeth of elephants, walrus, and other animals.

J

jamb: vertical side of a window or doorway.

K

knop: small decorative swelling or knob on the stem of a cup or chalice.

L

lancet: in architecture, a tall narrow window surmounted by a pointed *arch.*

lapis lazuli: semiprecious blue stone ground to manufacture the *pigment* ultramarine.

lectern: stand used to support books for reading or singing during the *liturgy.*

lintel: horizontal member spanning the top of a door or window opening.

liturgical instruments: objects used in the *liturgy,* especially during the *Mass,* such as the *chalice, paten,* and *censer.*

liturgy: communal prayers and other rituals prescribed by the church.

Lowlands: historical region corresponding roughly to modern Luxembourg, Belgium, and the Netherlands.

luster: iridescent metallic decoration of ceramics.

M

Magi (sing. Magus): the three "wise men" who followed a mysterious star to Bethlehem, where they presented gifts to the Christ Child. See *Epiphany*.

maiolica: Italian term originally describing tin-glazed Islamic ceramics shipped from Spain to Italy and later referring to tin-glazed vessels of Italian manufacture.

mandorla (Italian, "almond"): literally an almond shape that in visual representations often surrounds the image of Christ or the Virgin to indicate their holiness.

Man of Sorrows: devotional image depicting the dead Christ, who is usually shown in a frontal position and often flanked by the Virgin Mary or *angels* and the *Instruments of the Passion.*

Mass: principal service of the church, the centerpiece of which is the celebration of the *Eucharist*; also includes scriptural readings and sermons, all of which are offered for the welfare and communion of the living and the dead.

Maundy Thursday: Thursday before Easter Sunday, when the Last Supper attended by Christ and his disciples is commemorated.

meander: a decorative pattern, used since antiquity, consisting of a continuous line formed into interlocking rectangular shapes.

memento mori: visual image that serves as a reminder of the inevitability of death.

Mendicant (Latin, from the verb meaning "to beg"): type of religious order whose members take a vow of poverty and live by begging. Unlike the monastic orders, which seclude themselves from the outside world, Mendicants (such as the Franciscans and Dominicans) are not bound by a promise of confinement.

Middle Ages: in general, the period between the end of the western Roman Empire and the beginning of the Renaissance in Europe.

millefleurs (French, "thousand flowers"): popular decorative motif that uses a dense field of flowers as a background, especially for tapestries.

miter: tall, pointed ceremonial headdress worn by *bishops* (and sometimes *abbots*).

monastery: usually a reclusive community of monks or nuns living under religious vows and according to certain rules.

monasticism: devotional lifestyle of monks or nuns who live, to some degree, in seclusion under religious vows and who are subject to a fixed rule, or code of conduct.

mordant: substance that chemically fixes dyes to textiles.

mortise and tenon: joint in which a hole (mortise) is cut to receive a projecting tenon.

mother-of-pearl: iridescent lining of some shells used for carving and *inlay*.

mullion: vertical stone element within a window frame.

N

nave: in a *cruciform* church, the central aisle used by the congregation that intersects the shorter horizontal arm of the *transept*; comparable to the long vertical arm of a *cross*.

The Netherlands: historical region in northwestern Europe (not to be confused with today's kingdom of the Netherlands) around the delta of the Rhine, Scheldt, and Meuse rivers, bordering the Holy Roman Empire to the east and France to the south. The region was ruled in the later Middle Ages by many noble houses, including the French royal house of Valois, and encompassed today's Netherlands, Belgium, Luxembourg, part of northern France, and western Germany. Fluid boundaries divided the region into southern (including the counties of Flanders and Hainaut and the duchy of Brabant) and northern (including the counties of Holland and Zeeland) Netherlands. See *Burgundian territories*.

niello: black substance composed of powdered silver, lead, copper, and sulfur that is fused by heat to engraved metal surfaces.

O

oculus: a round window.

opus anglicanum (Latin, "English work"): luxurious embroideries produced in England between the thirteenth and fifteenth centuries.

Ottonian: period from 936, when Otto I became king of Saxony, to 1024, when Henry II died. These German kings were crowned emperors of the Holy Roman Empire, as were most German kings after them, until 1806. The Ottonian territories included part of today's Germany, eastern France, and northern Italy.

P

palmette: decorative motif derived from the form of a palm leaf.

parchment: animal skin that has been prepared for use in the production of manuscripts.

pasteboard: layers of paper pressed together to create a rigid surface.

paten: circular shallow dish used to hold the *host*.

pigment: coloring agent for paint, dye, etc.

pilaster: vertical architectural member. Unlike the *column,* which is round, the pilaster is often square or rectangular in section.

pilgrimage: journey made to a holy place as an act of religious devotion. The three major pilgrimage destinations in the *Middle Ages* were Rome, Santiago de Compostela, and Jerusalem.

polylobed: design that is ringed with petal-like projections; scalloped.

pope: *bishop* of Rome and head of the western church (today the Roman Catholic Church).

pot-metal glass: glass with color produced by adding metallic oxides to the molten glass during production.

predella: horizontal zone below the main panels of an *altarpiece* that is often decorated with painting or carving.

Premonstratensian order: monastic order founded in 1120 by Saint Norbert (ca. 1080–1134) at Prémontré near Laon, in northern France. The order observes the Rule of Saint Augustine, with considerable influence from the *Cistercians.*

priest: member of the *clergy* who has the authority to administer the *sacraments.*

pulpit: elevated structure in a church reserved for scriptural readings and preaching.

Q

quatrefoil: four-leaf design.

R

refectory: communal dining room in a *monastery.*

relic: any object associated with a *saint,* including bodily remains, regarded as a memorial after his/her death and held in esteem or venerated.

reliquary: receptacle for the preservation and sometimes display of *relics.*

repoussé: surface relief decoration created by hammering the reverse side of a metal object.

retable: see *altarpiece.*

rib vault: type of masonry *vault* whose surface is articulated by veinlike stone ridges (ribs).

rock crystal: transparent and extremely hard quartz.

Romanesque (French *roman,* "Roman-like"): descriptive term from the early nineteenth century for an architectural style that made prevalent use of the round *arches* found in Roman buildings. In general, Romanesque refers to the architectural and artistic style in western Europe from about 950 to 1150, when monumental art forms such as *fresco* and relief sculpture were revived.

rose window: large, circular *stained-glass* window often filled with intricate *tracery* designs.

S

sacrament: religious act that confers divine grace on the participant through the performance of certain rituals, for example, communion, baptism, and matrimony.

saint: in general, a holy person, the meaning and extent of which varied throughout the *Middle Ages.* See *canonize.*

sarcophagus: stone coffin.

shrine: in western Europe, a receptacle for the body or *relics* of *saints.* The term is often applied to spaces made holy by that receptacle, or to a place of worship where devotions are paid to a saint.

silver-stain: application of a silver compound to the back of *stained glass* that produces a yellow color; first used in western Europe in the fourteenth century.

socle: projecting pedestal of a *column.*

spandrel: wall areas between *arches.*

stained glass: colored and painted glass pieces assembled with lead channels to form a decorative panel or window.

stigmata: marks replicating the wounds of Christ from the Crucifixion.

surcoat: short tunic worn over armor.

T

tang: connecting element that holds together the vertical and horizontal elements of a *cross*.

tapestry: hangings woven on a loom with *warp* and *weft* threads.

tempera: generally refers to egg tempera, a paint made using egg yolk to bind *pigments*.

terracotta (Italian, "baked earth"): fired clay.

tonsure: shaved crown of the head of a *priest* or monk.

tracery: stone elements, often arranged in a decorative pattern, that hold glass in place (as in a stained-glass window). Tracery first emerged in the late twelfth century and became a prominent feature of Gothic architecture. Tracery patterns were also employed by artists working in a variety of other media, from wood sculpture and metalwork to furniture.

transept: in a *cruciform* church, a corridor-like space near the sanctuary that transverses the *nave*.

treasury: in a church or *monastery,* a storage room for precious objects (most of which are liturgical or devotional in nature).

trefoil: three-leaf design.

Trinity: theological concept of the existence of one God in three persons: God the Father, God the Son, and the *Holy Ghost* or *Holy Spirit.*

triptych: three hinged panels, carved or painted. See *diptych.*

True Cross: *cross* reputedly discovered in the fourth century by Helena, mother of Constantine the Great, that was thought to be the cross on which Christ was crucified.

tympanum: flat field above a doorway between the *lintel* and the *archivolt,* often decorated with carvings.

typology: method of associating the Old and New Testaments in which episodes and figures in the Old Testament are seen to prefigure those of the New Testament.

U

unicorn: mythological animal with the body of a horse (or kid) and a single horn on its forehead. In the *Middle Ages,* it was often considered a symbol of Christ, and its horn was believed to possess therapeutic and magical powers.

V

vault: in general, a concave ceiling often constructed of masonry; variations include *barrel vault* and *rib vault.*

vellum: high-quality *parchment.*

velvet: woven textile with a raised pile.

vermiculé: scroll-like decorative design that imitates the patterns of worm-eaten wood.

vestment: liturgical garment worn by those performing the *Mass.*

voussoir: one of the wedge-shaped stone blocks of which an *arch* is composed.

W

warp: in *tapestry* weaving, often undyed threads stretched across a loom to form the base structure of a hanging.

wattle: panels made of tree branches and twigs interwoven with stakes or rods; used as material for constructing fences, walls, or sometimes roofs.

weft: in *tapestry* weaving, dyed or metallic threads that run above and below the *warp* threads to form the design of a hanging.

Suggested Readings

The following titles are recommended for those interested in medieval art in general and The Cloisters collection in particular. It was prepared with the general reader in mind, with preference given to recent, accessible publications in English. The reader is also encouraged to consult the Museum's website, www.metmuseum.org, for additional information about the collection, including special features on selected works at The Cloisters; thematic discussions of medieval art can be found on the website in the Timeline of Art History.

Primary Sources

Davis-Weyer, Caecilia, comp. *Early Medieval Art, 300–1150: Sources and Documents*. Englewood Cliffs, N.J., 1971.

Frisch, Teresa G. *Gothic Art, 1140–c. 1450: Sources and Documents*. Englewood Cliffs, N.J., 1971; reprint, Toronto, 1987.

The Holy Bible, translated from the Latin Vulgate (Douay-Rheims Version). . . . Rockford, Ill., 1989.

Jacobus de Voragine. *The Golden Legend: Readings on the Saints*. Translated by William Granger Ryan. Princeton, N.J., 1993.

Saint Benedict. *Rule for Monasteries*. Translated by Leonard J. Doyle. Collegeville, Minn., 1948.

Theophilus. *On Divers Arts*. Translated by John G. Hawthorne and Cyril Stanley Smith. Chicago, 1963.

The Cloisters' History and Collection

Bayard, Tania. *Sweet Herbs and Sundry Flowers: Medieval Gardens and the Gardens of The Cloisters*. New York, 1985; reprint, 1997.

Cavallo, Adolfo Salvatore. *The Unicorn Tapestries at The Metropolitan Museum of Art*. New York, 1998.

Dickson, Harold E. "The Origin of 'The Cloisters.'" *The Art Quarterly* 28 (1965), pp. 253–74.

Freeman, Margaret B. *The Unicorn Tapestries*. New York, 1976; reprint, 1983.

Husband, Timothy B. *The Art of Illumination: The Limbourg Brothers and the Belles Heures of Jean de France, Duc de Berry*. Exh. cat. Los Angeles, J. Paul Getty Museum; New York, The Metropolitan Museum of Art. New York, 2008.

———. *The Metropolitan Museum of Art Bulletin* 70, no. 4 (Spring 2013), forthcoming.

Larkin, Deirdre. *The Medieval Garden Enclosed: The Cloisters Museum and Gardens* (blog), 2008– , http://blog.metmuseum.org/cloistersgardens/.

Leuchak, Mary Rebecca. "'Old World for the New': Developing the Design for The Cloisters." *The Metropolitan Museum Journal* 23 (1988), pp. 257–77.

Mumford, Lewis. "Pax in Urbe." *The New Yorker*, May 21, 1938. Reprinted in *Sidewalk Critic: Lewis Mumford's Writings on New York*, edited by Robert Wojtowicz, pp. 213–16. New York, 1998.

Parker, Elizabeth C., and Charles T. Little. *The Cloisters Cross: Its Art and Meaning*. New York, 1994.

Parker, Elizabeth C., ed., with the assistance of Mary B. Shepard. *The Cloisters: Studies in Honor of the Fiftieth Anniversary*. New York, 1992. A volume with more than twenty essays contributed by leading scholars on the history and major works of art of The Cloisters.

Rorimer, James J. *The Cloisters: The Building and the Collection of Mediaeval Art in Fort Tryon Park*. New York, 1938; reprint, 1963.

———. *Medieval Monuments at The Cloisters as They Were and as They Are*. Rev. ed. New York, 1972.

Schrader, J. L. "George Grey Barnard: The Cloisters and The Abbaye." *The Metropolitan Museum of Art Bulletin* 37, no. 1 (Summer 1979), pp. 1–52.

———. "A Medieval Bestiary." *The Metropolitan Museum of Art Bulletin* 44, no. 1 (Summer 1986), pp. 3–56.Shepard, Mary B. "The Cuxa Cloister" and "The Campin Room." In *Period Rooms in The*

Metropolitan Museum of Art. New York, 1996.

Smith, Elizabeth Bradford. "George Grey Barnard: Artist/Collector/ Dealer/Curator." In *Medieval Art in America: Patterns of Collecting, 1800–1940*. Exh. cat. University Park, Pa., Palmer Museum of Art. University Park, Pa., 1996.

Tomkins, Calvin. *Merchants and Masterpieces: The Story of The Metropolitan Museum of Art*. New York, 1970; reprint, 1989. See chapter 19.

Wixom, William D. "Medieval Sculpture at The Cloisters." *The Metropolitan Museum of Art Bulletin* 46, no. 3 (Winter 1988–89), pp. 3–64.

———, ed. *Mirror of the Medieval World*. Exh. cat. New York, The Metropolitan Museum of Art. New York, 1999.

———, and Margaret Lawson. "Picturing the Apocalypse: Illustrated Leaves from a Medieval Spanish Manuscript." *The Metropolitan Museum of Art Bulletin* 59, no. 3 (Winter 2002), pp. 1–56.

Wu, Nancy. "Teaching Medieval Architecture at The Cloisters." In *Perspectives on Medieval Art: Learning through Looking*. New York, 2009.

Young, Bonnie. *A Walk Through The Cloisters*. New York, 1979; reprint, 1988.

Medieval Art at the Metropolitan Museum

Ainsworth, Maryan W., and Keith Christiansen, eds. *From Van Eyck to Bruegel: Early Netherlandish Paintings in The Metropolitan Museum of Art*. Exh. cat. New York, The Metropolitan Museum of Art. New York, 1998.

Barnet, Peter, and Pete Dandridge. *Lions, Dragons, and Other Beasts: Aquamanilia of the Middle Ages, Vessels for Church and Table*. Exh. cat. New York, Bard Graduate Center. New Haven, 2006.

Boehm, Barbara Drake. *Enamels of Limoges 1100–1350*. Exh. cat. Paris, Musée du Louvre; New York, The Metropolitan Museum of Art. New York, 1996.

———. *Prague: The Crown of Bohemia, 1347–1437*. Exh. cat. New York, The Metropolitan Museum of Art; Prague Castle. New York, 2005.

Castelnuovo-Tedesco, Lisbeth, and Jack Soultanian, with Richard Y. Tayar. *Italian Medieval Sculpture in The Metropolitan Museum of Art and The Cloisters*. New York, 2010.

Cavallo, Adolfo Salvatore. *Medieval Tapestries in The Metropolitan Museum of Art*. New York, 1993.

Chapuis, Julien, et al. *Tilman Riemenschneider: Master Sculptor of the Late Middle Ages*. Exh. cat. New York, The Metropolitan Museum of Art. New Haven, 1999.

Deuchler, Florens, ed. *The Year 1200: A Background Survey*. Exh. cat. New York, The Metropolitan Museum of Art. New York, 1970.

Gómez-Moreno, Carmen. *Medieval Art from Private Collections*. Exh. cat. New York, The Metropolitan Museum of Art. New York, 1968.

Hayward, Jane. *English and French Medieval Stained Glass in the Collection of The Metropolitan Museum of Art*. Revised and edited by Mary B. Shepard and Cynthia Clark. 2 vols. New York, 2003.

Husband, Timothy B. *The Luminous Image: Painted Glass Roundels in the Lowlands, 1480–1560*. Exh. cat. New York, The Metropolitan Museum of Art. New York, 1995.

———, and Jane Hayward. *The Secular Spirit: Life and Art at the End of the Middle Ages*. Exh. cat. New York, The Metropolitan Museum of Art, The Cloisters. New York, 1975.

———, with the assistance of Gloria Gilmore-House. *The Wild Man: Medieval Myth and Symbolism*. Exh. cat. New York, The Metropolitan Museum of Art. New York, 1980.

Kargère, Lucretia, and Adriana Rizzo, "Twelfth-Century French Polychrome Sculpture in The

Metropolitan Museum of Art: Materials and Techniques." *Metropolitan Museum Studies in Art, Science, and Technology* 1 (2010), pp. 39–70.

Little, Charles T., ed. *The Art of Medieval Spain, A.D. 500–1200.* Exh. cat. New York, The Metropolitan Museum of Art. New York, 1993.

Little, Charles T., et al. *Set in Stone: The Face in Medieval Sculpture.* Exh. cat. New York, The Metropolitan Museum of Art. New York, 2006.

The Metropolitan Museum of Art. *Europe in the Middle Ages.* Introductions by Charles T. Little and Timothy B. Husband. New York, 1987.

———. *Gothic and Renaissance Art in Nuremberg, 1300–1550.* Exh. cat. New York, The Metropolitan Museum of Art; Nuremberg, Germanisches Nationalmuseum. New York, 1986.

Ostoia, Vera K. *The Middle Ages: Treasures from The Cloisters and The Metropolitan Museum of Art.* Exh. cat. Los Angeles County Museum of Art. Los Angeles, 1969.

Medieval Art and Architecture in General

Alexander, Jonathan J. G. *Medieval Illuminators and Their Methods of Work.* New Haven, 1992.

Bagnoli, Martina, et al. *Treasures of Heaven: Saints, Relics, and Devotion in Medieval Europe.* Exh. cat. Cleveland Museum of Art; Baltimore, Walters Art Museum; London, The British Museum. New Haven, 2010.

Barnet, Peter, ed. *Images in Ivory: Precious Objects of the Gothic Age.* Exh. cat. Detroit Institute of Arts; Baltimore, Walters Art Gallery. Detroit, 1997.

Baxandall, Michael. *The Limewood Sculptors of Renaissance Germany.* New Haven, 1980.

Camille, Michael. *Gothic Art: Glorious Visions.* New York, 1996.

Coldstream, Nicola. *Medieval Architecture.* New York, 2002.

Cross, F. L., ed. *The Oxford Dictionary of the Christian Church.* 3d ed. New York, 1997.

De Hamel, Christopher. *A History of Illuminated Manuscripts.* 2d ed., rev. and enl. London, 1994.

Duby, Georges. *The Age of the Cathedrals: Art and Society, 980–1420.* Translated by Eleanor Levieux and Barbara Thompson. Chicago, 1981.

Erlande-Brandenburg, Alain. *Cathedrals and Castles: Building in the Middle Ages.* Translated by Rosemary Stonehewer. New York, 1995.

Frankl, Paul. *Gothic Architecture.* Revised by Paul Crossley. New Haven, 2000.

Freeman, Margaret B. *Herbs for the Mediaeval Household, for Cooking, Healing and Divers Uses.* 2d ed. New York, 1997.

Gerli, E. Michael, ed. *Medieval Iberia: An Encyclopedia.* New York, 2003.

Gesta (1963–). A scholarly journal devoted exclusively to the study of medieval art. Of interest are special issues such as "The Renaissance of the Twelfth Century" (1970/72), "Paradisus Claustralis" (1973/71–72), and occasional publications of medieval objects at The Metropolitan Museum of Art.

Hearn, M. F. *Romanesque Sculpture: The Revival of Monumental Stone Sculpture in the Eleventh and Twelfth Centuries.* Ithaca, N.Y., 1981.

Hourihane, Colum, ed. *Gothic Art and Thought in the Later Medieval Period: Essays in Honor of Willibald Sauerländer.* [Princeton, N.J., and] University Park, Pa., 2011.

———. *Romanesque Art and Thought in the Twelfth Century: Essays in Honor of Walter Cahn.* University Park, Pa., 2008.

Jeep, John M., ed. *Medieval Germany: An Encyclopedia.* New York, 2001.

Kibler, William W., et al., eds. *Medieval France: An Encyclopedia.* New York, 1995.

Medieval Craftsmen Series

Binski, Paul. *Painters*. London, 1991.

Brown, Sarah, and David O'Connor. *Glass-Painters*. London, 1991.

Cherry, John. *Goldsmiths*. London, 1992.

Coldstream, Nicola. *Masons and Sculptors*. Toronto, 1991.

De Hamel, Christopher. *Scribes and Illuminators*. Toronto, 1992.

Pfaffenbichler, Matthias. *Armourers*. Toronto, 1992.

Staniland, Kay. *Embroiderers*. London, 1991.

Nees, Lawrence. *Early Medieval Art*. Oxford History of Art series. Oxford, 2002.

Raguin, Virginia Chieffo, with Mary Clerkin Higgins. *Stained Glass: From Its Origins to the Present*. New York, 2003.

Rudolph, Conrad, ed. *A Companion to Medieval Art: Romanesque and Gothic in Northern Europe*. Malden, Mass., 2006.

Sauerländer, Willibald. *Gothic Sculpture in France, 1140–1270*. Translated by Janet Sondheimer. New York, 1972.

Schapiro, Meyer. *Romanesque Art*. New York, 1977.

Sears, Elizabeth, and Thelma K. Thomas, eds. *Reading Medieval Images: The Art Historian and the Object*. Ann Arbor, 2002.

Snyder, James. *Medieval Art: Painting–Sculpture–Architecture, 4th–14th Century*. New York, 1989.

Stalley, Roger. *Early Medieval Architecture*. Oxford History of Art series. Oxford, 1999.

Stokstad, Marilyn. *Medieval Art*. 2d ed. Boulder, 2004.

Strayer, Joseph R., ed. *Dictionary of the Middle Ages*. 14 vols. New York, 1982–2004.

Szarmach, Paul E., et al., eds. *Medieval England: An Encyclopedia*. New York, 1998.

Williamson, Paul. *Gothic Sculpture, 1140–1300*. New Haven, 1995.

Selected References

References are arranged by object in order of appearance and are listed in chronological order within each entry. Omitted works of art do not have accompanying references. Frequently cited references have been abbreviated below; full bibliographic data for these is provided at the end of the list.

Plaque with Saint John the Evangelist (p. 22)
Wixom 1999.

Plaque with Scenes at Emmaus (p. 23)
Hermann Schnitzler, "Eine Metzer Emmaustafel," *Wallraf-Richartz-Jahrbuch* 20 (1958), pp. 41–54; Victor H. Elbern, "Vier karolingische Elfenbeinkästen: Historische, symbolische und liturgische Elemente in der spätkarolingischen Bildkunst," *Zeitschrift des deutschen Vereins für Kunstwissenschaft* 20, nos. 1–2 (1966), pp. 1–16.

Bursa Reliquary (p. 24)
Hermann Fillitz and Martina Pippal, *Schatzkunst: Die Goldschmiede- und Elfenbeinarbeiten aus österreichischen Schatzkammern des Hochmittelalters* (Salzburg, 1987).

Plaque with the Holy Women at the Tomb (p. 25)
Wixom 1999.

Ring (p. 26)
"Recent Acquisitions, A Selection: 2004–2005," *The Metropolitan Museum of Art Bulletin* 63, no. 2 (Fall 2005), p. 11; Charles T. Little, "New Gold Cloisonné Enamel Ottonian Rings," in *'Luft unter die Flügel . . .'—Beiträge zur mittelalterlichen Kunst: Festschrift für Hiltrud Westermann-Angerhausen*, edited by Andrea von Hülsen-Esch and Dagmar Täube, pp. 48–55 (Hildesheim and New York, 2010).

Plaque with Saint Aemilian (p. 27)
Little 1993; Wixom 1999.

Cloister from Saint-Michel-de-Cuxa (p. 28)
Rorimer 1972; Thomas E. A. Dale, "Monsters, Corporeal Deformities, and Phantasms in the Cloister of St-Michel-de-Cuxa," *Art Bulletin* 83, no. 3 (September 2001), pp. 402–36.

Narbonne Arch (p. 30)
J. L. Schrader, "A Medieval Bestiary," *The Metropolitan Museum of Art Bulletin* 44, no. 1 (Summer 1986), pp. 3–56; Little 1987a.

Angel from Saint-Lazare at Autun (p. 31)
Denis Grivot and George Zarnecki, *Gislebertus, Sculptor of Autun* (New York, 1961); Little 1987b.

Enthroned Virgin and Child (p. 32)
Forsyth 1982; Little 1987b; Lucretia Kargère and Adriana Rizzo, "Twelfth-Century French Polychrome Sculpture in The Metropolitan Museum of Art: Materials and Techniques." *Metropolitan Museum Studies in Art, Science, and Technology* 1 (2010), pp. 39–70.

Enthroned Virgin and Child (p. 33)
Forsyth 1982; Little 1987b; Lucretia Kargère and Adriana Rizzo, "Twelfth-Century French Polychrome Sculpture in The Metropolitan Museum of Art: Materials and Techniques," *Metropolitan Museum Studies in Art, Science, and Technology* 1 (2010), pp. 39–70.

Apse from San Martín at Fuentidueña (p. 35)
James J. Rorimer, Carmen Gómez-Moreno, and Margaret B. Freeman, "The Apse from San Martín at Fuentidueña," *The Metropolitan Museum of Art Bulletin* 19, no. 10 (June 1961), pp. 265–96; David L. Simon, "Romanesque Art in American Collections. XXI. The Metropolitan Museum of Art. Part 1: Spain," *Gesta* 23, no. 2 (1984), pp. 145–59; The Metropolitan Museum of Art, *The Fuentidueña Apse: A Journey from Castile to New York*, directed by Christopher Noey (New York, 2012), www.metmuseum.org.

Crucifix (p. 36)
Little 1993.

The Virgin and Child in Majesty and the Adoration of the Magi (p. 37)
Juan Ainaud de Lasarte, *Catalan Painting* (New York, 1990).

The Adoration of the Magi (p. 38)
Rorimer 1972; Elizabeth Valdez del Álamo, "The Epiphany Relief from Cerezo de Riotirón," in Parker 1992, pp. 110–45.

Commentary on the Apocalypse of Saint John (p. 39)
William D. Wixom and Margaret Lawson, "Picturing the Apocalypse: Illustrated Leaves from a Medieval Spanish Manuscript," *The Metropolitan Museum of Art Bulletin* 59, no. 3 (Winter 2002), pp. 1–56.

Game Piece with Hercules Slaying the Three-Headed Geryon (p. 41)
Vivian B. Mann, "Samson vs. Hercules: A Carved Cycle of the Twelfth Century, in the High Middle Ages," *ACTA* 7 (1980), pp. 1–38.

Doorway from San Leonardo al Frigido (p. 41)
Rorimer 1972; Castelnuovo-Tedesco and Soultanian 2010; Gigetta Dalli Regoli, "Il tema dell'Entrata in Gerusalemme nelle interpretazioni di Biduino," in *Forme e storia: Scritti di arte medievale e moderna per Francesco Gandolfo*, pp. 223–32 (Rome, 2011).

Plaque with the Pentecost (p. 42)
Peter Lasko, *Ars Sacra, 800–1200*, 2d ed. (New Haven, 1994).

Chapel from Notre-Dame-du-Bourg at Langon (p. 44)
Rorimer 1972; Jacques Gardelles, "Notre-Dame-du-Bourg à

Langon: État des questions," *Cahiers du Bazadais* 17 (1977), pp. 27–42.

Chapter House from Notre-Dame-de-Pontaut (p. 47)
Rorimer 1972.

Cross (p. 50)
Elizabeth C. Parker and Charles T. Little, *The Cloisters Cross: Its Art and Meaning* (New York, 1994); Elizabeth C. Parker, "Editing the Cloisters Cross," *Gesta* 45, no. 2 (2006), pp. 147–60.

Martyrdom of Saint Lawrence (p. 52)
Hayward 2003.

Plaque with Censing Angels (p. 53)
"Recent Acquisitions, A Selection: 2001–2002," *The Metropolitan Museum of Art Bulletin* 60, no. 2 (Fall 2002), p. 11.

Initial *V* from a Bible (p. 54)
Walter Cahn, *Romanesque Manuscripts: The Twelfth Century* (London, 1996); "Recent Acquisitions, A Selection: 1999–2000," *The Metropolitan Museum of Art Bulletin* 58, no. 2 (Fall 2000), p. 17.

Reliquary Cross (p. 55)
Pete Dandridge, "Reconsidering a Romanesque Reliquary Cross," *Met Objectives: Treatment and Research Notes* 4, no. 1 (Fall 2002), pp. 5–7; "Recent Acquisitions, A Selection: 2001–2002," *The Metropolitan Museum of Art Bulletin* 60, no. 2 (Fall 2002), p. 12; Martina Bagnoli et al., *Treasures of Heaven: Saints, Relics, and Devotion in Medieval Europe*, exh. cat., Cleveland Museum of Art; Baltimore, Walters Art Museum; London, The British Museum (New Haven, 2010).

Cloister from Saint-Guilhem-le-Désert (p. 56)
Rorimer 1972; Hélène Palouzié and Géraldine Mallet, *Le cloître de Saint-Guilhem-le-Désert* (Arles, 2009).

Corbel (p. 59)
Walter Cahn, ed., *Romanesque Sculpture in American Collections*, vol. 2, *New York and New Jersey, Middle and South Atlantic States, the Midwest, Western and Pacific States* (Turnhout, 1999); Christian Bougoux, *L'imagerie romane figurée de la Sauve-Majeure: L'iconographie romane au risque de la sémantique* (Bordeaux, 2002).

Torso of Christ (p. 60)
Little 1987b; François Avril et al., *La France romane au temps des premiers Capétiens, 987–1152*, exh. cat., Paris, Musée du Louvre (Paris, 2005); Lucretia Kargère and Adriana Rizzo, "Twelfth-Century French Polychrome Sculpture in The Metropolitan Museum of Art: Materials and Techniques," *Metropolitan Museum Studies in Art, Science, and Technology* 1 (2010), pp. 39–70.

Altar Frontal (p. 61)
Walter W. S. Cook, "The Stucco Altar-Frontals of Catalonia," *Art Studies* 2 (1924), pp. 41–81.

Segment of a Crosier Shaft (p. 62)
Wixom 1999; Charles T. Little, "Along the Pilgrimage Road: Ivories and the Role of Compostela," in *Patrimonio artístico de Galicia y otros estudios: Homenaje al Prof. Dr. Serafín Moralejo Álvarez*, edited by Ángela Franco Mata, vol. 3, pp. 159–66 (Santiago de Compostela, 2004).

Bowl of a Drinking Cup (p. 63)
George Zarnecki, Janet Holt, and Tristram Holland, eds., *English Romanesque Art, 1066–1200*, exh. cat., London, Hayward Gallery (London, 1984).

Clasp (p. 63)
Herbert Broderick, "Solomon and Sheba Revisited," *Gesta* 16, no. 1 (1977), pp. 45–48.

Relief with the Annunciation (p. 64)
Rorimer 1972; Lisbeth Castelnuovo-Tedesco, "Romanesque Sculpture in North American Collections. XXII. The Metropolitan Museum of Art. Part II: Italy (1)," *Gesta* 24, no. 1 (1985), pp. 61–76; Castelnuovo-Tedesco and Soultanian 2010.

Lion (p. 64)
Rorimer 1972; Walter Cahn, "The Frescoes of San Pedro de Arlanza," in Parker 1992, pp. 86–109.

Doorway from Notre-Dame at Reugny (p. 66)
Rorimer 1972; Anne Courtillé, *Auvergne et Bourbonnais gothiques, les débuts* (Nonette, 1990).

Doorway from Moutiers-Saint-Jean (p. 68)
Rorimer 1972; Neil Stratford, "The Moutiers-Saint-Jean Portal in The Cloisters," in Parker 1992, pp. 260–81.

Theodosius Arrives at Ephesus (p. 70)
Michael Cothren, "The Seven Sleepers and the Seven Kneelers: Prolegomena to a Study of the 'Belles Verrières' of the Cathedral of Rouen," *Gesta* 25 (1986), pp. 203–26; Hayward 2003.

Scene from the Life of Saint Nicholas (p. 71)
Suse Childs, "Two Scenes from the Life of St. Nicholas and Their Relationship to the Glazing Program of the Chevet Chapels at Soissons Cathedral," in Caviness and Husband 1985, pp. 25–33; Hayward 2003.

Evangelists Mark and Luke (p. 72)
Enamels of Limoges, 1100–1350, exh. cat., Paris, Musée du Louvre; New York, The Metropolitan Museum of Art (New York, 1996); Marie-Amélie Carlier, *Art médiéval: Exposition à l'occasion du centenaire de Brimo de Laroussilhe*, exh. cat., Paris, Brimo de Laroussilhe (Paris, 2008).

Chalice (p. 73)
McLachlan 2001, Didier and Toussaint 2003.

Arm Reliquary (p. 74)
Cynthia Hahn, "The Voices of the Saints: Speaking Reliquaries," *Gesta* 36, no. 1 (1997), pp. 20–31; Didier and Toussaint 2003.

Chalice, Paten, and Straw (p. 75)
McLachlan 2001.

Virgin (p. 76)
Rorimer 1972; *Iconoclasme: Vie et mort de l'image médiévale*, exh. cat., Berne, Musée d'Histoire; Strasbourg, Musée de l'Oeuvre Notre-Dame (Paris, 2001).

Head (p. 77)
Wixom 1999; Charles T. Little et al., *Set in Stone: The Face in Medieval Sculpture*, exh. cat., New York, The Metropolitan Museum of Art (New York, 2006).

Two Scenes from the Legend of Saint Germain of Paris (p. 78)
Mary B. Shepard, "The St. Germain Windows from the Thirteenth-Century Lady Chapel at Saint-Germain-des-Prés," in Parker 1992, pp. 282–301; Hayward 2003.

Enthroned Virgin and Child (p. 79)
Sarah M. Guérin, "An Ivory Virgin at the Metropolitan Museum, New York, in a Gothic Sculptor's Oeuvre," *The Burlington Magazine* 154, no. 1311 (June 2012), pp. 394–402.

Diptych with the Coronation of the Virgin and the Last Judgment (p. 80)
Barnet 1997.

Enthroned Virgin and Child (p. 81)
Wixom 1999.

The Crucified Christ (p. 82)
"Recent Acquisitions, A Selection: 2005–2006," *The Metropolitan Museum of Art Bulletin* 64, no. 2 (Fall 2006), p. 26; Peter Barnet, "Recent Acquisitions (1999–2008) of Medieval Art at The Metropolitan Museum of Art and The Cloisters, New York," *The Burlington Magazine* 150, no. 1268 (November 2008), p. 798, fig. 17.

Head of an Apostle (p. 82)
Charles T. Little et al., *Set in Stone: The Face in Medieval Sculpture*, exh. cat., New York, The Metropolitan Museum of Art (New York, 2006).

Cloister (p. 84)
Rorimer 1972.

Tomb Effigy of Jean d'Alluye (p. 88)
Rorimer 1972; Helmut Nickel, "A Crusader's Sword: Concerning the Effigy of Jean d'Alluye," *The Metropolitan Museum Journal* 26 (1991), pp. 123–28.

Tomb of Ermengol VII, Count of Urgell (p. 90)
Rorimer 1972; Timothy B. Husband, "'Sancti Nicolai de fontibus amoenis' or 'Sti. Nicolai et Fontium Amenorum': The Making of Monastic History," in Parker 1992, pp. 354–83.

Stained Glass with Emperor Henry II and Queen Kunigunde (p. 91)
Eva Frodl-Kraft, "Problems of Gothic Workshop Practices in Light of a Group of Mid-Fourteenth-Century Austrian Stained-Glass Panels," in Caviness and Husband 1985, pp. 107–23.

Stained Glass with the Baptism of Christ and the Agony in the Garden (p. 92)
Eva Frodl-Kraft, "The Stained Glass from Ebreichsdorf and the Austrian 'Ducal Workshop,'" in Parker 1992, pp. 384–407.

Diptych with Scenes of the Life of Christ and the Virgin, Saint Michael, John the Baptist, Thomas Becket, and the Trinity (p. 94)
Barnet 1997.

Pair of Altar Angels (p. 95)
Françoise Baron, *L'art au temps des rois maudits: Philippe le Bel et ses fils, 1285–1328*, exh. cat., Paris, Grand Palais (Paris, 1998).

Standing Virgin and Child (p. 96)
Wixom 1988–89.

Mirror Case with Scenes of the Attack on the Castle of Love (p. 97)
Barnet 1997; "Recent Acquisitions, A Selection: 2002–2003," *The Metropolitan Museum of Art Bulletin* 61, no. 2 (Fall 2003), p. 12.

Panel with Hunting Scenes (p. 97)
Barnet 1997; "Recent Acquisitions, A Selection: 2002–2003," *The Metropolitan Museum of Art Bulletin* 61, no. 2 (Fall 2003), pp. 12, 13.

Coffret (*Minnekästchen*) (p. 98)
Timothy B. Husband and Jane Hayward, *The Secular Spirit: Life and Art at the End of the Middle Ages*, exh. cat., New York, The Metropolitan Museum of Art, The Cloisters (New York, 1975).

Support Figure of a Seated Cleric or Friar (p. 98)
William D. Wixom, "A Thirteenth-Century Support Figure of a Seated Friar," *Wiener Jahrbuch für Kunstgeschichte* 46–47 (1993–94), pp. 797– 802; Wixom 1999.

The Hours of Jeanne d'Evreux, Queen of France (p. 99)
Das Stundenbuch der Jeanne d'Evreux / The Hours of Jeanne d'Evreux / Le livre d'heures de Jeanne d'Evreux, facsimile, with commentary by Barbara Drake Boehm, Abigail Quandt, and William D. Wixom (Lucerne, 2000); Barbara Drake Boehm,

"Perfect Penmanship: Pucelle's Creativity in the Margins of the Hours of Jeanne d'Evreux" in *Jean Pucelle: Innovation and Collaboration in Manuscript Painting* (Turnhout, 2012).

Reliquary Shrine (p. 100)
Danielle Gaborit-Chopin, "The Reliquary of Elizabeth of Hungary at The Cloisters," in Parker 1992, pp. 326–53; Boehm 2005.

The Cloisters Apocalypse (p. 101)
Florens Deuchler, J[effrey] M. Hoffeld, and Helmut Nickel, *The Cloisters Apocalypse: An Early Fourteenth-Century Manuscript in Facsimile* (New York, 1971).

Double Cup (p. 102)
Wixom 1999; Boehm 2005.

Covered Beaker (p. 103)
Wixom 1999.

Enthroned Virgin (p. 104)
Wixom 1999; Castelnuovo-Tedesco and Soultanian 2010.

Relief with Saint Peter Martyr and Three Donors (p. 105)
"Recent Acquisitions, A Selection: 2000–2001," *The Metropolitan Museum of Art Bulletin* 59, no. 2 (Fall 2001), pp. 18, 19; Castelnuovo-Tedesco and Soultanian 2010.

The Crucifixion and the Lamentation (p. 106)
Laurence B. Kanter et al., *Painting and Illumination in Early Renaissance Florence, 1300–1450*, exh. cat., New York, The Metropolitan Museum of Art (New York, 1994).

Leaf from a *Laudario* with the Martyrdom of Saint Bartholomew (p. 107)
Barbara Drake Boehm, *Choirs of Angels: Painting in Italian Choir Books, 1300–1500*, exh. cat., New York, The Metropolitan Museum of Art (New York, 2008).

The Adoration of the Shepherds (p. 108)
Keith Christiansen, "Fourteenth-Century Italian Altarpieces," *The Metropolitan Museum of Art Bulletin* 40, no. 1 (Summer 1982), pp. 38, 39, 41; Bruce Boucher and Francesca Fiorani, eds., *Bartolo di Fredi: The Adoration of the Magi, a Masterpiece Reconstructed*, exh. cat., Charlottesville, University of Virginia Art Museum; New York, Museum of Biblical Art (Charlottesville, 2012).

Chalice (p. 109)
Wixom 1999.

Aquamanile in the Form of a Dragon (p. 110)
Barnet and Dandridge 2006.

Aquamanile in the Form of a Ram (p. 111)
"Recent Acquisitions, A Selection: 2007–2008," *The Metropolitan Museum of Art Bulletin* 66, no. 2 (Fall 2008),

p. 14; Peter Barnet, "An English Pottery Aquamanile in the Form of a Ram," in *'Luft unter die Flügel . . .'—Beiträge zur mittelalterlichen Kunst: Festschrift für Hiltrud Westermann-Angerhausen*, edited by Andrea von Hülsen-Esch and Dagmar Täube, pp. 66–70 (Hildesheim and New York, 2010).

Aquamanile in the Form of a Cock (p. 112)
Barnet and Dandridge 2006.

Aquamanile in the Form of a Lion (p. 113)
Barnet and Dandridge 2006.

Altar Cruet (p. 114)
Wixom 1999.

Brooch (p. 114)
Wixom 1999.

The Bishop of Assisi Giving a Palm to Saint Clare (p. 115)
Nuremberg 1986; Wixom 1999.

Embroidered Hanging (p. 117)
Bonnie Young, "Needlework by Nuns: A Medieval Religious Embroidery," *The Metropolitan Museum of Art Bulletin* 28, no. 6 (February 1970), pp. 262–77; Kay Staniland, *Embroiderers*, Medieval Craftsmen series (London, 1991).

Bust of the Virgin (p. 118)
"Recent Acquisitions, A Selection: 2005–2006," *The Metropolitan Museum of Art Bulletin* 64, no. 2 (Fall 2006), p. 26; Julien Chapuis, "Tonbüste einer gekrönten Jungfrau," in *Karl IV. Kaiser von Gottes Gnaden: Kunst und Repräsentation des Hauses Luxemburg, 1310–1437*, edited by Jiří Fajt, pp. 519–20 (Munich and Berlin, 2006).

Pietà (*Vesperbild*) (p. 119)
"Recent Acquisitions, A Selection: 2000–2001," *The Metropolitan Museum of Art Bulletin* 59, no. 2 (Fall 2001), p. 20; Boehm 2005.

Credenza (p. 120)
Luisa Bandera, *Il mobile emiliano* (Milan, 1972); Graziano Manni, *Mobili in Emilia: Con una indagine sulla civiltà dell'arredo alla corte degli Estensi* (Modena, 1986).

Plate with the Arms of Blanche of Navarre (p. 121)
Timothy B. Husband, "Valencian Lustreware of the Fifteenth Century: An Exhibition at The Cloisters," *The Metropolitan Museum of Art Bulletin* 29, no. 1 (Summer 1970), pp. 20–32; Timothy B. Husband, "Valencian Lustreware of the Fifteenth Century: Notes and Documents," *The Metropolitan Museum of Art Bulletin* 29, no. 1 (Summer 1970), pp. 11–19.

Julius Caesar and Attendants, from the Nine Heroes Tapestries (p. 122)
Cavallo 1993.

The Belles Heures of Jean de France, Duc de Berry (p. 123)

Millard Meiss, with Sharon Off Dunlap Smith and Elizabeth Home Beatson, *French Painting in the Time of Jean de Berry: The Limbourgs and Their Contemporaries*, 2 vols. (New York, 1974); John Plummer, "The Beginnings of the Belles Heures," in Parker 1992, pp. 420–39; *Paris 1400: Les arts sous Charles VI*, exh. cat., Paris, Musée du Louvre (Paris, 2004); Timothy B. Husband, *The Art of Illumination: The Limbourg Brothers and the Belles Heures of Jean de France, Duc de Berry*, exh. cat., Los Angeles, J. Paul Getty Museum; New York, The Metropolitan Museum of Art (New York, 2008).

Beaker with Apes (p. 124)

Timothy B. Husband and Jane Hayward, *The Secular Spirit: Life and Art at the End of the Middle Ages*, exh. cat., New York, The Metropolitan Museum of Art, The Cloisters (New York, 1975); Reinhold Baumstark, ed., *Schatzkammerstücke aus der Herbstzeit des Mittelalters: Das Regensburger Emailkästchen und sein Umkreis*, exh. cat., Munich, Bayerisches Nationalmuseum (Munich, 1992).

Altarpiece with Christ, Saint John the Baptist, and Saint Margaret (p. 126)

Lisbeth Castelnuovo-Tedesco, "A Late Gothic Sculpture from Italy: The Savona Altarpiece in The Cloisters," in Parker 1992, pp. 440–59; Castelnuovo-Tedesco and Soultanian 2010.

Fragment of a Tapestry Hanging (p. 127)

Cavallo 1993; Wixom 1999.

Altar Frontal with Man of Sorrows and Saints (p. 128)

Nuremberg 1986; Wixom 1999.

Altarpiece with Scenes from the Life of Saint Andrew (p. 129)

Charles D. Cuttler, *Northern Painting from Pucelle to Bruegel*, rev. and updated ed. (Fort Worth, 1991).

Annunciation Triptych (Merode Altarpiece) (p. 130)

Stephan Kemperdick, *Der Meister von Flémalle: Die Werkstatt Robert Campins und Rogier van der Weyden* (Turnhout, 1997); Maryan W. Ainsworth and Keith Christiansen, eds., *From Van Eyck to Bruegel: Early Netherlandish Paintings in The Metropolitan Museum of Art*, exh. cat., New York, The Metropolitan Museum of Art (New York, 1998); Felix Thürlemann, *Robert Campin: A Monographic Study with Critical Catalogue* (Munich, 2002); Stephan Kemperdick and Jochen Sander et al., *The Master of Flémalle and Rogier van der Weyden*, exh. cat., Frankfurt am Main, Städel Museum; Berlin, Gemäldegalerie, Staatliche Museen zu Berlin (Ostfildern, 2009).

The Virgin Mary and Five Standing Saints Above Predella Panels (p. 134)

Jane Hayward, "Stained-Glass Windows from the Carmelite Church at Boppard-am-Rhein: A Reconstruction of the Glazing Program of the North Nave," *The Metropolitan Museum Journal* 2 (1969), pp. 75–114; Rorimer 1972.

Kneeling Angel (p. 136)

Timothy B. Husband, "Tilman Riemenschneider and the Tradition of Alabaster Carving," in *Tilman Riemenschneider, c. 1460–1531*, edited by Julien Chapuis, pp. 64–81 (New Haven, 2004).

Paschal Candlestick (p. 137)

Margaret B. Freeman, "Lighting the Paschal Candlestick," *The Metropolitan Museum of Art Bulletin* 3, no. 8 (April 1945), pp. 194–200.

Altar Predella and Socle of Archbishop Don Dalmau de Mur y Cervelló (p. 138)

R. Steven Janke, "The Retable of Don Dalmau de Mur y Cervelló from the Archbishop's Palace at Saragossa: A Documented Work by Francí Gomar and Tomás Giner," *The Metropolitan Museum Journal* 18 (1983), pp. 65–80.

Saint James the Greater (p. 140)

María Jesús Gómez Barcena, *Escultura gótica funeraria en Burgos* (Burgos, 1988); Jay A. Levenson, ed., *Circa 1492: Art in the Age of Exploration*, exh. cat., Washington, D.C., National Gallery of Art (Washington, D.C., 1991).

Standing Virgin and Child (p. 141)

Chapuis 1999; Wixom 1999; Stefan Roller et al., *Niclaus Gerhaert: Der Bildhauer des Späten Mittelalters*, exh. cat., Frankfurt am Main, Liebieghaus Skulpturensammlung; Strasbourg, Musée de l'Oeuvre Notre Dame (Petersberg, 2011).

Saint Barbara (p. 141)

Eva Zimmermann, "Zur Rekonstruktion des ehemaligen Hochaltares der Kippenheimer St. Mauritiuskirche," in *Festschrift für Peter Bloch zum 11. Juli 1990*, edited by Hartmut Krohm and Christian Theuerkauff, pp. 121–33 (Mainz am Rhein, 1990).

The Death of the Virgin (The Dormition) (p. 142)

Wixom 1988–89; Dagmar Täube et al., *Glanz und Grösse des Mittelalters: Kölner Meisterwerke aus den grossen Sammlungen der Welt*, exh. cat., Cologne, Museum Schnütgen (Munich, 2011).

Triptych with the Passion of Christ (p. 143)

"Recent Acquisitions, A Selection: 2006–2007," *The Metropolitan Museum of Art Bulletin* 65, no. 2 (Fall 2007), p. 18.

The Lamentation (p. 145)

Theodor Müller, *Sculpture in the Netherlands, Germany, France, and Spain: 1400 to 1500* (Baltimore, 1966); Mojmír

Frinta, "Identified Shutters of a Sculptured Shrine at The Cloisters," *Gesta* 6 (January 1967), pp. 40–45.

Tau Cross (p. 145)
Timothy B. Husband, "The Winteringham Tau Cross and Ignis Sacer," *The Metropolitan Museum Journal* 27 (1992), pp. 19–35; Wixom 1999.

Set of Fifty-Two Playing Cards (p. 146)
Wixom 1999.

Armorial Bearings and Badges of John, Lord Dynham (p. 146)
Cavallo 1993; Richard Marks and Paul Williamson, eds., *Gothic: Art for England 1400–1547*, exh. cat., London, Victoria and Albert Museum (London, 2003).

Fragment of a Chasuble (p. 148)
Wixom 1999.

Seated Bishop (p. 148)
Chapuis 1999.

Three Kings from an Adoration Group (p. 150)
Spätgotik am Oberrhein: Meisterwerke der Plastik und des Kunsthandwerks, 1450–1530, exh. cat., Badisches Landesmuseum (Karlsruhe, 1970); Wixom 1988–89.

Saint Anthony Abbot (p. 151)
Wixom 1999.

Covered Beaker (p. 152)
Heinrich Kohlhaussen, *Nürnberger Goldschmiedekunst des Mittelalters und der Dürerzeit 1240 bis 1540* (Berlin, 1968); Wixom 1999.

Covered Chalice (p. 153)
José Manuel Cruz Valdovinos, *Platería en la época de los Reyes Católicos*, exh. cat., Madrid, Fundación Central Hispano (Madrid, 1992).

Triptych with Scenes from the Passion of Christ (p. 154)
Johannes Neuhardt, ed., *Gold + Silber: Kostbarkeiten aus Salzburg*, exh. cat., Dommuseum zu Salzburg (Salzburg, 1984).

Cloister from Trie-sur-Baïse (p. 157)
Rorimer 1972.

Doorway and Staircase Enclosure (p. 160)
Rorimer 1972; Pantxika Béguerie-De Paepe, *La sculpture picarde à Abbeville vers 1500* (Tournai, 2001).

One of a Pair of Ewers (p. 162)
Timothy B. Husband, *The Wild Man: Medieval Myth and Symbolism*, exh. cat., New York, The Metropolitan Museum of Art, The Cloisters (New York, 1980); Nuremberg 1986.

Paten with Abraham and Melchizedek (p. 163)
Peter Barnet, "Recent Acquisitions (1999–2008) of Medieval Art at The Metropolitan Museum of Art and The Cloisters, New York," *The Burlington Magazine* 150, no. 1268 (November 2008), p. 799, fig. 20; "Recent Acquisitions, A Selection: 2008–2010," *The Metropolitan Museum of Art Bulletin* 68, no. 2 (Fall 2010), p. 20.

Lectern in the Form of an Eagle (p. 164)
Jan Crab, "The Great Copper Pelican in the Choir: The Lectern from the Church of St. Peter in Louvain," *The Metropolitan Museum of Art Bulletin* 26, no. 10 (June 1968), pp. 401–9.

Man of Sorrows (p. 165)
Peter Barnet, "An Ivory Relief of the 'Man of Sorrows' in New York," *The Sculpture Journal* 4 (2000), pp. 1–6.

Memento Mori (Dives in Hell) (p. 165)
Wixom 1999.

The Mater Dolorosa (p. 166)
Wixom 1999.

Quatrefoil Panel with Secular Scenes (p. 168)
Nuremberg 1986.

The Unicorn Tapestries (pp. 168–75)
Cavallo 1993; Adolfo Salvatore Cavallo, *The Unicorn Tapestries at The Metropolitan Museum of Art* (New York, 1998); Thomas P. Campbell et al., *Tapestry in the Renaissance: Art and Magnificence*, exh. cat., New York, The Metropolitan Museum of Art (New York, 2002).

Panels with Scenes from the Life and Passion of Christ (p. 177)
Margaret B. Freeman, "Late Gothic Woodcarvings from Normandy," *The Metropolitan Museum of Art Bulletin* 9, no. 10 (June 1951), pp. 260–69.

Sorgheloos (Carefree) in Poverty (p. 177)
Timothy B. Husband, *The Luminous Image: Painted Glass Roundels in the Lowlands, 1480–1560*, exh. cat., New York, The Metropolitan Museum of Art (New York, 1995).

Christ Blessing (p. 178)
"Recent Acquisitions, A Selection: 2008–2010," *The Metropolitan Museum of Art Bulletin* 68 (Fall 2010), pp. 20–21.

Saint Michael (p. 178)
Suzanne L. Stratton, ed., *Spanish Polychrome Sculpture, 1500–1800, in United States Collections*, exh. cat., New York, The Spanish Institute; Dallas, Meadows Museum, Southern Methodist University; Los Angeles County Museum of Art (New York, 1993).

Episode from the Story of the Redemption of Man: Christ Is Born as Man's Redeemer (p. 180)
Cavallo 1993.

ABBREVIATIONS

Barnet 1997. Peter Barnet, ed. *Images in Ivory: Precious Objects of the Gothic Age*. Exh. cat. Detroit Institute of Arts; Baltimore, Walters Art Gallery. Detroit, 1997.

Barnet and Dandridge 2006. Peter Barnet and Pete Dandridge. *Lions, Dragons, and Other Beasts: Aquamanilia of the Middle Ages, Vessels for Church and Table*. Exh. cat. New York, Bard Graduate Center. New Haven, 2006.

Boehm 2005. Barbara Drake Boehm. *Prague: The Crown of Bohemia, 1347–1437*. Exh. cat. New York, The Metropolitan Museum of Art; Prague Castle. New York, 2005.

Castelnuovo-Tedesco and Soultanian 2010. Lisbeth Castelnuovo-Tedesco and Jack Soultanian, with Richard Y. Tayar. *Italian Medieval Sculpture in The Metropolitan Museum of Art and The Cloisters*. New York, 2010.

Cavallo 1993. Adolfo Salvatore Cavallo. *Medieval Tapestries in The Metropolitan Museum of Art*. New York, 1993.

Caviness and Husband 1985. Madeline H. Caviness and Timothy B. Husband, eds. *Corpus Vitrearum: Selected Papers from the XIth International Colloquium of the Corpus Vitrearum, New York, 1–6 June 1982*. New York, 1985.

Chapuis 1999. Julien Chapuis et al. *Tilman Riemenschneider: Master Sculptor of the Late Middle Ages*. Exh. cat. New York, The Metropolitan Museum of Art. New Haven, 1999.

Didier and Toussaint 2003. Robert Didier and Jacques Toussaint, eds. *Autour de Hugo d'Oignies*. Exh. cat. Namur, Musée des Arts Anciens du Namurois. Namur, 2003.

Forsyth 1982. Ilene H. Forsyth. *Throne of Wisdom: Wood Sculptures of the Madonna in Romanesque France*. Princeton, N.J., 1982.

Hayward 2003. Jane Hayward. *English and French Medieval Stained Glass in the Collection of The Metropolitan Museum of Art*. Revised and edited by Mary B. Shepard and Cynthia Clark. 2 vols. New York, 2003.

Little 1987a. Charles T. Little, with David L. Simon and Leslie Bussis. "Romanesque Sculpture in North American Collections. XXV. The Metropolitan Museum of Art. Part V. Southwestern France." *Gesta* 26, no. 1 (1987), pp. 61–76.

Little 1987b. Charles T. Little. "Romanesque Sculpture in North American Collections. XXVI. The Metropolitan Museum of Art. Part VI. Auvergne, Burgundy, Central France, Meuse Valley, Germany." *Gesta* 26, no. 2 (1987), pp. 153–68.

Little 1993. Charles T. Little, ed. *The Art of Medieval Spain, A.D. 500–1200*. Exh. cat. New York, The Metropolitan Museum of Art. New York, 1993.

McLachlan 2001. Elizabeth Parker McLachlan. "Liturgical Vessels and Implements." In *The Liturgy of the Medieval Church*, edited by Thomas J. Heffernan and E. Ann Matter, pp. 369–429. Kalamazoo, Mich., 2001.

Nuremberg 1986. *Gothic and Renaissance Art in Nuremberg, 1300–1550*. Exh. cat. New York, The Metropolitan Museum of Art; Nuremberg, Germanisches National-museum. New York, 1986.

Parker 1992. Elizabeth C. Parker, ed., with the assistance of Mary B. Shepard. *The Cloisters: Studies in Honor of the Fiftieth Anniversary*. New York, 1992.

Rorimer 1972. James J. Rorimer. *Medieval Monuments at The Cloisters as They Were and as They Are*. Rev. ed. New York, 1972.

Wixom 1988–89. William D. Wixom. "Medieval Sculpture at The Cloisters." *The Metropolitan Museum of Art Bulletin* 46, no. 3 (Winter 1988–89), pp. 3–64.

Wixom 1999. William Wixom, ed. *Mirror of the Medieval World*. Exh. cat. New York, The Metropolitan Museum of Art. New York, 1999.

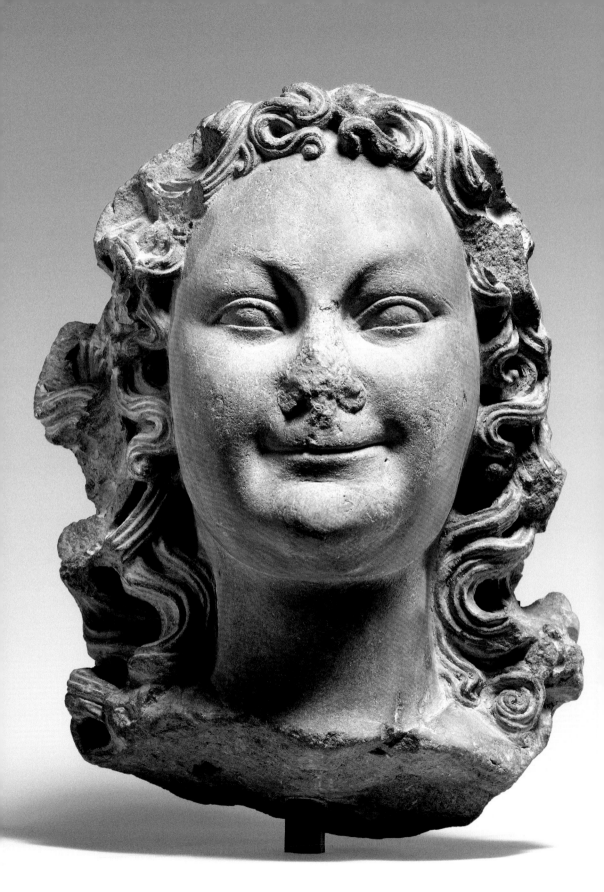

Acknowledgments

This book and its prior edition are the result of the cooperation and encouragement of many. We owe an enormous debt to our fellow curators and educators in the Department of Medieval Art and The Cloisters, past and present, who tirelessly read drafts of the texts and made many helpful suggestions. They are: Barbara Drake Boehm, Julien Chapuis, Helen C. Evans, Meredith Fluke, Melanie Holcomb, Timothy Husband, Charles T. Little, and Leslie Bussis Tait. Many other current and former staff members and friends made valuable contributions. We are especially grateful to Maryan Ainsworth, Christina Alphonso, Drew Anderson, Sylvan Barnet, Carrie Rebora Barratt, Emeline Baude, Christine Brennan, Céline Brugeat, Michael Carter, Lisbeth Castelnuovo-Tedesco, Dorothy Glass, Keith Glutting, Sigrid Goldiner, Penny Jones, Lucretia Kargère, Deirdre Larkin, Marlene Lieu, Theo Margelony, Susan Moody, Thom Morin, John P. O'Neill, Nadine Orenstein, José Ortiz, Doralynn Pines, Xavier Seubert, Lisa Skogh, Tiffany Sprague, Dale Tucker, Tom Vinton, Ann Webster, Emma Wegner, Andrew Winslow, and Elizabeth Zechella. Christine McDermott expertly coordinated the revised edition at The Cloisters. Barbara Bridgers and Museum photographers Joe Coscia, Oi-Cheong Lee, and Karin Willis produced the superb photographs used throughout. Mark Polizzotti, Publisher and Editor in Chief, and his staff, including Peter Antony, Chief Production Manager, and Michael Sittenfeld, Managing Editor, were responsible for the high standards of editing, design, and production, overseen by our editor, Cynthia Clark. Steven Schoenfelder created the handsome design of the book, with a new floor plan of The Cloisters by Kamomi Solidum. Finally, we are grateful to Philippe de Montebello, Director Emeritus, and Thomas P. Campbell, Director, for their leadership and support of this guidebook from its inception.

Index

PHOTOGRAPH CREDITS

The Metropolitan Museum of Art
endeavors to respect copyright in a
manner consistent with its nonprofit
educational mission. If you believe
any material has been included in
this publication improperly, please
contact the Editorial Department.

New color photography of The
Cloisters and of works in the
Metropolitan Museum collection
is by Karin Willis and Oi-Cheong
Lee, The Photograph Studio, The
Metropolitan Museum of Art.

Additional photograph credits:
The Cloisters Library and Archives,
The Metropolitan Museum of Art:
p. 8 (photograph by Irving
Underhill); p. 12 (top, photograph
by L. H. Dreyer); pp. 13, 16, 29
(bottom), 35 (top and bottom), 41
(bottom), 47, 56, 66, 68. Joseph
Coscia Jr., The Photograph Studio,
The Metropolitan Museum of
Art: pp. 166–75. From *Spanish
Romanesque Sculpture*, by A. K. Porter
(New York: Pantheon, ca. 1928):
p. 38 (top), copyprint by Mark
Morosse, The Photograph Studio,
The Metropolitan Museum of Art;
p. 45 (middle)

Published by
The Metropolitan Museum of Art, New York

Mark Polizzotti, Publisher and Editor in Chief
Gwen Roginsky, Associate Publisher and General
    Manager of Publications
Peter Antony, Chief Production Manager
Michael Sittenfeld, Managing Editor
Robert Weisberg, Senior Project Manager

Edited by Cynthia Clark
Designed by Steven Schoenfelder
Production by Peter Antony

Typeset in Centaur and Chaparral
Printed on 150 gsm Galerie Art Silk
Printed and bound by Ofset Yapimevi,
    Istanbul

Floor plan of The Cloisters (pp. 18–19) by
    Kamomi Solidum
Map (inside covers) by Anandaroop Roy

Cover illustrations: front, view into the Cloister
from Saint-Michel-de-Cuxa (p. 28) from the Chapter
House from Notre-Dame-de-Pontaut (p. 47); back,
detail of *The Falcon's Bath* (p. 125)

p. 1, detail of *The Unicorn in Captivity* (p. 175); p. 2, view
into the Cloister from Saint-Guilhem-le-Désert (p. 56);
p. 4, detail of stained glass with *The Gathering of Manna*
(p. 167); p. 6, *The Evangelist Mark* (p. 72); pp. 20–21,
detail of a fragment of a tapestry hanging (p. 127);
p. 182, upper driveway entrance to The Cloisters in
winter, with the Froville arcade and Sens windows
visible at center (pp. 13, 17); p. 202, head, possibly of
an angel (p. 77); p. 212, view from the Early Gothic
Hall into the Gothic Chapel at The Cloisters

The Metropolitan Museum of Art
1000 Fifth Avenue
New York, New York 10028
metmuseum.org

Distributed by
Yale University Press, New Haven and London
yalebooks.com/art
yalebooks.co.uk

Library of Congress Cataloging-in-Publication Data
Barnet, Peter.
The Cloisters : Medieval art and architecture /
Peter Barnet and Nancy Wu. —
75th Anniv. ed., rev. and expanded
p. cm.
Includes bibliographical references and index.
ISBN 978-1-58839-477-4 (Metropolitan Museum
of Art)—ISBN 978-0-300-18720-5
(Yale University Press) 1. Cloisters (Museum)—
Guidebooks. 2. Art, Medieval—Guidebooks. 3. Art—
New York (State)—New York—Guidebooks. I. Wu,
Nancy Y. II. Cloisters (Museum) III. Title.
N611.C6A85 2012
709.02'0747471—dc23
2012036640

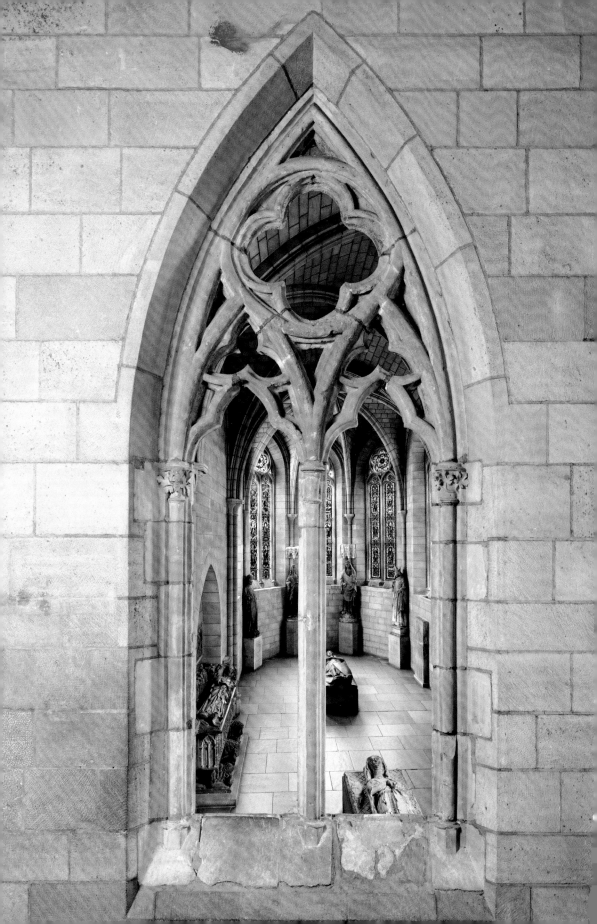